LIFE IN
MEDIEVAL FRANCE

BY JOAN EVANS

Frontispiece: THE LILIES OF FRANCE
Miniature from the Book of Hours of the
Duke of Bedford. London, British Museum

Coment-n̄t sez̄ par son ange enuoia les trois fleurs de lis dor en vn escu disant au roy clouis.

LIFE
IN MEDIEVAL
FRANCE

BY JOAN EVANS

PHAIDON

PHAIDON PUBLISHERS INC · NEW YORK

DISTRIBUTORS IN THE UNITED STATES: FREDERICK A. PRAEGER INC

111 FOURTH AVENUE · NEW YORK · N.Y. 10003

LIBRARY OF CONGRESS CATALOG CARD NUMBER 69–19801

SBN 7148 1373 7 (CLOTH)

SBN 7148 1374 5 (PAPER)

MADE IN GREAT BRITAIN

PLATES PRINTED BY LONSDALE & BARTHOLOMEW LTD · LEICESTER

TEXT PRINTED AT THE PITMAN PRESS · BATH

CONTENTS

Preface

MEDIEVAL HISTORY is like a great tapestry, on which many figures—some splendid, some humble, some sinister, and some beautiful—appear against a shadowy background. A crabbed inscription gives to some a name and a story; many remain nameless and unknown. But all are in artistic relation with the background, and a close study of its shadows reveals a thousand details that help to explain their significance.

It is this background which I have tried to describe; my concern is with neither the political nor the literary history of France, but with the elements of her medieval civilization. The background is full of detail; yet much is obscured by shadow or darkened by time, and distance that softens the familiar may add the greater emphasis of mystery to the unusual and the strange. Yet however misty and remote the Middle Ages may seem to us, however much governed by ways of thought that time has made unfamiliar, it should not be hard to study them with sympathy and comprehension. The men of medieval France were men of like passions with ourselves; they knew pleasure and pain, freedom and limitation as we do; like us they were uncertain of the road they trod, yet ever went forward in hope.

For Englishmen they have a peculiar interest. They belong to the time when England held provinces in France; when in the palaces and law courts of England French was the common speech; when English poets wrote in a dialect of French, or, first attempting the rhythms of English verse, found their matter in the romances and *chansons de geste* of France. In literature, in art, in learning, England is the daughter of France; if there had been no such French civilization in the Middle Ages there could have been no such English Renaissance. Indeed, a critic, writing on the life of the French seigneurial class in the thirteenth century, finds that in their passion for sport, in their rural pleasures, in the relations at once free and courteous between men and women, this medieval society resembles nothing so closely as that of the England of a generation or two ago. 'Ways of living and acting', he says, 'as well as modes of speech, once very common . . . that were originally derived from medieval France, have survived until our days only in England. The traces of them that can still be perceived help to give English life its peculiar character. But we must not forget that it is the antiquity of these customs which makes them seem, to us, original.'[1]

I therefore venture to beg indulgence for a book, written with a medieval want of originality, that aims only at describing some aspects of the civilization of Medieval France.

I desire to express my indebtedness to the teaching of Dr. Ernest Barker, to encouragement and help received from the late Miss E. F. Jourdain, Principal of my College, and to the kindness of Professor Studer, who read the book in proof.

Oxford, 1925   J.E.

I reprint this book almost as it stands, with the omission of the chapter on medieval art, since I have treated this more fully in a book published in 1948.[2] Literature, too, only figures illustratively, and the theatre has likewise been omitted. Much work has been done on the subject since my book on life in medieval France was written, but to such work it may, I hope, still serve as an introduction.

Wotton under Edge, 1956   J.E.

I am happy to know that this book should still meet a continuing need, and that a new edition is now being published. No changes have been made in the text or the illustrations, but the Bibliography has been brought up to date by Mrs. J. G. Russell, Librarian of St. Hugh's College, Oxford, to whom I am most grateful.

London, 1969   J.E.

[1]Langlois, *La Société française au XIIIe siècle*, Introduction.
[2]*Art in Mediaeval France*, Oxford University Press.

I

France in the Early Middle Ages

Touching, or almost touching, Spain, Italy, Switzerland, Germany, the Low Countries, and England, France is for ever rich in that force which arises from the contact and clash of nations. Her own strength has always been great enough to transmute and absorb external impulses into her national being; her own race, unchanging yet never exhausted, has made her for more than seven centuries the focus of civilization for the countries of Europe. Always seeing civilization as social congruity, art as the expression of life, learning as a precious heritage, she has never failed in 'le courage spirituel et l'esprit courageux', and has never ceased to unite a respect for fact to a capacity for philosophic thought.

She is the true heir of Rome in law, in clear thinking, in philosophy; in the urbanity of her civilization, in the relation between social function and position, and in the fitting pageantry that lends splendour to practical things.

There is no country more conscious of the continuity of her history, in spite of invasion, resettlement, and revolution; she brings to the Middle Ages the heritages of Roman Gaul. Caesar's *Commentaries* remain the best mirror of the Gallic temperament: 'swiftly and easily inflamed to war or revolution, hating the servile state, unstable, quick-witted, talkative, ingenious'. Yet politically France is neither Roman nor Celtic; she dates from the dark age of barbarism that followed the Roman Empire, when the medieval peoples emerged from the chaos of warring races, and the world gradually came to rest on a new balance.

If the history of medieval Europe begins with the coronation of Charlemagne, the history of the medieval nations begins with the partition of his empire after his death. In thirty years it was divided no less than five times; with the final Treaty of Verdun in 843 the State of France was established.[1] It is a significant fact that the earliest monument of the French language, the Strasburg Oaths, dates from 842. Even the divisions and dissensions of the early Middle Ages did not destroy the sense of the solidarity of France; the bard of the *Chanson de Roland* already sings of

---

[1]This is a general book and I use 'France' to mean the entity we know rather than the realm with constantly changing frontiers that was under royal domination in the Middle Ages.

'dulce France', and the name comes again and again as a refrain to point the distance and peril of Roncesvalles.[1] *Cleomadès* tells us that to love France is natural and right,

> *Car en anciens escris*
> *Trueve on que tousjours a esté*
> *France la flours et la purté*
> *D'armes, d'onnour, de gentillece,*
> *De courtoisie et de largece.*
> *Ce est la touche et l'exemplaire*
> *De ce c'on doit laissier et faire.*

In *Jerusalem* the Count of Flanders goes so far as to say that he wonders that Christ should have chosen to live in the desert of Syria. For his part,

> *Miex aim del' borc d'Arras la grant castelerie*
> *Et d'Aire et de Saint Pol la grant caroierie*
> *Et de mes biaus viviers la riche pescherie*
> *Quo tote ceste terre, ne la chité antie.*

The many political divisions of France after the death of Charlemagne are of considerable importance for its political history, but for considering the growth of its medieval civilization they are of secondary interest. Its social, intellectual, and artistic history—and even the history of its legal institutions—naturally group themselves round four centres: Provence in the south, Burgundy in the east, the Île de France in central France, and Normandy in the north-west. Each of these was the centre of a civilization with characteristics of its own, and though interaction between them became more and more frequent a close assimilation was not reached until after the end of the Middle Ages.

Provence is the part of France that has the most ancient and the most continuous recorded history. Marseilles itself was founded as a colony from Hellenic Phocaea about 600 B.C., and Provence owes its name to its foundation as a Roman *Provincia* in 118 B.C. When the rest of Gaul was still under military rule as an occupied territory, Provence was administered directly by the Roman Senate. Pliny calls it 'Italia verius quam provincia', and whether by sea or by the mountain passes it finds easy acess to Italy. Christianity, too, came to Latin- and Greek-speaking Provence in the course of the original dissemination of the faith, to meet with a temporary check only when it encountered a barrier of Celtic speech beyond Lyons.

[1]The word appears 170 times in the Oxford MS.

Thus in spite of serious Teutonic inroads classical traditions endured there in laws and institutions, architecture and way of life, in a degree that is only surpassed in Italy. The form of Roman legal institutions survived. In Southern France alone can the medieval municipalities be considered direct descendants of the Roman *municipia*. They have the Italian tradition: the noble as well as the merchant lives within the city. They are *municipalités consulaires*; their officers have the title of consul—eight at Avignon, twelve at Marseilles, twenty-four at Toulouse. Roman Law was early studied at Montpellier, Toulouse, and Avignon, and it is remarkable that in the fourteenth century, when Provençal civilization was under an eclipse, the great jurists of Philippe le Bel—Pierre Flotte, Guillaume de Nogaret, Pierre de Belle Perche—were all graduates of Toulouse. Sir Paul Vinogradoff considered the most interesting contribution of France to the revival of Roman Law to be a summary of the Code of Justinian written in Provençal in 1149 for the use of the local judges; it is the first treatise on Roman Law to be written in a modern language, and is clearly intended not for academic use, but for that of laymen acting as presiding judges or arbitrators. It is an intelligent and practical work of reference for a region where Roman Law was recognized as the principal legal authority.

But Roman influence in Provence was not confined to law: because there were there many small schools of classical learning rather than a single great one, it is easy to forget that it was a centre of humanistic studies. Guiot de Provins reminds us of the writers studied at Arles:

> *A Arle oï conter molt gent*
> *Lor vie en l'estoire sanz troffe*
> *Dont furent né le Philosofe—*

of whom he cites twenty—Plato, Seneca, Aristotle, Virgil, Socrates, Lucan, Diogenes, Priscian, Aristippus, Cleobulus, Ovid, Statius, Pythagorus, and others. It was in the south that the classical love of beauty and pleasure came most strongly into conflict with the monastic ideal. The Prior of Montaudon leaves his cloister, and keeping his religious habit, wanders about as a troubadour, till in the end he drifts to the Court of his friend Alphonso II of Aragon. His poems express his attitude to life.

'The other day I was in Paradise, because I am merry and joyful, and because I love well the good God whom all things obey—earth, sea, valley, and mountain. And God said to me, "Monk, why comest thou here? And how dost thou fare at Montaudon with all thy brethren?"'

'Lord, I stayed a year or two in the cloister, which was enough to lose me the barons' love; but it is you alone whom I love and would serve.'

' "Monk," replied God, "think not thou gavest me pleasure in shutting thyself up in the abbey; why desist from war and singing? I would rather hear thee laugh and sing. It makes princes more generous, and the priory of Montaudon can only gain by it." '

In the whole of Provençal life there is something of the Italian feeling of the Renaissance: the country surrounds the town, and the citizens go, Italian fashion, to work or to play there in the day, and return singing to the city at nightfall. Life is insecure, and city and country have alike their dangers, but through everything runs a strain of Lorenzo's 'Quant' è bella gioventù'. There is the same Italian note in Provençal architecture, but this is directly attributable to the influence of the splendid classical buildings of Roman times that survived in Arles, Nîmes, Orange, and the other Roman cities. The monastic carvers of the cloister of Saint Trophime at Arles decorated their work with the figures of Jupiter, Juno, Hercules, Silvanus (with oak leaves for hair), Faunus, Diana, Neptune, Ceres, Bacchus, Pan, Venus, Paris, and Helen. As late as the middle of the twelfth century the characteristic Provençal church was constructed like a classical temple with a single nave, walls unpierced by windows, fluted columns crowned with the Corinthian acanthus, and pediments, entablatures, and mouldings that in their form as in their proportion are classical and Roman.

In all the territory once belonging to *Provincia Narbonensis*, including Toulouse and a part of Guyenne, Roman influence is strong, but there is also a second influence, the influence of the East. The Mediterranean brought the whole coast from Nice to Perpignan and the country behind it into close connexion with half-Eastern Spain and even with Africa and the commercial cities of Asia Minor; the sea might be stormy, but it was safer than the highways of France. As early as the time of Charlemagne the coast towns had relations with the Bagdad of Haroun-el-Raschid, with Byzantium, Egypt, and Syria, and imported purple stuffs, spices, Indian pearls, Egyptian papyrus, and even monkeys and elephants. Benjamin of Tudela, writing in 1160, describes Montpellier as a very good city for commerce to which Christians and Mohammedans come from all quarters to trade, so that its streets are thronged with Arabs of North Africa, merchants of Syria, Lombardy, Rome, Genoa, Pisa, and England.

Even when Southern France found herself in conflict with an Eastern people, as she did in 1018 when a Crusade was undertaken against the Moors, conquest only preceded assimilation. The leaders of the army gained great riches, and stayed to lead an Oriental life in Moorish palaces. A Jewish merchant has left a story of waiting upon one of these

French leaders in his palace at Barbastro, and finding him in Eastern garments seated upon a divan, surrounded by evidences of his riches, while a tearful Arab girl played the lute and sang songs in a language that he could not understand.

Thus the Eastern element was important in the development of the life of the south-western cities in particular. Indeed, the foundation of Montpellier itself is traditionally ascribed to fugitives from the Saracen city of Maguelone, destroyed by Charles Martel in 737. From its considerable Arabic and Jewish population may be derived the tradition of medical knowledge, which in the twelfth century made Montpellier second only to Salerno as a University of Medicine. Another sign of Eastern influence is the Oriental character of the architecture of Périgord, as Eastern as that of St. Mark's at Venice. Saint Front de Périgueux, built after 1120, shows the classical single nave, without divisions or side chapels, surmounted by a characteristically Eastern series of cupolas.

It is in Provence that the first efforts were made to bring the perpetual warfare of feudalism within the control of the Church. The *Pax Dei* and the *Pactum Pacis* are characteristic of Southern France. They were the first expressions of that almost Hellenic feeling for the gentler side of life, that wish, not for strength alone, but for strength allied with grace, which Provence shared with Greece, 'that made gracious the life of the world'. They were its contribution to the early military chivalry of the Middle Ages; and Provence remained the home of *courtoisie*.

This is not the place to consider the history of Provençal literature, which, like that of Greece, rose, blossomed, and died in a short three hundred years, between the end of the tenth and the end of the thirteenth century. It is possible that Provençal lyric art may have owed something to the great tenth-century Arab school of lyric poetry, and that the Provençal troubadours may have gained some of the complexity of their versification from this source.

Another influence of the East helped to bring Provençal civilization to a violent and an untimely end. The Eastern conception of a dualistic religion, of a Spirit of Good and a Spirit of Evil inherent in all things and ever at war, had influenced the Manichaeans of Early Christian times. In the early Middle Ages the belief flourished in the Balkan peninsula, and during the eleventh century it reached Provence. The sect of Cathari, later called Albigensians from their headquarters at Albi, maintained that all physical and material things pertained to the Spirit of Evil, and that all who wished for salvation must utterly renounce them. Their dualism denied the Christian doctrine of Redemption, and by 1163 the

Council of Tours denounced them as heretics. In 1199 Innocent III seriously took up the work of suppressing the heresy, and with it the Provençal free spirit which had found a more orthodox expression in such sects as the Vaudois. His Albigensian Crusade hastened the end of Provençal chivalry and Provençal civilization, already menaced by the centralizing influence of Paris. The Crusade, indeed, was not only the expression of hostility between the established order and heresy, but also of the instinctive and resentful envy that always lies between north and south. Hundreds of helpless women and children were killed in the church of St. Mary Magdalene at Béziers alone, and the chivalry and peasantry of the Midi, Catholics and Cathari alike, were killed by the Crusaders 'avec un extrême allégresse'. The *Chanson de la Croisade* tells us that the grass of the fields was dyed red as roses, since no prisoners were taken.

Provence and the surrounding country is then an entity of which the lines of demarcation from the rest of France can be established. It finds a pendant in the north, but one of which every characteristic is different. Provence has a history going back to Rome and even to Greece: Normandy enters history, to all intents and purposes, when it is granted to Rollo and his followers in 911. The Norman expansion from the ninth to the twelfth century may be thought of as the last wave of the Great Migrations. But whereas Goth and Vandal, Hun and Frank, had been nomads on the land, the Northmen were driven by the configuration of their land to become nomads upon the waters, 'nageans par l'Océan en manière de pyrates'. Three sea routes lead from Scandinavia, apart from any in the Baltic itself: the first leads direct to Iceland, the second to the eastern shores of Britain, and the third, skirting the Frisian coasts, reaches the northern coast of France. Therefore it is natural that the migrations of the Northmen should have led to the establishment of a Scandinavian principality in Iceland, the Danelaw in England, and Normandy in France.

Their tendency was naturally enough to settle at the mouths of great rivers: the Humber, Elbe, Weser, Rhine, Meuse, Scheldt, Seine, Loire, Garonne, and Guadalquivir. Theirs was a genius for colonization. Their contemporary Geoffrey Malaterra has described them, balancing light and shadow in the portrait: they are a cunning and revengeful race, he says, despising their own inheritance in the hope of winning a greater elsewhere, eager for gain and eager for power, quick to imitate whatever they see, at once lavish and greedy; given to hunting and hawking, delighting in horses and accoutrements and fine clothing, yet ready if need be to bear labour and hunger and cold; skilful in flattery and the use of fine words, but unbridled unless held down by the yoke of justice. This quickness and eagerness, this gift for imitation without loss of their own personality, made it possible for them to assimilate much that was French while retaining many northern characteristics. In spite of continued migration from the north, by the eleventh century Normandy had become French in law and language, recognizing federation if not feudation to the King at Paris. The second Duke, William Longsword, had to send his son to learn Norse at Bayeux, for it was no longer spoken at Rouen.[1]

But Normandy was not French in outlook; rather was it the centre of an Atlantic Empire that stretched from Scotland to the Pyrenees. It sent its knights to fight the Moors in Spain, its crusaders to Jerusalem, and its younger sons to Sicily. There a handful of Normans so dealt with the problem of a mixed population of Mohammedans, Greek and Roman Christians and Jews in a country which had never been the home of a single nation or a single speech that they gave Sicily the most brilliant epoch in her history since classical Syracuse. Such a feat shows great administrative ability and a gift for dealing with the forms of law: a code of Lombard and Roman law and Norman custom had to be administered to a mixed population so that Greek, Saracen, Lombard, Norman, and Jew should be alike protected; and an Arab, Latin, and Greek Chancery had to invent and administer a system of exchequer and administrative writs. The love of legal action is a Norse characteristic, and is early shown in such sagas as that of Burnt Njal. The *Coutume de Normandie* was the connecting link between the Frankish law of the Continent and English Common Law. Trial by jury, for instance, is of Frankish origin, but was developed and disseminated by the Normans.

It is characteristic of the Norman habit of order and organization that the military service of nobles was there exactly and systematically defined earlier than elsewhere. The military service owing to the Duke was assessed in units of five or ten knights, representing so much land, and the amounts of service were fixed by custom and regularly enforced. The unit of life was thus the knight's fee and the castle. These castles could not be built without the Duke's licence; they were all built for defence, and the life of their inhabitants was narrowed by defensive necessities. Further, the Duke had the power of limiting private wars and blood-feuds, and a large monopoly of jurisdiction was reserved for him.

The Norman gift for administration is notably shown in the financial system. Taxes and dues were collected more in money and less in kind

---

[1]Scandinavian survivals remained chiefly in the language of the sea, whence they crept into the naval vocabulary of modern French.

than in Capetian France; their collection, checking and administration were in the hands of skilled officers. The English Chancery under Henry II—then the most advanced in Europe—was typically Norman.

The Normans, then, were a practical people, immediately concerned with concrete things. Ways and means and not ideas were their pre-occupation; their literature deals in fact and not in speculation. History in the vernacular, which developed earlier in France then elsewhere, developed earliest in Normandy and in the English lands which shared Norman speech. Its first production, the *Histoire des Engles* of Gaimar, was written between 1147 and 1151 at the Court of Henry II and Eleanor of Aquitaine, to whom are also dedicated the histories of Wace and Benoît de St. More.

The same tendencies achieve greatness in Norman architecture; breadth, space, a certain grand manner from which not even a certain crudity of ornament can detract; solid reasoning and powerful will lie behind it, and give an effect curiously reminiscent of the Dorian architecture of the Spartan Peloponnese. As conditions became more settled in the eleventh century there was an immense amount of church building done by the bishops. The chronicler shows Geoffrey de Mowbray, for instance, labouring night and day for the enlargement and beautification of his church at Coutances, which was dedicated in 1056. He bought the better half of the city from the Duke to get a clear space for his cathedral and palace, he travelled as far as Apulia to secure for it gold and gems and vestments from Robert Giuscard and his fellow Normans, and he maintained from his rents a force of sculptors, masons, goldsmiths, and workers in glass. Nearly forty years later, when the church had been damaged by earthquake and tempest, he brought a plumber from England to restore the leaden roof and the fallen stones of the towers and to replace the gilded cock which crowned the whole; and when he saw the cock once more shining at the summit, he gave thanks to God and died, pronouncing eternal maledictions upon those who should injure his church.

In 1204 the Duchy of Normandy became a part of the Kingdom of France. Powicke's *Loss of Normandy* concludes: 'When the Normans became French they did a great deal more than bring their national epic to a close. They permitted the English once more to become a nation, and they established the French nation for all time.' They kept their own spirit of enterprise: it was Norman seamen who visited Senegal and Guinea and established the Gold and Ivory Coasts in 1365; and it was a Norman gentleman who was Lord of the Canary Islands in 1402. They added something to the national heritage of enlightened common sense,

PORTRAIT OF KING CHARLES VII. *Painting by Fouquet, about 1445. Paris, Louvre*

they aided the development of an adequate financial system and of the Parlement of Paris, and thus did their share in the gradual centralization of authority and power in the monarchy and the capital.

If the vitality of Normandy flows through the channels of the seas, the life of Burgundy runs through the ways of the land. Michelet has said, 'France has no element more binding than Burgundy, more capable of reconciling North and South.' It lies at the centre of the river-system of France, and so has been from time immemorial a centre of trade. The fairs of Châlon, Autun, Dijon, Auxonne, Beaune, Châtillon, and Tonnerre carried on a commercial tradition dating from Carolingian and even from Roman times. But besides being the home of commerce, it was the home of religion; its abbeys—Cluny, Cîteaux, Clairvaux, Vézelay, Flavigny, Tournus, St. Pierre de Bèze, Pothières, Saint Benigne de Dijon, and the rest—were not only important in themselves but did much to bring religion into feudal life. Cluny made Burgundy the land of crusaders and pilgrims. The first Capetian Duke, Hugh I (1076–9), fought the Saracens in Spain; Odo I besieged Tudela for two years; Hugh II died in 1143 after making the pilgrimage to Compostella; Hugh III was at the taking of Saint Jean d'Acre and died at Tyre; Odo III took a prominent part in the Albigensian Crusade; Hugh IV fought the infidels in Palestine and Egypt, and then in 1258 made the pilgrimage to Compostella; his successor, Hugh V, was King of Thessalonica; and Odo IV, Prince of Achaea. Even in 1436 Philippe le Bon still has the idea of crusade, and the Byzantine ambassadors have faith 'after God in him only'; and only the Pope's death brings the last Burgundian Crusade of 1465 to nothing.

The story of the core of France—the Île de France that has its centre at Paris—is bound up with the story of the Capetian monarchy. Intellectual argument has flourished in the atmosphere of Paris at least since the time of Julian the Apostate, and intellectual argument kept the idea of sovereignty alive. Here Law and Theology flourished, and the lawyers and the clergy were the two sections of society least dependent upon feudalism and most addicted to theory. The clergy held that the King through an eighth sacrament of coronation received a divine commission, different in kind from the power of any feudatory[1]; that he alone was Defender of the Church, and that to him pertained the execution of justice throughout the kingdom. The lawyers, fresh from the study of Roman Law, not only exalted the principle of his prerogative but also found legal methods and formulas to extend his power. Because the tradition of the

[1] The King wore the dalmatic beneath the royal mantle, as the kings of England still do, at their coronation.

Roman idea of sovereignty survived, monarchical feeling remained strong enough to give that centralized force to feudalism without which disintegration would have been inevitable.

The coronation oath of Hugh Capet and his successors concludes: 'I promise to grant to the people who are entrusted to my care Justice according to their rights'; and down to the end of the monarchy the King of France is the only sovereign in Europe who holds, besides the sceptre, not a sword but the 'main de justice'. As early as the tenth century Abbo could describe the monarchy as 'the incarnation of justice'.

So it is as Justiciar that the King consolidates his power, and by ecclesiastical and legal help that he attains and keeps it. The elevation of the Capetian dynasty had been due neither to a national movement nor a feudal movement, but to the ecclesiastical support given to the King by the French clergy, led by the Archbishop of Rheims. The Capetian monarch justly held the title of 'Eldest Son of the Church and most Christian King', and, though in friendly relation with the Papacy, remained a strong supporter of Gallicanism. The history of the French Church in the late eleventh century is the history of its bishoprics, and thus the King found in the bishoprics a counterbalance to the power of lay feudalism. But a third power arose, that of the people, and it was in allying itself with this power that the French monarchy attained a really national position.

The strength of this monarchy lay not only in its relations with Church and people—that made it less dependent upon the support of its feudatories—but also in its possession of a compact royal domain, with Paris as its centre. Every other monarchy in Europe owned scattered tracts of land, which afforded no strong *point d'appui* for the royal struggle against the barons. But the Île de France formed a core, round which, by purchase, marriage, and conquest an ever-increasing royal domain was built up, and it is owing to this possession that the centralization of power in Paris and in the monarchy was possible. In the administration of the first Capetians the provosts and the mayors combined all functions, giving the King a fixed yield and retaining the rest of the dues and taxes. Not until Norman methods of administration were introduced were the royal revenues increased. Further, the justice of the King became sovereign in a gradually widening area, while its seat in Paris made the city a true metropolis.

With the accession of Louis VI in 1108, a certain balance of power appears to restrain the unbridled forces of early feudalism. It is royal justice that modifies the feudal order and makes France a nation. From the royal domain, compacted into a central demesne round Paris, the monarchy made itself the centre of a modification of feudalism: one in which the Church, while becoming national, was to a great extent de-feudalized; in which the bourgeoisie of the towns was given a place in society, and became the King's allies at the expense of the nobles; in which the rural population was gradually permitted to escape from the servitude of the glebe. By the time of St. Louis the monarchy was already the fundamental institution of the realm. Its divine origin was recognized; 'The King holds his power from God and his sword alone'; the dynastic succession was established. But its true consecration lay in the justice it administered; the friar, Hugues de Digne, could preach to St. Louis: 'I have never seen in the Scriptures or any other book that a kingdom or a lordship of any kind has ever passed from one House to another, except for default of justice.' The best title-deeds of the monarchy are such edicts as the *Grande Ordonnance* of 1254:

'*The seneschals and other royal officers shall swear and observe the oath, under pain of punishment by the King himself, to give justice without distinction of persons, according to the approved customs and uses; to protect the rights of the King without encroaching on those of private persons; to receive no gift, neither they, nor their wives, nor their children, and to give back any they may have taken; never to borrow from those under their jurisdiction a sum over twenty livres, and to repay within two months; not to take any share in the proceeds of sale or appointment to subordinate posts, of rents due to the King, &c.; not to protect their subordinates who may be guilty of peculations or abuse of power . . . but on the contrary to punish them. . . . They shall not buy any house within the area of their jurisdiction without the King's consent, under pain of confiscation. . . . They shall not make the monasteries admit their relations or their servants, or procure for them ecclesiastical benefices. . . . They shall take neither bed nor board in monastic houses without the King's authoriza-tion. . . . They shall only have a small number of bedels and sergeants to execute their judgements. . . . The seneschals and bailiffs and their servants shall cause no man to be arrested for debt, unless the money be due to the King. They shall not be able to detain a man accused of crime who may be in a position to clear himself. . . . Persons of good reputation, however poor, shall not be put to the question on the evidence of a single witness. . . . They shall not collect any imposition. . . . They shall not forbid the exportation of corn, wine, and other provisions except after the Council has debated the question. . . . The royal officers, after their term of office has expired, shall remain for fifty days on the spot to answer any complaints which may be laid against them.*'

St. Louis endowed the monarchy with an added dignity, a dignity of moral greatness which survived even the lower standards of his successors.

When he was ill he said to his son, 'Fair son, I pray you that you make yourself beloved of your people; for truly I would rather that a Scot should come from Scotland and govern the Kingdom loyally and well than that you should govern it ill.' This good government he defines in the testament addressed to the same son, the future Philippe III: not to take away the goods or the rights of another, to do everything to enable his subjects to live in peace and righteousness, not to make war against Christians unless forced to do so, to appease quarrels, 'as St. Martin did', and to do his best to stamp out sin and heresy. This policy was not invariably followed by his successors, but the tradition of it made such a dictum as Beaumanoir's 'What the King pleases should be Law' the subject of less controversy that it would have been if St. Louis had not invested the monarchical power with the dignity of saintliness. In Joinville's words, 'As a scribe who has written a book illuminated with blue and gold, so did the King illuminate his realm'.

Under this policy the prosperity of the royal demesne increased. Private war was there more strictly limited, and the *droit coutumier* more carefully codified and corrected.[1] But it was definitely *royal* France; the right of ennobling, taxing, and striking money was insisted on as a royal prerogative, and there were no sovereign republics, no elected magistrates, no town belfries, no town seals, no independent militia, no justice but royal justice. But the *corvées* due to the King were carefully determined by *chartes octroyées*, and privileges thus granted were precious, since they were directly guaranteed by the monarchy. *Les Libertés de Lorris*, quite a small town, served as a model;[2] under such a charter it was more advantageous to be a *bourgeois du roi* than to be the member of a commune with rights of making war and peace: to be the citizen of a kingdom rather than of a single township.[3] At first residence in the royal city was necessary, but as the jurists of Philippe le Bel accustomed men's minds to accept legal theory as well as fact, by 1288 it was decided that it sufficed to make a formal disavowal of the old lord and to avow the King as master. Thus an important bourgeois class was created directly dependent on the King, who recruited from them his civil service. Further, they played a part in political life; the first exclusively bourgeois assemblage was summoned by Philip Augustus in 1185, and a century later began the political development of the États Généraux.

The reign of Philippe le Bel is an era of change. The Parlement of Paris

---

[1] The *royal* rights were not codified, and therefore they could grow gradually.

[2] It even influenced town charters in the west of England.

[3] Private war was forbidden: every dangerous conflict was an attempt against public security, and as such punishable by the King.

was given a regular constitution and made a real court of justice, with political, judicial, and financial functions, and met twice a year for a session of two months in the Palais de la Cité, afterwards called the Palais de Justice. An additional Chambre des Enquêtes was formed for extra-feudal jurisdiction. As Boutaric remarks, 'There was thenceforth a nobility in France but not an aristocracy.'

Philippe le Bel not only added considerably to the privileges of the *bourgeois du roi*, but also did much to encourage trade. The great fair *du Lendit*, held on land belonging to St. Denis and dating back to Frankish times, was regulated by him in 1295; already every town and craft in France was represented at it each year, but it was now opened to foreigners also, on the payment of certain dues. Further, merchants going to the *foires franches* of Champagne—at Troyes, Provins, Bar-sur-Aube, and Lagny—at the junction of the trade routes of the north and south, were declared exempt from local tolls on their way. Thus companies of Italian merchants came to frequent the fairs, and occasionally to found fixed establishments. It was through them that Villani, Boccaccio, Brunetto Latino, Francesco da Barberino, and the rest came to visit France; and it was through the position of the great Lombard merchants as financiers to the King that the financial basis of the monarchy made it more independent of its feudal vassals.

Further, the monarchy took political advantage of a growing feeling against arbitrary servitude. There was a preference to engage men into definite contracted service; it was more consistent with Christian principles, and on the whole it yielded better work: a charitable act was justified by its economic results. Such freedom, however, was usually bought, and when Louis X, in 1315, freed all the serfs of the royal domain, on the ground that according to natural law every man should be born free, such freedom had compulsorily to be bought at a fairly high price.

From the time of Philip Augustus the power of the monarchy was supported by legal opinion. This duty of law—customary, Canon, and especially Roman—is one of the characteristic developments of Capetian France, though its elements are not in the first instance Parisian. Roman Law was the heritage of the south, and Canon Law, in so far as it had a local source, sprang from Lorraine and the eleventh-century jurists of Lorraine such as Bruno of Toul, Cardinal Humbert, and Wazo of Liége. But under St. Louis juristic study was encouraged in the royal demesne, the Digest was translated into French, and schools of Roman Law were established at Orléans and Angers. Legal power appears unchecked by piety or any moral consideration under Philippe le Bel. Guillaume de

Nogaret and his colleagues were Roman in their juristic education and feudal in their violence: they had no consideration for the rights of any one but their master. By legal process they wrested Guyenne from Edward I, more territory from the Count of Flanders, more power from Pope Boniface VIII, and more money from the Order of the Temple. The jurist du Bois, in his 'Inquiry touching the power of the Pope', says that the Pope is evidently the temporal lord of the Emperor, for the latter needs to be confirmed and crowned by him; but no such authorization is needed in France, and no such authority should be recognized. He decides that it would be the best thing for society that the whole world should be subject to French rule, for 'it is a peculiar merit of the French to have a surer judgement than other nations, not to act without consideration, nor to place themselves in opposition to right reason'.

Philippe le Bel was the last King of France to be excommunicated, and he had his revenge. The captivity of the Popes at Avignon from 1308 to 1378 put even the papal power in the hands of the monarchy.

Paris and the Île de France, through the King's relations with Church and people, thus became the seat of a monarchy, backed by a system of burgess administration and supported by a system of legal theory. Thus Paris and the privileged provinces came to be the seat of order and authority. Though the west and the south might be plunged in anarchy, and the country in general a prey to superstition, vagabondage, robbery, and feudal guerilla warfare, none the less in Paris and the royal demesne life was civilized, urbane, and comparatively speaking secure. The Dominican André de Châalis, preaching in 1272, said that while everywhere the wife called her husband 'Monseigneur', at Paris he in his turn called her 'Madame'. The centre of the Île de France was Paris, the seat of monarchy and university: a city thus described by Gui de Bazoches between 1175 and 1190, at the time when it had first reached political importance under Philip Augustus:

'I am in Paris,' he writes, 'in that royal city where abundance of natural wealth not only holds those who live there, but also attracts those from afar. Just as the moon outshines the stars in brilliance, so does this city, the seat of the monarchy, lift her proud head above the rest. She lies in the embrace of an enchanting valley, surrounded by a crown of hills which Ceres and Bacchus make fruitful. The Seine, proud river of the East, runs there a brimming stream, and holds in its arms an island which is the head, the heart, the marrow of the whole city. Two suburbs extend to right and left, of which the lesser alone rivals many cities. Each of these suburbs communicates with the island by two bridges of stone; the Grand Pont towards the north, on the side of* *the English Channel, and the Petit Pont towards the Loire. The first—great, rich, trading—is the scene of seething activity; innumerable ships surround it, filled with merchandise and riches. The Petit Pont belongs to the dialecticians, who walk there deep in argument. In the island, by the side of the King's palace that dominates the whole city, is seen the palace of philosophy, where study reigns as sole sovereign in a citadel of light and immortality.'*

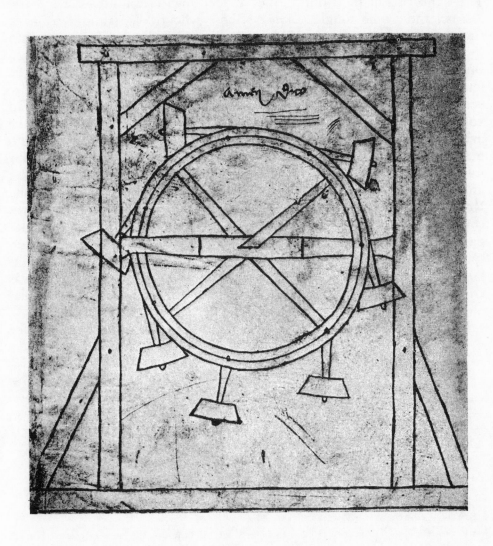

II

Feudal Society

T<small>HE</small> theorists of the Middle Ages divided men into three classes: *bella-tores*, those who fought; *oratores*, those who prayed; and *laboratores*, those who worked with their hands; and in fact in France from the ninth to the twelfth century there were three such classes living side by side on the same soil under three different laws: the nobles, living under the feudal government in right of their tenure of land; the clerics, living under ecclesiastical government and under the rule or canons to which they had voluntarily subjugated themselves; and the people, living under the arbitrary law of the lord of the domain in which they lived. The strength of feudalism lay in the fact that it recognized and established the peculiar function of each of these classes and of its individual members in the State, and thus both justified their existence and assured their livelihood. When Robert of Courçon in the time of Philip Augustus announced that reform could only come when each member of the State should be forced under pain of excommunication and of civil condemnation to work either spiritually or manually, 'so that none may eat bread not gained by his labour', instead of bringing forward a doctrine of revolution, he was emphasizing the doctrine, obscured by time, that is as much the spiritual basis of feudal society as a system of land tenure is its material basis.

The early thirteenth-century poem *Miserere* expresses the truth:

> *Labours de clerc est Dieu prïer*
> *Et justice de chevalier.*
> *Pain lor truevent li laborier.*
> *Chil paist, chil prie, et chil deffent.*
> *Au camp, a le vile, au moustier*
> *S'entreaïdent de lor mestier*
> *Chil troi par bel ordenement.*[1]

Feudal society, indeed, ultimately rests on the necessity for mutual help between men whose powers and needs are different. During the centuries

---

[1]'It is the work of a clerk to pray to God, and of a knight to do justice, the labourer gets their bread. This man labours, this prays, and that defends. In field, in town, and in church these three help one another by a beautiful dispensation.'

when there was no strong central government the poor and the weak had to seek the protection of those who could give it, and protection meant dependence. As the *Chanson de Guillaume* says, 'Gent senz seignur sunt malement bailli'.[1] So feudalism arose in some sense as a defence against the dangers of the Dark Ages, invasions by Huns, Arabs, and Northmen; internecine strife and unjust oppression. *Sidrach* tells us that if there were not authority and lordship, men would live like fishes; the strong would eat the weak and the great the little. All justice must be strong. The medieval view of the feudal pact recognized its historic basis; the *Coutume de Bayonne*, of about 1273, states:

> '*The people come before lords; it is the lesser folk, more numerous than the others, who, wishing to live in peace, create lords to restrain and defeat the strong and to maintain each man in his rights, so that each may live according to his condition, the poor with their poverty and the rich with their wealth. And to assure this in perpetuity, the populace has submitted itself to a lord, has given him what he holds, and has kept what the people hold for themselves. It is in witness of this that the lord should take the oath to his people before the people take it to their lord; and this oath taken by the people to their lord is only binding so long as the lord keeps his oath.*'

By the time of the death of Charles the Bald in 887 the State was definitely feudal,[2] but its feudalism was of a different spirit from that which was to develop round the increasing power of the French monarchy. At this early date the vassal limited his freedom by a free contract, and recognized no authority that he had not in the first instance voluntarily imposed upon himself. He still had the rights of waging war and concluding peace, that in a more developed society fall to the King alone; his 'bonne épée' was still the best guardian of his privileges, and he could be judged in law only by his equals.

The social conditions of the age forced men to live by the land and not by commerce or industry, and since this involved a 'natural' economy and the absence of a money economy,[3] this land was held by individuals conditionally on their rendering service for it. Such service fell into two classes, depending on the size of the fief and the relations of the tenant and his lord. The first, and most important, was political service; the land was held conditionally on the tenant doing government work, both military and civil. He owed *auxilium* in war, and thus supplied the army; and

[1]'Men without a lord are ill provided for.'
[2]In 853 he ordered that the old manors should be rebuilt and fortified, and that others should be erected, in order to check the invasions of Normans, Danes, and Saracens.
[3]Money became increasingly scarce from the later days of the Roman Empire. Even as early as Diocletian (300) taxes were paid in kind, as they continued to be for eight centuries more.

concilium in peace,[1] and thus supplied the deliberative assembly. Incidentally, since tenants did justice on their own holdings, feudalism supplied executive officers for the law.

The second class of service was economic; a manor was divided into small agricultural tenements held by peasants, rendering service not with the sword but with the plough, not in political service but in produce. Thus the edifice of the whole commonwealth rested upon the land, and since public duties were incidents of land tenure the constitution was part of the land laws. Gradually the feudal relationship between lord and vassal, which had at first been for life only, became hereditary, and with the right to be a lord's vassal descended the right to hold the fief from him. Such descent was generally recognized by the tenth century, and in token of it family names were lost in the territorial appellations that descended from father to son.

In this system, as in all the political theory of the Middle Ages, two elements can be distinguished: a Teutonic and a Roman. These elements had been acting one upon the other long before the Middle or even the Dark Ages. The Gallo-Roman kept his language and his property, and continued to live under the Roman law; the Frank lived under his own Salic or Ripuarian system of tribal custom. A gradual assimilation of the two elements eventually made it impossible to distinguish between the two, and a territorial law superseded the law of race. Clovis was a Teutonic king, yet he accepted the title of Consul and put the effigy of the Eastern Emperor on his coins. It is this double power welded by custom into one that made it possible for Hugh Capet, elected monarch in 987, to establish an hereditary dynasty. Similarly, both Roman and Teutonic institutions had prepared men's minds for the establishment of a feudal State. On the one hand the old Germanic levy of freemen serving the King is the precursor of his successor's bodyguard of knights; and on the other the Roman system of land tenure on the frontiers by men who owed military service for their land,[2] and were attached to the administrative service of the Empire, is a precedent for the conditions of medieval feudalism. So the Middle Ages were able to invest feudalism with the glamour of antiquity, and the *Image du Monde* of 1247 can explain that the three 'Manières de gens' were established by the philosophers at Athens, that they taught it to Rome, and Rome to France.

Caesar states[3] that 'In all Gaul there are but two classes of men who are

---

[1] By custom the vassal went three times a year to the King's court, at Christmas, Easter, and Whitsun.
[2] When Probus re-colonized the two Germanies he let the German colonists (Laeti) into Flanders in this way, and the Ripuarian Franks held the Rhineland on a similar tenure.
[3] *de Bell. Gall.* vi, 13.

of honour and account; for the common folk are reckoned as but little better than slaves, dare nothing of themselves and have no voice in council. . . . The two classes left are the nobles and the knights.' They keep their precedence in the Middle Ages; not only do they hold the land, but they also fight for it. In the early Middle Ages, indeed, it is as *bellator* pure and simple that the knight takes his place. His two virtues are courage and wisdom,

> *Rollant est proz e Oliver est sage,*

and their balance makes the 'prud'homme'. It is by his courage and wisdom that the structure of society is maintained:

> *Itel valor deit aveir chevaler*
> *Ki armes portet e en bon cheval set;*
> *En bataille deit estre forz et fiers,*
> *U altrement ne valt ·iiij· deners,*
> *Einz deit monie estre en un de ces mustiers,*
> *Se prierat tuz jurz por noz peccez.*[1]

Further, it is through battle that he has a strong link with his dependents; there they fight as one united household, and there the lord loves his men as he does his family. *Raoul de Cambrai* describes the Count of Artois' grief when he sees the men of his 'mesnie' lying dead on the field of battle: 'His household is there, dead and covered with blood; with his right hand he blesses them; over them he mourns and weeps, and the tears roll down to his girdle.' Even at Mansourah the old spirit was not dead, and Joinville tells us that Guy Mauvoisin covered himself and his men with glory, 'nor is this to be marvelled at, that he and his people should approve themselves well on that day; for it was told to me, by those who had knowledge of his affairs, that all his company, save but few, were knights of his own lineage or knights who were his liegemen.'

If Roland is the perfect *bellator* of epic, William the Marshal is of history. Fighting was the dominant interest of his life. When not engaged in war, he found occupation in fighting in tournaments;[2] at one time he tourneyed every fortnight. These tournaments were very different from the chivalric contests of the fourteenth and fifteenth centuries; there was no *courtoisie* to inspire them and no elaborate rules and conditions to regulate their risks. They were fought like battles in the open, with all the arms and weapons

---

[1]'Such valour should the knight have, who bears arms and bestrides a good horse; in battle he must be strong and brave, or else he is not worth a groat. Otherwise let him rather be a monk in a monastery and pray every day for our sins.' (*Chanson de Roland.*)
[2]Tournaments were a French invention; Matthew Paris calls them 'Conflictus Gallici'.

of war and all its manœuvres and ferocity of attack; they differed from it mainly in being voluntary, in lasting for a single day, and in doing comparatively little damage to the country in which they were waged. Even in scale they resembled real warfare; at the tournament of Lagny over three thousand knights were engaged at once. Nor were the blows given and received less hard; when William the Marshal was sought after one tourney to be acclaimed victor he was eventually found in a smithy, with his head on the anvil and the smith working with hammer and pincers to remove his battered helmet.

This purely military knighthood was modified in two directions. Firstly, the actual ceremony of bestowing knighthood was brought into the province of the Church. The ancient Germanic usage had been, as Tacitus tells us, for no man to bear arms until he had reached the age of citizenship. 'Tum, in ipso concilio, vel principum aliquis, vel pater, vel propinquus scuto frameaque juvenem ornant. Hoc apud illos toga; hoc primus juventae honos.' In early feudal days the boy was dubbed knight by the accolade; so, when in *Ogier le Danois* Charles dubs his son Louis knight,

> *Haucha le palme, ens el col li assist:*
> *'Chevaliers soies,' dist li peres, 'biaus fix,*
> *Et corageus envers tes anemis'.*[1]

By the end of the eleventh century this ceremony was greatly changed; the initiate received a ritual bath, spent a night in solitary prayer in the church, made his Confession and received Communion, heard a sermon on the duties of knighthood—to be pure, honest, and faithful; to protect the Church, widows and orphans, and all that are desolate and oppressed. Finally he received the honour of knighthood in the name of the Trinity.

The *Pontifical* of Guillaume Durand describes the ceremony. At the pontifical mass, as the last Alleluias of the Gradual die away, the bishop, laying the naked sword upon the altar, says: 'Bless this sword, that Thy servant may henceforth defend churches, widows, orphans, and all those who serve God, against the cruelty of heretics and infidels. Bless this sword Holy Lord, Almighty Father, Eternal God; Bless it in the name of the coming of Christ and by the gift of the Holy Ghost the Comforter. And may Thy servant, armed with Thy love, tread all his visible enemies underfoot, and, master of victory, rest for ever protected from all attack.' Then the bishop reads from the Old Testament: 'Blessed be the Lord

---

[1]'He raised his palm, and brought it down upon his neck. "Be a knight," said the father, "fair son, and show courage in the face of thine enemies." '

God who formeth my hands for battle and my fingers for war. He is my salvation, he is my refuge, he setteth me free.' After further prayer, the bishop puts the sword in the knight's right hand, saying, 'Take it in the name of the Father, and of the Son, and of the Holy Ghost.' Then he girds it on him as he kneels before him. The knight brandishes it three times, and sets it back in the scabbard. Then the bishop gives him the kiss of peace, and bids him 'Be a soldier peaceful, courageous, faithful, and devoted to God'. Then he blesses the knightly banner; 'and these things being done, the new knight goes in peace.' This consecration added not only to the moral force of chivalry but also to that of feudalism, for knight and vassal were almost synonymous terms, and the knight often received the accolade from the lord whose vassal he was. So strong was this force, indeed, that it modified even the virtues of feudalism. Not only did it increase that respect for the sanctity of the oath on which the fabric of society rested, but it also modified the idea of feudal duty. *Legalitas* was originally the feudatory's discharge of the legal duties of his position as defined by custom; but *legalitas*, under the influence of Christian chivalry, became *loiauté*: a fine idea of generous obligation owed by one man to another. Further, under the influence of this moral force, the feudal duty developed into the knightly *devoir*.

The second force that modified the purely military form of chivalry was the second class of duties that the vassal owed his lord: that of *concilium* in peace, and of administration of the lands held. Justice and mercy came to be added to the tale of feudal virtues; the thirteenth-century poem 'Carité' tells the lord:

> *Tu ki des lois tiens le droiture,*
> *Quant avient si gries aventure*
> *Ke damner t'estuet par besoigne*
> *Un hom por se forfaiture,*
> *Et destruire le Dieu faiture,*
> *Soiés discrés en tel essoigne*
> *Que pietés au cuer te poigne! . . .*
> *Toi le convient amer et pendre;*
> *Amer por chou qu'il est tes frere,*
> *Pendre por chou ke il est lere.*[1]

In the twelfth century a great system of ducal castles was created in Normandy; new strongholds were built on the frontiers, and those of

[1]'Do thou, who upholdest the rights of the law, when the hard hap befalls that it is thy work to condemn a man for his crime and to destroy the handiwork of God, do thou have care for thy justification that pity move thy heart! It behoves thee to love him and hang him: to love him because he is thy brother, and to hang him because he is a thief.'

Rouen, Caen, Falaise, and Argentan were enlarged. They did not remain merely a system of frontier defence, but under Henry II became the chief administrative centres of his domain. Their *châtelains* were royal officers rather than feudal vassals; the baronial system has in it the germ of a royal bureaucracy. It is they who develop the communications of their region:

> *Bons pons fist faire, chemins haus,*
> *De piere, de sablon, de caus,*

and it is they who, for certain dues, protect the traveller. Thus with a more developed society the fighting knight gradually became the administrator; and the rough-and-tumble of the *mêlée* was superseded by the political and tactical strategy involved in the taking of an enemy's stronghold without loss of control over the assailant's own castle and domain. The King in this respect is the archetype of baron; the *Livre des Manières*, written by Étienne de Fougères in 1178, shows him:

> *Ça et la veit, sovent se torne,*
> *Ne repose ne ne sejorne.*
> *Chasteaus abat, chasteaus aorne,*
> *Sovent haitié, plus sovent morne.*
> *Ça et la veit, pas ne repose*
> *Que sa marche ne seit desclose.*[1]

The same author again shows what importance was attributed to the judicial functions of the lord when he upbraids Henry II (Plantagenet) for spending too much time in hunting. Such a pursuit, he says, is not worthy of one who has been anointed with the holy oil. It is better to be at all times at the disposition of those who need justice, and to be ready to punish those who seek after war or discord.

The castle, then, is the crystallization of developed feudalism. It emphasizes the fact that the suzerainty of the lord is a local fact, based on the possession of land; it is the symbol of his force, which if it sometimes serves as a weapon of oppression yet also serves as a weapon of defence for the neighbouring villages. Its great hall, where lord and vassal, servant and peasant, dine together according to their degree, is an expression of the fact that they form a community within the State bound together by mutual obligations. Moreover, practically every man belonged to such a

---

[1]'He goes here and there, often turning his path, neither resting nor staying in one place. He destroys castles and he adorns them, and is often merry and more often sad. He goes here and there, and rests not that his line of march may not be revealed.'

community; the story of *Les Quatre Fils Aymon* tells that from Senlis to
Orleans, from Orleans to Paris, and from Laon to Rheims, in fact in the
real core of France:

> *N'i trovissiés nul homme qui de mere fust nés*
> *Qui ne soit en chastel ou en tor enserés.*[1]

The development of feudalism is reflected in the development of the castle.
In the tenth century it is a wooden tower[2] with a moat; a fortified farm, in
which the lord's family leads a life like that described by Lambert
d'Ardres, where the first son of the lord is a fighter, the second a hunter,
the third a farmer, and the fourth a stock-raiser. In the next century wood
gives place to stone, and the house becomes the fortified donjon. Jean de
Colmieu, Archdeacon of Thérouanne, who died in 1130, describes such a
castle:

'*They throw up a little hill of earth as high as they can; they surround it by a
fosse of considerable width and awful depth. On the inside edge of the fosse they set a
palisade of squared logs of wood, closely bound together, which is as strong as a wall.
If it is possible they strengthen this palisade by towers built at various points. On the
top of the little hill they build a house, or rather a citadel, whence a man can see on
all sides. No one can reach its door except by a bridge, which, thrown across the fosse
and resting on coupled pillars, starts from the lowest part of the fosse and gradually
rises until it reaches the top of the little hill and the door of the house, from which the
master can control the whole of it.*'

In the twelfth century the donjon is retained for purely defensive purposes (as at Coucy), and within the same fortified enclosure a second
building—the *palais*—becomes the home of the lord and his family. Later
in the century there is often a second enclosure, which affords shelter for
the lord's lesser dependents and for the 'retrahants' who seek a refuge at
the castle in time of danger. Even a fortress that was not the home of its
lord offered a similar plan; Guillaume le Breton describes Cœur-de-Lion's
Château Gaillard: 'He had the summit of the hill made round and walled
with strong fortifications; he cleared it of stones, and then, having flat-
tened the interior of the enclosure, he caused a number of small habitations to be built there, to hold many people, and only kept the centre for
the construction of the donjon.'

The creation of the *palais* shows more clearly than anything else how
the late twelfth and the thirteenth centuries were years in which men were

---

[1]'You will find no man born of a woman who is not shut up in a castle or a tower.'
[2]The first dateable stone donjon is that of Langeais, built by Foulques Nerra, Count of Anjou, in 992.

not entirely absorbed in the struggle to obtain a working scheme of life, but had time to seek grace as well as strength. In and for its hall were created not only courtesy and the refinements of honour, but also much that is of material beauty—wall-painting, tapestry, and the decorative arts of everyday life:

> *And beauty making beautiful old rhyme*
> *In praise of ladies dead and lovely knights.*

This medieval feeling for the graces of life appeared first in France; Brunetto Latino tells us in his *Livre dou Trésor* of 1265:

> '*Les Ytaliens, qui souvent guerroyent entre eux, se délitent à faire hautes tours et maisons de pierres; et, si c'est hors de ville, ils font fossés et palis, et murs, et tourelles, et ponts, et portes coulisses, et sont garnis de mangoniaux et de saiettes, et de toutes choses qui appartienent à la guerre. . . . Mais les français font maisons grandes et planières, et paintes, et chambres lées, pour avoir joie et délit sans noise et sans guerre. Et pour ce savent mieux faire préaux et vergers et pommiers autour de leur habitacle que autre gent.*'[1]

This new spirit made as great a modification in thirteenth-century chivalry as religion had made in the military knighthood of the early Middle Ages. The boy of noble birth comes to the castle to serve as a page; the *Ordene de Chevalerie* tells us that it befits him to serve before others serve him, for otherwise he will not understand the nobility of lordship. So, in the romance, Galeran goes to the Court of Lorraine and 'serves' there as squire, at table, in the chase, in the tourney, for two years. Then the time comes for him and his companions to be dubbed knights, and there is a great feast. Galeran puts on hauberk, shoes, and helmet; a cloak of blue samite, embroidered like his banner with his double eagle before and behind. The Duke does him the honour of putting on his right spur, and gives him a splendid Eastern sword, 'claire et lettrée, à pommeau d'or'. Then he asks a knight who is present 'lui faire honneur de l'épée', and the knight girds him with the sword, and then with his right hand gives him

> *La collée qui signifie*
> *L'Ordre de chevalerie;*
> *Et si li a dit au donner:*

---

[1]'The Italians, who often make war among themselves, delight in making high towers and houses of stone; and if they are outside the city, they make fosses and palisades and walls, turrets and bridges and portcullises, and furnish them with mangonels and arrows and all things that belong to war. . . . But the French build houses that are large and open and painted, with spacious rooms, to have joy and delight without injury and war. Wherefore they know better than other folk how to plant gardens and orchards and apple trees round their habitations.'

'*Chevalier, Dieux te puit tourner*
A si grand honneur en la somme
Qu'il face de ton corps proudomme
En penser, en dit et en fait.'[1]

Then the Duchess hangs the shield with the golden eagle round his neck
and all the company go to mass, which the newly dubbed knights hear in
helmet and armour. Together they receive the sacrament, and then,
taking off their armour and donning robes of silk, 'qui sont faites en la
terre aux Maures', sit down to feast. The next day they tourney for the
first time. Afterwards Galeran goes with a train of thirty white packhorses and ten Spanish chargers to Metz. The streets, strewn with herbs,
are full of knights on horseback, of squires carrying presents to ladies, of
young men airing their hawks. Coloured banners and shields hang out of
the windows, and the walls are gay with festival draperies. The market is
full: venison, game, fish in the cool corner, wax, pepper, and spice are
being sold. The shouting money-changers, with their wares of jewels and
plate; the wandering mountebanks, with their lions and leopards and
bears, the fiddlers and singers, and over all the church bells ringing
through the town, fill the air with gay and cheerful sounds, and give the
new knights spirit for the morrow's jousting.

But if we have to turn to the romances for the life of youth, more sober
sources describe the life of the *châtelain* who has settled down. The *Quatre
Ages de l'homme* advises him how he is to spend the day. He is to begin with
a triple sign of the Cross and prayer; then, before getting up, he is to think
of what is to be done in the course of the day for himself, for others, or for
'un commun profit de païs', and to repeat it to himself three times that he
may not forget. Then he is to hear mass; to give alms, if only a little; to
dress very carefully, and to see that his nails are clean; and then to proceed with his business diligently. At midday it should be finished, so that
he may eat and drink in peace. The sort of meal he had we may guess from
Fra Salimbene's account of St. Louis' dinner on a *maigre* day in 1248:
first, crayfish, then bread and wine, then new beans cooked in milk; fish
and crabs, eel pies; rice with milk of almonds and powdered cinnamon;
stewed eels with an excellent sauce; tarts and junkets; and finally, fruit.
Then, having eaten, he is to rest an hour, and afterwards is the time to
amuse himself, 'por avoir remède et repos in son cuer'. The *Roman de
Joufroi* describes Madame Agnès de Tonnerre, shut up in a tower by a

---

[1]'The accolade which signifies the order of knighthood; and as he gives it he says, "Knight, may God so
dispose you to high honour in all things that He may make you a *prud'homme* in thought, in word, and in
deed".'

jealous husband, consoling herself by looking from her window into the
square below. There, under the shade of a splendid pear tree,

> joent li chevalier
> As dez et autres jous divers.
> Enqui est tot an li josters
> Et les dances et les caroeles.
> Enqui vienent et fous et foles
> Et menestreil et jugleor.[1]

There the story-tellers tell of Priam and Pyramus; of fair Helen, of
Ulysses, Hector, Achilles, Aeneas and weeping Dido; of Lavinia, Tydeus
and Eteocles, Alexander, Cadmus, Jason, Narcissus, Pluto and Orpheus,
Hero and Leander, Daedalus and Icarus, Goliath and David, Samson and
Delilah; of Julius Caesar, who was so brave that he crossed the sea without invoking the name of Christ; of the Round Table and of Charlemagne;
of the squire of Nanteuil and of Olivier de Verdun.[2] One plays the 'lai de
chèvrefeuille', another the song of Tintagel; one plays the harp, another
the lute; one the flute, another the fife; one makes his marionettes dance,
another juggles with knives.

The development of château life had no less effect on women, since their
lives were bound up with those of the fighting nobles. In the early days of
chivalry their life was almost incredibly hard; they lived exposed to every
discomfort and danger. They shared in the victories and defeats of their
lords and masters, and helped them with advice. In the *Chanson de
Guillaume* the hero comes back, beaten and despairing, to his wife:

> 'Or m'en fuirai en estrange regné
> A saint Michiel al Peril de la mer
> U a Saint Piere, le bon apostre Deu,
> U en un guast ou ne soie trovez:
> La devendrai hermites ordenez
> Et tu nonein, si fait tun chief veler.
> 'Sire', dist ele, 'Ço ferum nus assez,
> Quant nos avrom nostre siecle mené.'[3]

But gradually, as life grew more settled and more civilized, the castle

---

[1]'The knights play at dice and other games. There, all the year round, is jousting and dancing and carolling.
There come fools and jesters and minstrels and jongleurs.'
[2]The list is taken from *Flamenca* (1234).
[3]'So will I flee into a strange land, to St. Michael by the peril of the sea, or to St. Peter the good apostle
of God, or to some desert where I shall not be found: there will I become an ordained hermit, and thou
shalt be a nun and shalt veil thy head.' 'Sire,' said she, 'we shall do those things soon enough when we
have finished our life in the world.'

became the woman's sphere. Over their wheels and frames they sang the
Chansons de Toile, with the rhythm of the clashing loom:

> *Bele Yolanz en chambre coie*
> *Sur ses genouz pailes desploie,*
> *Cost un fil d'or, l'autre de soie.*
> *Sa male mere la chastoie*
> > *'Chastoi vos en*
> > *Bele Yolanz . . .'*
>
> *'Mere de coi me chastoiez?*
> *Est ceu de coudre ou de taillier*
> *Ou de filer ou de broissier?*
> *Ou se c'est de trop sommillier?'* —
> > *'Chastoi vos en*
> > *Bele Yolanz.*
>
> *Ne de coudre, ne de taillier,*
> *Ne de filer, ne de broissier*
> *Ne ce n'est de trop sommillier . . .*
> *Mais trop parlez au chevalier.*
> > *Chastoi vos en*
> > *Bele Yolanz.'*

By the thirteenth century the *Chansons de Toile* had fallen out of use, and
the life of the *jeune fille comme il faut* could be thus described in *Galeran*:

> *Que je ne face aultre mestier*
> *Le jour fors lire mon saultier*
> *Et faire œuvre d'or ou de soie,*
> *Oïr de Thebes ou de Troye*
> *Et en ma herpe lays noter*
> *Et aux echez autruy mater*
> *Ou mon oisel sur mon poign mestre.*
> *Souvent ouy dire a mon maistre*
> *Que tel us vient de gentilesse.*[1]

The women of the house helped to receive and entertain distinguished
guests. The romance of *Guillaume de Dôle*, written about 1200, describes the

---

[1] 'I should do no other work in the day but read my psalter, work in gold or silk, hear the story of Thebes
or Troy, play tunes on my harp, checkmate some one at chess, or feed the hawk on my wrist. I have often
heard my master say that such a way of life was gentle.'

Emperor's messenger paying a polite visit after dinner to Guillaume's mother. She tells him:

> *'Biaus filz, ce fu ça en arriers*
> *Que les dames et les roïnes*
> *Soloient fere lor cortines,*
> *Et chanter les chançons d'istoire.'*
> *'Ha! ma très douce dame, voire,*
> *Dites nous en, se vos volez . . .'*
> *Quant ele ot sa chanson chantée,*
> *'Certes, mout s'est bien aquitée',*
> *Fet cil, 'madame votre mere.'*[1]

Already a century earlier Guibert de Nogent had been lamenting the advent of new manners:

> *'Alas, how miserably . . . maidenly modesty and honour have fallen off, and the mothers' guardianship hath decayed both in appearance and in fact, so that in all their behaviour nothing can be noted but unseemly mirth, wherein are no sounds but of jest, with winking eyes, and babbling tongues, and wanton gait, and most ridiculous manners. The quality of their garments is so unlike to that frugality of the past that in the widening of their sleeves, the tightening of their bodices, their shoes of cordovan morocco with twisted beaks—nay, in their whole person, we may see how shame is cast aside. Each thinketh to have touched the lowest step of misery if she lack the regard of lovers and measureth her glory of nobility or courtliness by the ampler number of such suitors. . . . Thus and in such-like ways is our modern age corrupted.'*

His laments are echoed with equal force and futility by Bernard, but occasionally the Church took a more practical view. Etienne de Bourbon tells us that he knew a holy man who had the gift of working miracles, who lived in the monastery of Saint Antoine at Paris. One day some ladies came to him to ask him to pray for a lady of the Countess of Montfort's household who suffered from dreadful headaches. He consented, but asked to see her. When she came, he said, 'Promise me first, madam, to take off those vain adornments, all that proud scaffolding which surmounts your head, and then I will pray Our Lord for you in full confidence.' The lady refused; the sacrifice was too great. But her headaches grew worse and worse, until she resigned herself and laid before the servant of God her false hair, her golden circlet, and all the rest, promising that she would

---

[1]'Fair son, it was in past times that ladies and queens used to make their hangings and sing songs spinning.' 'Indeed, sweet lady, sing us some, if you will.' When she had sung her song, 'In truth your lady mother has acquitted herself well,' said he.

CHARLES VI, SALMON, AND PRINCES. *Miniature by the Boucicaut Master, 1412. Geneva, Bibl. publique et universitaire, ms. fr. 165, fol. 4.*

never wear anything of the kind again. The holy man at once began to pray; but the miracle had already been effected, and the pain was gone.

The preachers must not be allowed to make us forget the part played by the feudal noblewoman in medieval history; and, indeed, the preachers who hurl the most violent diatribes against women in general are loudest in praise of the saintliness of their own mothers. In all the historic dramas of the Middle Ages women play leading and often noble parts:

> *Où est la tres sage Helloïs*
> *Pour qui fut chastré et puis moyne*
> *Pierre Esbaillart à Saint Denis?*
> *Pour son amour ot cest essoyne.*
> *Semblablement, où est la royne*
> *Qui commanda que Buridan*
> *Fust gecté en ung sac en Saine?*
> *Mais où sont les neiges d'antan!*
>
> *La royne Blanche comme lis,*
> *Qui chantoit à voix de seraine;*
> *Berte au grant pié, Bietris, Allis;*
> *Haremburgis qui tint le Maine,*
> *Et Jehanne, la bonne Lorraine,*
> *Qu'Englois brulerent à Rouan;*
> *Où sont elles, Vierge souvraine?*
> *Mais où sont les neiges d'antan!*

The *oratores*, those whose life is devoted to prayer, may seem at first to be outside the sphere of feudalism. But the Church grew up sufficiently under the shadow of the Roman Empire for its organization to rest upon a land basis; the lords of the ecclesiastical provinces—in other words the bishops—stood side by side, feudally speaking, with the seigneurs of the King. The 'Twelve Peers of France' at the coronation of Philip Augustus were six laymen: the Dukes of Normandy, Burgundy, and Guienne, and the Counts of Champagne, Flanders, and Toulouse; and six ecclesiastics: the Archbishop of Rheims, and the Bishops of Laon, Noyon, Châlons, Beauvais, and Langres. Even the theory of the organization of the Church became influenced by feudalism, and we find the bishop holding certain offices to be 'fiefs incorporeal' and demanding liege-homage from his dean, chancellor, precentor, and other officers. So Bishop Robert of Coutances, who died in 1048, gave the prebends of his cathedral to his relations and made them do homage for them. Moreover, in much disturbed times there was a tendency for royal lands to be added, as it were for safe custody, to the bishop's domain, which generally lay compactly, in comparative security round his cathedral city. Therefore he held land not only as bishop, exercising ecclesiastical rights, but also as lord, exercising seigneurial rights. The Bishop of Le Puy, as Count of Velay, holds on his seal not only the pastoral crozier, but also the naked sword of secular jurisdiction; the Chapter of Roye in Picardy has on its seal an armed and mounted knight. Up to 1788 the Count-Bishop of Cahors had the right, when he said mass in state, to have upon the altar his helmet, cuirass, and sword.

The Church, indeed, took its place in the feudal system, and though its functions were extra-feudal, its activities were sometimes those of feudalism. Turpin, the fighting archbishop of the *Chanson de Roland*, is the type of many:

> *Par le camp vait Turpin, li arcesvesque,*
> *Tel coronet ne chantat unches messe*
> *Ki de sun cors feïst tantes' proecces.*
> *Dist al paien: 'Deus tut mal te tramette*
> *Tel as ocis dunt al coer me regrette.'*
> *Sun bon ceval i ad fait esdemetre*
> *Si l'ad ferut sur l'escut de Tulette*
> *Qui mort l'abat desur l'herbe verte.*[1]

Hugh de Noyers, Bishop of Auxerre in the late twelfth century, took up arms against the nobles and resisted even the King. His palace was 'surrounded by wide fosses, to which water is brought from afar at great expense, bounded by huge palisades, dominated by a donjon with ramparts and turrets and a drawbridge.' When Richard Cœur-de-Lion was asked by one of the papal legates to free Philippe de Dreux, Bishop of Beauvais, whom he held prisoner, he indignantly replied that Philip had not been captured as a bishop but as a knight in full armour, a knight, moreover, who was 'a robber, tyrant, and incendiary, who did nothing but devastate Richard's lands day and night'. So in 1356 the Bishops of Châlons, Sens, and Melun cover themselves with glory at Poitiers, and the Archbishop of Sens dies sword in hand on the field of Agincourt. It is because they formed part of feudal society, because they shouldered their

---

[1]'Over the field went Turpin the archbishop. Never did a clerk sing mass who in his own person had done such gallant deeds. He said to the infidel: "God send you all ill. You have killed one whom my heart mourns." He drives his good horse foward and strikes the infidel on his shield of Toledo with such a blow that he lays him dead on the green grass.'

share of feudal duties and responsibilities, that the bishops of France were able to christianize feudalism.

There remain the people: *laboratores*, men who worked with their hands. We have seen how far the feudal obligations of the lord to the King affected his life, and we shall find the obligations of the villein to his lord moulding his life even more straitly. The serf was not even free in person, and his dues were arbitrary and fixed by his master. The relation between serf and master is indeed in a sense unfeudal, since it rests upon no contract; its origin is to be sought in the Roman institution of slavery. So even the serf's children were not his own, as is shown by many deeds for the division of families of servile birth.

'We, the monks of Marmoutier and Gautier Renaud, held in common men and women serfs, who were to be divided between us. Therefore, in the year of the Incarnation of Our Lord 1087, on the sixth day of June, in the time of Abbot Bernard, we proceeded to the division of the male and female children of several families. We have received for our share, among the children of Renaud de Villana, a boy, Barthélemi, and three girls, Hersende, Milesende, and Letgarde; and among the children of Guascelin, a girl, Aremburge, and a boy, Gautier. There was excepted from the division one very young girl-child, who remained in her cradle. If she lives, she is to be our common property until the conclusion of an agreement that shall assign her to one or other lordship.'

Even in the time of Robert the Pious, Adalberon of Laon was preaching: 'This unhappy class owns nothing which is not bought by hard toil. Who can estimate, in counting on the beads of an abacus, the sorrows, the toil, the weariness which the poor serfs have to endure?' Sometimes the lord took the view that they came of a class from which nothing could be expected. Robert of Blois, like many another thirteenth-century moralist, warns the knight to have no confidence in his serfs: 'Serf sont por que servir doivent', and they have no sense of fidelity:

> *A lor gré voudroient chascun jor*
> *Tel genz avoir noveaul siegnor,*
> *Qu'il ne sevent de cuer amer.*[1]

This point of view led to the diminution of serfdom by enfranchisement, whether individual, collective, or regional;[2] the lord gained considerable sums of money from those he freed, and the better feeling and more

---

[1] 'Such men would like each day to have a new lord, for they know not how to love sincerely.'
[2] Philip Augustus freed those of Chambly, Beaumont-sur-Oise, Orleans, and other fiefs; St. Louis many more. His brother the Count of Poitiers freed all upon his domain. Many more were freed by the great abbeys, Saint Germain and the rest.

defined relation of the villein made for better administration on his estate. By the end of the Middle Ages serfdom was dead. The free villein was free in person, but was bound—*adscriptus*—to cultivate a particular piece of land belonging to some one else, and owed fixed dues and service at fixed seasons. The *Conte des Vilains de Verson* gives an account of such service.

'*In June the peasants must cut and pile the hay and carry it to the manor house. In August they must reap and carry in the convent's grain; their own grain lies exposed to wind and rain while they hunt out the assessor of the harvest dues and carry his share to the barn. On the Nativity of the Virgin the villein owes the pork-due, one pig in eight; at St. Denis's day the manorial dues; at Christmas the fowl, fine and good, and thereafter the grain-due of two measures of barley and three quarters of wheat; on Palm Sunday the sheep-due; at Easter he must plough, sow, and harrow. When there is building the tenant must bring stone and serve the masons; he must also haul the convent's wood for two deniers a day. If he sell his land, he owes the lord a thirteenth of its value: if he marries his daughter outside the seigniory, he pays a fine. He must grind his corn at the seigneurial mill and bake his bread at the seigneurial oven, where the customary charges do not satisfy the attendants, who grumble and threaten to leave his bread unbaked.*'

Garin le Lorrain describes the typical villein, Rigaut[1]: with enormous arms and massive limbs, his eyes separated from each other by a hand's breadth, his shoulders large, his chest deep, his hair bristling, and his face black as coal. He goes for six months without washing, and no water but rain ever touches his face. The sculptured and illuminated calendars show the brighter side of his life. January is a month of rest and feast days; he drinks in peace. February is a dull month; he sits by the fire at home to dry himself after his work. In March he tends the vines. April is for him, as for the noble, the best month in the year, and the villein sees the corn sprout and prunes the vines. In May, while the gentleman walks, and hunts and hawks, the villein rests in the shade. In June he is busy with the hay-making, in July and August with the harvest, and in September with the vintage. In October the wine is made and the sowing is done; in November he takes the pigs to gather acorns in the forest and gets in his own store of wood for the winter; and then at Christmas there is once more feasting. The villeins live in a *villete* or hamlet of scattered *mesnils* or cottages, such as is described in *Galeran*: each house alone in its little field, shut in with an old thorn hedge and a ditch bridged by a plank. The *manse* or cottage has three separate buildings; one for grain, one for fodder, and

---

[1] A similar description is to be found in *Aucassin et Nicolette*.

one for the family. There a fire of peat and faggots crackles in an immense chimney. There is a pothook for the kettle, a trivet, a shovel, and heavy fire-dogs; a saucepan and a ladle, by the side an oven, and next to it a huge bed that can shelter all the family at once. On the other side are a cupboard, a table, a bench, a cheese-press, a crock and some baskets. Besides such furniture the villein owns a mortar, a ladder, fishing tackle, hedging gloves, a plough, a billhook, spade, knife, shears and harrow, and a little cart. He has a small garden with a dog for watchman, and at least one cow.[1] The thirteenth-century *Dit des vingt-trois manières de vilains* describes types that we all know. Some say to the wayfarer who asks his way 'You know it better than I do'; some sit at their cottage doors on Sunday to mock at passers-by, and some are against everybody—God, the saints, the Church, and the gentry. There is the poacher; the man who is always bringing his case before the bailiff, saying that his grandfather had rights of pasturage over such and such fields; the miser, and the wastrel.

The villeins were by no means crushed by knightly oppression. In 987 those of Normandy rose against their lords to demand rights of chase, of fishery, and of administration of their own affairs, legal and judicial; and this was the first of many such revolts. The *Roman de Rou* describes

> *Li paisan et li vilain,*
> *Cil del boscage et cil del plain*

saying of their lords

> *Nus somes homes cum il sunt,*
> *Tex membres avum cum ils unt;*
> *Et altresi grans cors avum;*
> *Et altretant sofrir povum.*[2]

The *Besant de Dieu*, written about 1230, describes the sins of clerk and noble, but does not consider the peasant blameless:

> *Car il ne prenent mie a gré*
> *Lor sofreite e lor povreté*
> *Et sont felons et envios*
> *Et mesdisant et orguillos*
> *Et plains d'envie et de luxure.*

---

[1]The description is taken from the thirteenth-century *fabliau* '*Del' Houstillement au vilain*'. The resemblance between the villein's *manse* and a cottage in the remoter parts of modern Finland is striking.

[2]'The peasant and the villein from the woods and the plain [say] "We are men as they are, with limbs like theirs, and bodies as tall; and can suffer as they do".'

[Tosjors] li est avis por veir
Que se il puet del riche aveir,
Coment que seit, n'est pas pecché.[1]

None the less, many men held a high ideal of what the relations between lord and man should be. Etienne de Fougères in 1178 said:

Grainour fei deit sire a son home
Que non a seignor et a dome;
Molt devon chiers aveir nos homes,
Quar li vilein portent les somes
Dont nos vivon, quant que nos summes,
Et chevaliers et cleres et domes'.[2]

Though he admits that the poor peasant grumbles too much against God and man, and cheats the Church and his lord of their dues when it is possible, he pities his lot:

Terres arer, norrir aumaille,
Sor le vilain est la bataile.
Quar chevalier et clerc sanz faille
Vivent de ce que il travaille.[3]

In the time of Philip Augustus Jacques de Vitry preached:

'*All the peasant amasses in a year by stubborn work, the knight, the noble, devours in an hour. Not content with his pay as soldier, not content with his revenues and with the annual tax levied upon his subjects, he furthers despoils them by illicit taxes and heavy exactions. The poor are exhausted, the fruit of their years of pain and sorrow is extorted from them. . . . The great must make themselves loved by the small. They must be careful not to inspire hate. The humble must not be scorned: if they can aid us, they can also do us harm. You know that many serfs have killed their masters or have burnt their houses.*'

But the great movements in which both lord and peasant played their parts side by side helped to heal the breach between them, and we find the Lord of Borlaymont saying to Joinville: 'You are going oversea; now take heed how you come back; for no knight, be he poor or be he rich, can

---

[1]'For they do not take cheerfully their need and poverty, and are dishonest and envious, and backbiting, and proud and full of envy and vice. Indeed, he [the peasant] thinks that if he can get anything from the rich man, by whatever means, it is no sin.'
[2]'A lord owes greater loyalty to a tenant than to a lord or a lady; very dear should we hold our men, for the villeins bear the burdens by which we live whether we be knights, clerks, or ladies.'
[3]'To plough the fields and feed the beasts is the struggle for the peasant, for the knight and the priest live on his work.'

come back without dishonour if he leaves in the hands of the Saracens the meaner folk of Our Lord, in whose company he went forth.'

The feudal order was established to meet a national need; like knighthood, it became ennobled by the feudal virtues, 'souffrance, service, valeur, honneur'; and like all social systems it had its good and bad points. Its chief source of weakness was that while definite relations were assured vertically between lord and vassal, and between vassals and their dependents, the horizontal relations *inter pares* were not regulated at all. As a consequence twelfth-century France was divided into provinces, of which the inhabitants formed so many small nations living in a state of mutual hatred; these provinces were divided into a multitude of seigneuries and fiefs, whose owners lived in a perpetual state of private war, and further rivalries were prolonged between city and city, village and village, valley and valley, until war seemed to spring spontaneously from the soil itself. It was in an attempt to mitigate this evil that the Church for the first time played an important part in the feudal world. It did not attempt the impossible task of bringing war to an end, but strove to impose on feudalism the Augustinian view, 'Pacem habere debet voluntas, bellum necessitas'. The Archbishop of Bordeaux in 969 at the Council of Charroux initiated the *Pax Dei* by anathematizing all those who in the course of a private war broke into churches, stole goods from the poor, or struck a clerk. The movement came from the Church, and first concerned those who served her or were her dependents. But in the next year the ordinance was repeated, and infringed on the temporal sphere, for merchants and their goods were included under its protection. Gradually it grew into a *pactum pacis*, a league not of nations but of seigneurs, bound together to keep its rules. The oath administered at Beauvais in 1023 is typical:

'*I will not invade in any way churches, or the crypts of churches, unless it be to seize malefactors who have broken the peace or committed homicide; I will not assault clerks or monks not bearing secular arms. I will carry off neither ox, nor cow, nor any other beast of burden. I will do nothing to cause men to lose their possessions on account of their lord's war, and I will not beat them to make them give up their property. From the first day of May until All Saints' Day I will seize neither horse, nor mare, nor foal from the pastures. I will neither destroy nor burn houses, nor root up nor cut down the vines under pretext of war.*'

The great development of the *pactum pacis* was in Berri; by 1038 every man at the age of fifteen, whether clerk or layman, was sworn into the diocesan forces for keeping the peace. For the first time the whole population of a district was enrolled as a *garde nationale*. A fresh development was the *Truga Dei*, or Truce of God, which ordained a close time in which private war might not be waged. At the Council of Elne in 1027 this truce was proclaimed from the ninth hour of Saturday to the first of Monday, to leave Sunday free. By 1041 it was extended from Wednesday night to Monday morning: Thursday, the Council of Nice declared, was sacred as the day of the Ascension; Friday as that of the Passion; Saturday as that of the Adoration at the Tomb; and Sunday as the day of the Resurrection. In the same year private war was interdicted from Advent to Epiphany and from Septuagesima till Easter. Thirteen years later this was extended to Pentecost, and the feasts of the Virgin, St. John Baptist, St. Peter in Vinculis, St. Lawrence, St. Michael, St. Martin, and the Ember days were also included. Further, a new sanction for its keeping was devised in addition to excommunication. When once a *forma pacis* had been legislated by a Council, *Judices pacis*, Justices of the Peace, were appointed to decide when it had been broken. Thus the Church appointed a new legislature, judicature, and executive to do the work which the temporal power was as yet too weak to undertake.

> *Gaudet lancea falx, gaudet spatha*
> *Devenire vomer :*
> *Pax ditat imos, pauperat superbos.*
> *Salve, summe Pater, fer et omnibus*
> *Integram salutem,*
> *Quicumque pacis diligunt quietum.*[1]

[1]'The lance is happy to become a scythe, the sword to be a ploughshare. Peace enriches the poor, impoverishes the proud. Hail, Almighty Father, give thy perfect well-being to all men who long for the rest of peace.' (Fulbert of Rheims, d. 1029.)

WOMAN SHEARING A SHEEP
Detail of a tapestry, about 1500. Paris, Louvre

III

Town Life

THE second half of the eleventh century witnessed a general revolution in Europe as widespread and as far reaching as that which began five generations ago with the French Revolution. In things spiritual the Gregorian movement sought to make the clergy dependent on the Papacy and independent of the local state, substituting for a territorial and proprietary Church one that should be universal and free; in things intellectual Anselm and Berengar of Tours, each the head of a flourishing school, were precursors of later scholastic thought; the Crusades enlarged the horizon of feudalism; and in temporal things the establishment of the Latin kingdom of Jerusalem and of the Norman kingdoms of England and Sicily led to a great awakening of communication and trade. All these combined to stimulate the growth of towns; the Gregorian movement helped to weaken the hold of bishops of the old type over the cities of their diocese; the growth of men's intellectual interests added scholars and students to the urban population; the Crusading Truce of God with its protection of merchants and its associations for keeping the peace improved economic conditions; and the Crusades themselves, and the Norman Conquest, opened up new routes; Western Europe began to communicate through its length and breadth along great highways of trade. It is along the line of these great trade routes that the towns develop; in Northern France, south of a line from Cologne to Bruges, and along the line of the Rhine into Northern Italy, from Cologne to Venice. The chief centres of development in France are the Oise, Aisne and Somme. The age was one of danger and instability; even the balance between production and population was precarious, and forty-eight years of the eleventh century were years of famine. Because of this there was movement; whatever the law, starvation will drive labourers to seek new fields of toil, artisans to found new centres of industry; troubled times when justice is rare will compel men from all parts to seek it where it can be found, whether in the cathedral city, the lord's castle, or the King's court.

Pilgrimage brought yet other cohorts upon the road, and helped to make the Church the protector of travellers against feudal oppression.

How necessary was such protection in the eleventh century is shown by such documents as this:

'I, Landru the Fat, seduced and tempted by the greed that often creeps into the hearts of worldly men, admit that I have stopped the merchants of Langres who passed through my domain. I took their merchandise from them and kept it until the day when the Bishop of Langres and the Abbot of Cluny came to me to demand reparation. I had kept for myself a part of what I had taken and restored the rest. The merchants to obtain this remainder, and to be able in the future to cross my land without fear, consented to pay me a certain sum for tribute. This first sin suggested to me the idea of a second, and I undertook to impose and to cause to be imposed by my officers, an exaction called a toll on all those who crossed my territory for business or for pilgrimage. The monks of Cluny, knowing that my predecessors had never levied a tax of this kind, complained strongly and asked me, through my brother Bernard, Chamberlain of their abbey, to give up this unjust exaction, hateful in the eyes of God. To buy it off and assure safety to travellers, they have given me the sum of three hundred sous.'

By the end of the twelfth century the town enters literature. The *Philippide* of Guillaume le Breton describes Ghent, proud of its turreted houses, of its treasures and its large population; Ypres, famous for its wool dyeing; Arras, an ancient city filled with riches and eager for prosperity; Lille with its wealthy merchants and the brilliant textiles it exports to foreign lands; Angers with its vineyards, Tours with its grain, and Nantes, carrying on a trade in salmon and lampreys with distant countries. Towns even invade the feudal *Chansons de geste*; in *Aubri le Bourguignon* are descriptions of Arras, Courtrai, and Lille, in *Aiol* of Poitiers and Orléans.

The eleventh century was an age of lordship and vassalage; the twelfth of brotherhood and equality. In every rank men lived in close and corporate association with their compeers; in the Church, in the Orders of monks and canons; in the battlefield, in the Orders of Templars and Hospitallers; in centres of learning, in the new guilds of masters; in town and village, in political and religious confraternities; and in street and workshop, in guilds of craftsmen and traders.

In the eleventh century a man had his proper place in a society that was feudal, ecclesiastical, or agricultural. But while the feudal structure regulated the relation between men and their lords, it left the relation between man and man undefined and unsanctified by an oath. Yet men were bound together on an equal footing by their very sufferings at the hands of their lord and their sense of comradeship was soon expressed in formal brotherhood. The Church, before whom all men were equal, by the institution of the *pactum pacis* enlisted men into a quasi-religious confraternity with the political aim of restraining the feudal abuse of war, and other such societies of men sworn together against feudal excesses soon came into being. Indeed such were the needs of the time that any confraternity of men sworn to give mutual aid was apt to become hostile to the feudal order. In 1182, for instance, the Virgin of Le Puy appeared to a carpenter of that town,[1] bearing the Child and a scroll with the legend 'Agnus Dei, qui tollis peccata mundi, dona nobis pacem'. She bade him go to the bishop and ask him to found a confraternity of all those who wished to keep the peace. The brotherhood was founded, each member wearing on his hood or capuchon the leaden pilgrim's sign of the Virgin of Le Puy. But this devout brotherhood of peace-lovers sought peace actively by exterminating the brigands of the Auvergne, Berri, Aquitaine, and Gascony. Then, when the brigands had been dealt with, they turned against the nobles who oppressed the countryside. The chronicler of Laon, who had at first been much impressed by their piety and usefulness, by 1184 has changed his note. The nobles, he tells us, trembled on every side; they no longer dared levy from their men any but the legal dues. 'This mad and undisciplined body had reached the crowning point of its insanity. Its members dared to inform the counts, viscounts, and princes that they must treat all those subject to them with greater kindness, under pain of feeling the effects of their anger.' But feudalism was too strong for the Capuchonnés, and suppressed them as they had suppressed the brigands.

None the less other confraternities were instituted, all avowedly religious in intention, and many working for political ends. For the most part they have left no written documents and have passed out of history;[2] but the traces of their work are clear enough to indicate their importance in securing collective rights. The merchant confraternity of the Assumption, for instance, founded about 1110, created the commune of Mantes; the brotherhood of the Holy Spirit acted as the governing body of the city of Marseilles, and similar corporations ruled Avignon, Arles, Digne, and many other cities of the south before they were formally enfranchised. At Poitiers in the time of St. Louis the 'confrérie de Saint Hilaire' included the hundred men who formed the corporation; it was in fact the municipal body, though its statutes were pious ones dealing only with such matters as the burial rites of its members. In many places the name given to the

---

[1] A contemporary chronicler states that the vision was stage-managed by the canons of Le Puy because brigands were diminishing the influx of pilgrims to the shrine.
[2] Exceptions are the Charité of Valenciennes, before 1070, and the guild of Saint Martin du Canigou, *c.* 1195.

commune in the eventual charter shows what its origin has been; that given by the Count of Flanders to the town of St. Omer in 1127 simply confirms the privileges of the guild without changing its name; the charter of Arras confirms its *Charité* and that of Lille its *Amitié*. Similarly the characteristic French institution of a rural commune which includes the villages and hamlets of the countryside, sometimes, as in Ponthieu and Laonnais, as many as fifteen in number, arises from a religious confraternity covering the same area. Pious brotherhoods, indeed, were so far identified with political activities that in some districts they came under the ban both of the Law and the Church. Philippe le Bel tried in vain to abolish all the confraternities of Paris and the other towns of his domain, and they were forbidden by the Councils of Toulouse (1229), Montpellier and Arles (1234), Valence (1248), and Avignon (1281 and 1326). The Council of 1326 stated: 'They meet under pretext of brotherhood once a year in a fortified place, and, taking a mutual oath, swear to defend each other against all comers, and to give each other aid in all circumstances. It often happens that they dress alike, with particular badges, and that they elect a head or mayor, whom they swear to obey in all things. Such misdeeds offend justice, entail murder and pillage, destroy peace and security, and end in the oppression of the poor and innocent.'

The communal movement started in 1076 at Cambrai and continued for two centuries until it died out with the death of Louis IX in 1270. It was a rising of commerce and industry against feudal exploitation, with the object of constituting a sworn association of townsmen as a collective feudatory.

The movement was in fact less destructive than constructive. The people were not anti-feudal in theory, however often in practice they might find themselves in conflict with their overlord. Indeed the lord, civil or ecclesiastical, alone made town life possible; the body of artisans who collected round the monastery, the cathedral, or the castle were as dependent upon its protection as any other vassals; they too were *laboratores*, but their only holdings were their cottages and gardens, and their labour lay not in the fields but in the workshops. In virtue of these differences they sought relief from the burdens of the agriculturists, forced labour, frequent payments, and restrictions upon freedom of movement and freedom of buying and selling. Their economic needs drew them together into industrial and commercial centres of population, and these demanded to be treated as communities. They did not ask for the overthrow of the feudal system, but for a place within it that should recognize their peculiar economic and political interests; and their efforts, when fully successful, established what has been called a collective seigneury,[1] standing as a community in the relation of vassal to lord or king, and owing the obligations of homage, fealty, and communal military service. Even this was often limited to the actual defence of the town; at Cambrai it was decreed that 'neither the bishop nor the emperor can impose tax or tribute, or can order out the militia, except for the good keeping and defence of the city, and that only between cockcrow and night'.

A full-grown commune aimed at more than obtaining fixed feudal payments. A civil code might enable the poorest class to escape servile dues, it might satisfy the merchants and the artisans who got fixed fines and tolls, but the leading townsmen, holders of burgage tenements and possibly even knights, realized that unless they got their own magistrates little was really gained. Something more was needed than their lord's plighted word, or even than guilds of merchants and artisans, which might form the basis of a successful rising, but could not maintain what had been thus secured. Thus by the explicit grant of the lord, with his tacit consent, or in opposition to his will, the townsmen endeavoured to secure by a constitution such a measure of self-government as was exemplified in the *établissements* of Rouen—by a mayor, by *jurats*, who formed an administrative council, and often also by *échevins*, judges in the town court of common law. Their real functions are those of the officers of the confraternity, for the commune is still a brotherhood. The charters of Senlis, Compiègne, and Soissons state: 'Within the limits of the commune, all men shall give mutual help according to their power, and shall in no wise suffer that any man whatsoever shall take any thing or impose payment of *tailles* on any one of them.' In France the medieval commune was the home of but one estate of commons, merchants, and artisans, and they had to struggle for freedom from the feudal nobles and their courts. Fra Salimbene of Parma notices with surprise, 'In France only the townspeople live in the towns; the knights and noble ladies stay in their castles and on their own domains.' The townsmen developed a borough custom for which they desired free working, adjusted to the mercantile and industrial character of their community; they did not aspire to be city states, but were franchises within the greater state. Sometimes—as at Laon—a sworn union might employ force, and the confraternity had usually a militant and military side. Thus the commune had its belfry to summon its citizens to resist attack; it maintained militia and fortified its walls, and had usually an armed horseman upon its seal.

---

[1]So the Hôtel de Ville is made like a noble house, with a machicolated tower, surmounted by a weathercock with the town arms, a great hall, chapel, and prison.

After the eleventh century two types of towns must be distinguished: the old towns, which had survived as centres of partly urban activity from antiquity (such as Paris, *Lutetia Parisiorum*), or had grown up round an abbey, cathedral, castle, fair, or market; and the new towns—*villes neuves*—of the twelfth century. In that century the old towns themselves developed, and in the last half of it are found to fall into two classes— towns which are free in that their inhabitants are freemen and not villeins, such as Paris; and towns enjoying certain privileges but under the authority of a lord, such as Rouen.

The beginnings of the political life of the city of Paris are obscure, but under Louis VII the privileges of the Hanse or Guild of Paris merchants, which under the name of *marchands de l'eau de Paris* had the monopoly of carrying goods from Saint Germain-en-Laye up the river, and of levying toll on all goods entering the city by river, were confirmed. Once more the continuity of tradition is manifested; the guild is as old as Roman times—its members dedicated an altar to Jupiter in the time of Tiberius— and it is their badge, a ship, with the motto, *Fluctuat nec mergitur*, which still appears as the arms of the city of Paris.

Twelfth-century Paris, like eighteenth-century Moscow, was an assem- blage of castles, each fortified and each with its gardens and dependencies, and of churches and monasteries all lying within the walls.[1] The lord or abbot held feudal rights over his own land, and there was no corporate city life. But Philip Augustus not only added to the defences and amenities of the city, but made its citizens *francs bourgeois*[2] with a provost and a council of six burghers. Men flocked to the city; numbers and prosperity alike increased. 'To be a free burgess', says *Renart le Contrefait*, 'is to be in the best estate of all; they live in a noble manner, wearing lordly garments, having falcons and sparrow-hawks, fine palfreys and fine chargers. When the vassals are obliged to join the host, the burgesses rest in their beds; when the vassals go to be massacred in battle, the burgesses go to picnic by the river.' Crafts, trades, and commerce flourished and continued to flourish, 'en l'an 1400, et quant la ville estoit en sa fleur, passoient tant de gens tout jour sur ce Grand Pont, que on y recontroit adéz ung blanc moine, ou ung blanc cheval'.[3]

Rouen was an 'old town' of a different kind, with a constitution dating from 1171. One hundred of its citizens met once a fortnight for judicial

---

[1]Even down to the time of Louis XIV thirty-four seigneurs owned half Paris, and each had the rights of justice on his land.
[2]The word 'bourgeois' first appears in an ordinance of 1134.
[3]Guillebert de Metz, *Description de Paris*, ch. xxii. 'In 1400, and so long as the city flourished, so many men passed every day over the Grand Pont that one always saw upon it either a white monk or a white horse.'

and other business, and chose each year from among themselves twelve *échevins* or magistrates and twelve councillors to assist them. They also chose three candidates for the mayoralty, from whom the King appointed one. Their administration, indeed, was felt to exercise its powers only by delegation of the royal authority; the King's presence, or a session of his assize, automatically suspended the communal powers of justice.

But if Rouen had fewer rights, its connexion with the King of England gave it many privileges. Except for one ship yearly from Cherbourg, it had the monopoly of the trade with Ireland. In England its merchandise was free of all the markets in the land. In London its merchants were quit of all payments except for wine and great fish, and had exclusive rights in their special wharf of Dowgate. In its own territory only a citizen might take a shipload of merchandise past Rouen or bring wine to a cellar in the town. These privileges led to a growing trade in leather, cloth, grain, and salt fish, and in the end recouped their royal donor, for under Henry II the ducal rights over the town were worth more than 3,000 livres annually.

The *établissements* of Rouen, that provided for government by a hundred of its citizens under the King's suzerainty, were copied by the chief towns of Western France—Tours, Poitiers, Angoulême, and La Rochelle, and even by Bayonne on the Spanish frontier.

Both Paris and Rouen, however many elements were represented among their citizens, achieved unity under their sovereign lords. Many cities were an agglomeration of townships each under a different jurisdiction. At Arles, for instance, there were four towns: the *cité*, under the archbishop; the *vieux bourg*, divided into three fiefs held by the archbishop, the Count of Provence, and the family of Porcellet; the *marché*, depending upon the archbishop but held by two vassals; and the *bourg neuf*, belonging to the Seigneur des Baux.

The new towns, or *villes neuves*, were in their beginnings a result of the Truce of God, by which abbeys or churches, being sacrosanct, were enabled to offer asylum and thus to attract settlers.[1] But in time the lay lords, attracted by the prospect of revenue, founded towns also, sometimes in alliance with the local bishop. Four crosses were set up at the four points of the compass to mark the town boundary, and within this the future town was traced upon the ground: the church, the market, the town hall, and the regular and symmetrical streets.[2] A typical *ville-neuve* charter, by the privileges it enumerates, explains the causes that brought citizens to the new towns:

[1] The first *ville neuve* is Vaucresson, founded by Abbot Suger in 1125.
[2] Montpazier and Montferrand are a good surviving example of such planning, which was also followed by Stephen of Penchester at Winchelsea.

'Know all men by these presents that I, Henry Count of Troyes, have established the customs defined below for the inhabitants of my Ville Neuve near Pont-sur-Seine between the highways of the bridges of Pugny: every man dwelling in the said town shall pay each year twelve deniers and a measure of barley for the price of his domicile; and if he wishes to have an allotment of land or meadow, he shall pay four deniers an acre as rent. The houses, vines, and fields can be sold or disposed of at the will of the buyer. Men dwelling in the said town shall neither go with the army in the field nor on any expedition if I do not myself lead them. I further accord them the right to have six échevins, who shall administer the common business of the town and shall assist my provost in hearing his pleas. I have decreed that no lord, knight or other, shall take away from the town any of its new citizens, for any reason whatsoever, unless the citizen be his "homme de corps", or unless he be in arrears with his taille. *Signed at Provins,* 1175.'

Breteuil, founded by a Norman lord in 1060, came to be a model followed as far away as Ireland and the Welsh marches. The privileges conferred by the *leges Britoliae* were three: a town-peace, protecting the settlers; a town market, with a court of *lex mercatoria*; and fixed and moderate tolls.

Since communes were most apt to arise in towns of a certain size, they were more often directed against the power of a bishop or an abbot than that of a lay lord, as the cathedral or monastery had usually proved a more secure focus for industry than the lord's castle. Consequently, however much the sworn unions that demanded the charter might approximate to religious confraternities, the Church condemned them out of hand. Jacques de Vitry laments:

'Not only do they crush and ruin the knights and the country side, taking away the lords' jurisdiction over their men; but they even usurp the rights of the Church; they demolish the independence of the clergy by their iniquitous statutes, contrary to all canonical law. This is not all; nearly all breed brotherly enmity, desire the destruction of neighbouring towns, or even attack them. They rejoice in the death of a neighbour, and women share these evil feelings with men. Strangers and travellers, defenceless against the communes, are made to pay new and illegal tolls; every one is envious, every one deceitful, every one selfish, every one destructive; without the walls there is battle, and within unceasing alarms.'

The dominant fact in the history of the communes of north-central France is their relation to the King, and the complement to this is their importance in the development of the monarchical power. Up to 1180 the policy of the monarchy towards the communes appears to be opportunist, but is really subordinated to the royal dependence on the bishops against the feudatories. If a commune arose in opposition to the bishop, his appeal to the King usually resulted in the suppression of the commune, but if it arose in opposition to a dangerous lay lord the King usually supported it, particularly if it had the favour of the Church. Thus it came about that in the next period, from 1180 to 1220, the natural policy of the monarchy was alliance with the communes against the feudatories.[1]

St. Louis on his deathbed exhorted his son: 'Especially maintain the good cities and commons of thy realm in the same estates and with the same franchises as they enjoyed under thy predecessors; and if there be aught to amend, amend and set it right, and keep them in thy favour and love. For because of the power and wealth of the great cities, thine own subjects, and especially thy peers and thy barons, and foreigners also, will fear to undertake aught against thee.'

The French communes had greatly developed under Philip Augustus, who granted seventy-eight communal charters in the course of his reign. One of the earliest, that granted to Corbie in 1180, reserves the lord's rights over the members of the commune: 'The inhabitants who hold fiefs shall acquit their ordinary services to their immediate lords, without prejudice to that which is due to the King and to the commune.' The charters of Voisines, Saint Quentin, and Athies have a clause forbidding serfs of the district to join the commune. But the royalty of Philip Augustus ended by being antagonistic to feudalism, and by 1223 the charter of Beaumont-sur-Oise contains the clause, 'There shall be included in this franchise all men, belonging to whatever seigneury, who shall wish to settle at Beaumont'; the only exception being the bondsmen and bondswomen of the King and his sons.

The administration of Philip Augustus introduced two new elements: jurists experienced in Roman Law, and burgesses from the free towns. It was by legal sentence that he deprived John of England of his French provinces, but it was by the towns who acted as fortified posts on the frontier that he held them, as it was by the help of their militia that he defeated John at Bouvines.[2] It was by the aid of his jurists that he declared that all communes were the King's, and by this elision of the feudatories gained a new source of power and revenue in granting and confirming charters to the communes throughout the kingdom. Beaumanoir in the *Coutumes de Beauvoisis* says that the King's intervention in communal affairs

---

[1] Here France resembled England, where the towns supported the Angevins, and differed from Germany, where Frederick II sacrificed the towns to gain the support of the bishops and princes; and from Italy, where the feudal nobles took their share in town life and thus in the struggle against the monarchy under Frederick I and II.

[2] Cf. the defeat of Frederick I by communal militia at Legnano.

is necessary because he is the natural guardian of all civil and religious associations established within his realm; because he only can create communes, and all 'nouvelletés' must be forbidden. The conduct of the mayors must be under his control in order that 'the poor inhabitants may earn their bread in peace'.

The King's most striking innovation appeared to be a temporary measure, but its results were lasting. Immediately before his departure on Crusade in 1190, he deputed authority to deal with city affairs in every city of the royal domain to a provost and four burgesses. In Paris there were six, and these were appointed guardians of the royal treasure and the royal seal. On his return he continued to use burgesses as officials, and ordered the officers of his demesne to act in co-operation with the townsmen where the towns had not communal rights. Thus with him the urban class reached political importance, and hence arose dynasties of *grands bourgeois* who dominated Paris and the great towns. But with this development of a bourgeois aristocracy communal democracy suffered, and after 1220 a period of decline begins. An oligarchical element appears in their government; the *parlement* or mass meeting of the burgesses disappears or becomes unimportant, and the whole power passes into the hands of a patriciate of wealthy townsmen, owners of land, merchants, or both, who by co-optation and influence gain a monopoly of the offices of mayor and jurats, which tend to become hereditary. This introduces two elements of weakness: internal strife within the oligarchy, and the disaffection of the excluded artisans. It was partly a question of economics; unorganized commerce had been succeeded by organized industry, and as a social institution the commune was out of date. The mercantile oligarchy tried to put the burden of the taxes on the artisan masses, and ran into debt rather than shift the burden when changing conditions made it intolerable.

Already by the end of the twelfth century, Lambert of Waterloo is lamenting the decline of the commune of Cambrai:

'*At the beginning it was greeted with favour, because it had been instituted by men held in high esteem, men whose lives were just, simple, honourable, and not avaricious. Each was content with what he had; justice and concord reigned among them; avarice was rare. Citizen respected citizen; the rich did not despise the poor; all shunned strife, discord, and lawsuits. Their only rivalry was in honour and justice. What a change has come over the commune! It has suddenly become dishonourable, such fair beginnings have led to such a state of shame and perversity for reasons that are only too clear. The citizens have become numbed by prosperity; they have risen one against the other; they have left sin and crime unpunished, each thinks of nothing*

but his own enrichment by dishonest means. Little by little the great have set them-
selves to oppress the poor by lies, perjury, and open force; right, equity, and honour
have disappeared; the very strength of the commune has vanished.'

Thus the communes of thirteenth-century France were centres of
struggle and bankruptcy, and the King was forced to interfere in the name
of order and of reputable finance and to destroy municipal liberty in
favour of government by royal officials. The commune came with revolt
against the financial oppression of the feudal lord, and it went in the
bankruptcy of an oligarchical government. The artisan and merchant had
exchanged the rule of a seigneur first for democracy and then for oligarchy
and hence passed to direct control by a strong monarchy.

The importance of the charter of the *Hanse des marchands de l'eau* in the
political development of the city of Paris has been mentioned. With the
twelfth century town life everywhere led to the organization of such corporations within the corporation of the city—guilds of traders, or merchants' guilds, since mutual association facilitated both transport and
exchange, especially when such exchange was more apt to be in kind than
in money; and secondly, manufacturing corporations, craft guilds, for the
protection and regulation both of trades carried on in every city—baking,
meat selling, and so on—and of skilled crafts more or less special to the
locality, such as enamelling at Limoges. But industry remained to a
certain extent under seigneurial control, since certain necessities—ovens,
wine presses, flour mills, cloth mills, and so on—were seigneurial mono-
polies, and the members of the guilds owed seigneurial dues. When they
had obtained a collective seigneury, whether as members of a commune
or as *bourgeois du roi* under a charter, this seigneurial power over industry
passed into municipal hands. Here, since the municipal potentates were
usually of commercial origin, it tended to be more intelligently employed
than under a feudal seigneur. In these cities, statutes such as those codified
by Étienne Boileau remained for a very long time the basis of French
industry. The root principle of apprenticeship and examination before
admittance is usually thus expressed: 'Whosoever wishes to practise the
craft as master, must know how to do it in all points, by himself, without
advice or aid from another, and he must therefore be examined by the
wardens of the craft.' Further, the members supervised the quality of
material used in the trade, and saw that its secrets were kept. Similarly,
partnerships and multiple shops were forbidden except with the consent
of the guild. Some crafts were even more strictly limited; no one, for
example, could be a weaver in Paris who was not a weaver's son. In few

instances was it permissible to have more than one apprentice outside the master's own family.

Up to the time of Philippe le Bel the number of masters in each *métier* was unlimited, and some industries—*métiers libres*—were not corporate. But by the end of the thirteenth century these also became guilds, and the existing *métiers* were further subdivided. The French guilds were not divided according to the thing produced, but according to the material of which it was made. The cutlers, for instance, were in two corporations, 'couteliers fabricants de lames' and 'couteliers faiseurs de manches', since blades and handles were of different material. On the other hand the lantern-makers and comb-makers were in one guild, since both worked in horn. In the thirteenth century the 'tailleurs de robes fourrées' were separated from the 'tailleurs de robes', and new corporations were formed for *métiers*—for example, embroidery—that had hitherto been free. The rosary-makers, again, were divided into those who made in bone and horn, those working in ivory and shell, and those working in amber and jet. A single object not only passed through several hands in the course of its manufacture, but through hands belonging to members of different corporations. This brought about difficulties similar to those in a modern industry of a complex kind—such as shipbuilding—through the overlapping of trade unions. Even thieves, assassins, beggars, and vagabonds were organized in corporations like honest men, and had their 'masterpieces' and *épreuves de maîtrise*.

Many of the guild regulations are of the sort that the cycle of the world has brought back upon the statute book; the number of hours a week are limited, and certain crafts—such as the weaving of tapestry on the *haute lisse*—are forbidden to women as being too fatiguing. Some *métiers*, on the other hand, are reserved for women; for instance the 'feserresses de chapeaux d'orfrois', or makers of embroidered head-dresses, had to be women; six years' apprenticeship was needed, and since the work to be well done must be done in a good light, 'nulle mestresse ne aprantice de ce mestier ne peuvent ouvrer en yver ne en esté au soir, ne au matin si ce n'est par la clarté de jour'.[1] The guilds are religious confraternities, and therefore owe a duty of almsgiving; each Sunday one goldsmith is to keep his shop open, and the proceeds of the day's sale are to go to provide a fine feast on Easter Sunday for the poor of the Hôtel Dieu. If a journeyman tailor spoils a piece of stuff, he is to give a day's work to mending the clothes of the poor. Strikes were not unknown; the jurist Beaumanoir defines the

---

[1]'No mistress nor apprentice in this craft may work in winter or summer at night, nor in the morning if it be not by daylight'.

'alliance which is made against the common good, when any sort of people swear or engage or covenant that they will not work any more at as low a wage as before . . . and so if they are permitted are they against the common good, for then will there never be cheap merchandise, since those of each trade will struggle to get higher wages than is reasonable and the public interest will not permit all work to stop.'

It is further admitted that the artisan works as little as he can, and has the time-worker's aptitude for knocking off work too punctually:

> *A tierce dit que il est none*
> *Et a none que il est nuit,*
> *Et si tost com il puet s'enfuit.*[1]

A sermon of the time of St. Louis suggests that even guild regulations did not do much to improve the moral standards of trade. 'The innkeepers and wine merchants secretly mix water with their wine, or bad wine with good. The innkeeper charges for a bad candle at six times its value, and demands extra payment if you use his dice. Wretched old women water the milk . . . and try to make their cheeses look richer by soaking them in broth. Flax which is to be sold by weight is left out all night on the damp grass, so that it may be heavier. Butchers blow out their meat. Before delivering a pig they drain away its blood and use it to redden the gills of stale and discoloured fish. The drapers make up on the baize what they lose on the scarlet cloth; they have one yard measure for selling and another for buying. They only display their goods in dark streets, so as to deceive the buyers as to its quality.' The butchers also sold cooked meat. The preacher tells the story of the old customer who asked to have his sausages cheaper as he had dealt only with the one butcher for seven years. 'Seven years!' cried the pork-butcher, 'and you're still alive!'

Paris soon outgrew the walls built by Philip Augustus, and on the side of the *ville* they eventually became an inner defence within the *enceinte* of Etienne Marcel. The *taille* rolls of 1292 enumerate 352 streets, 10 squares, 11 cross roads, and over 15,000 taxpayers. The narrow and unpaved streets were thronged and noisy; the shopkeepers cried their wares, and the street hawkers vied with them. The thirteenth-century *Dit des Crieries de Paris* gives all their cries; the apple woman

> *Primes ai pommes de ronviau*
> *Et d'Auvergne blanc duriau,*

---

[1]'At tierce (nine o'clock) he says it is three o'clock, and at three o'clock that it is night, and gets off as soon as he can.'

the chestnut seller from Lombardy; the fruit-seller with

> *Figue de Melités sans fin*
> *J'ai roisin d'outre mer, roisin . . .*

and the cheese hawker,

> *J'ai bon fromage de Champaigne;*
> *Or i a fromage de Brie!*

Each trade had its quarter: the apothecaries in the Cité; the literary trades—parchment sellers, scribes, illuminators, book-sellers—in the Latin Quarter; money changers and goldsmiths on the Grand Pont; butchers near the Grand Châtelet; Lombards near the Rue Saint Martin, and mercers near the Rue Saint Denis. Paris still has its Rues des Parche-miniers, des Écrivains, des Enlumineurs, de l'Ecorcherie, de la Buffleterie, de la Verrerie, de la Tannerie, des Lavandières-Sainte-Opportune. There were recognized hiring-places for every trade; men seeking work as fullers, for instance, congregated near the apse of Saint Gervais, in front of the house with the sign of the Eagle. Each shop had its gaily-painted sign; a few still survive in the names of the streets or alleys, du Chat qui pêche, du Coq-Héron, des Marmousets, des Trois Poissons, des Trois Canettes, des Trois Visages, du Pied de Boeuf. There were numerous markets, each with special wares and special privileges: one in the Place Maubert for bread, one near the Grand Châtelet for meat, one near Saint Germain l'Auxerrois for sausages, one on the Petit Pont for flowers and eggs; the herb market—the *grant orberie*—was on the quayside of the Ile de la Cité, near where the flower market is now. Saturday, when many of the shops were closed, was the great day for shopping in the Halles.[1] There each trade had its quarter and the provincial towns—Beauvais, Cambrai, Amiens, Douai, Pontoise, Lagny, Gonesse—each had its section.

Everywhere was movement, activity, and gaiety. A fourteenth-century manual of polite conversation tells us the proper salutations: to an equal you say, 'Mon Signour, Dieus vous donne bone matin et bonne aventure', or 'Mon amy, Dieus vois doint bon jour et bonne encontre'. To a priest or a monk the proper greeting is 'Dieus vous gart', while a workman or a labourer is saluted with 'Dieus vous ait, mon amy', or 'Dieus vous avance, mon compaignon'.

The class of the wealthy bourgeois became more and more important, and developed a society and standards of its own. An old bourgeois wrote

---

[1] The modern Halles are on the site of the famous Marché aux Innocents, which dates from the time of Philippe le Hardi.

the *Ménagier de Paris* between 1392 and 1394 for the instruction of his young wife, and his good counsels incidentally give an admirable picture of bourgeois life. He begins by telling her: 'Know that I am not displeased, but glad, that you should tend rose-bushes and grow violets and weave garlands, and that you should practise dancing and singing, and wish that you will continue so to do among our friends and equals, for it is right and proper so to pass your girlhood, though always without appearing at the feasts of lords too great for us, for that would not be fitting to your position, nor to mine.' She is to rise early, but not so early as the bell for matins, and to say her prayers. 'Take heed that ye be fitly dressed, without new-fangled devices or too much or too little show'; she is to be particularly careful that her chemise and underdress do not ride up at the back of her neck and appear above her collar. She is to go into town or to church properly accompanied by her duenna, 'walking with head up, eyes lowered and quiet and looking straight before you on the ground, regarding neither man nor woman and stopping to speak to no one in the street'. Arrived at the church she is to choose a quiet corner before a fine altar or image and to pray there with 'head up and lips always moving as they pray'. Her chief, and indeed her only, occupation is to be the supervision of her establishment. She must know how to garden and how to manage servants. Her *dispensier* or steward will help her to choose day labourers and people of special trades, such as bakers, furriers, and shoemakers; her *béguine* or duenna will advise her about the domestics. The work of the household must begin early in the morning; 'The entrance to your house, that is the parlour and the entrances whereby people come in to speak within the house, must be swept early in the morning and kept clean, and the stools, benches and cushions dusted and shapen; and thereafter the other rooms likewise, as befits our station'. The duenna is to remind her mistress to look after the domestic pets such as dogs and cage-birds, 'for they cannot speak and you must speak for them'. She must look after her own linen-chest and wardrobe, and at fitting times have her maid clean, air and look over the sheets, coverlets, feathers, furs and all such things.

Most important of all, she must see that the kitchen is kept clean, and that proper dinners are ordered. The anxious husband gives a systematic cookery book and many specimen menus for her guidance. She must see that the men and maids are set to work in different places, 'l'un a mont, l'autre a val, l'un aux champs, l'autre en la ville, l'un en chambre, l'autre en solier ou en cuisine . . . chascun selon son endroit et science'. The servants' meals must be regular, but at each they should have only one sort of meat and one of drink. 'And so soon as they begin to tell tales, or

ask riddles or to lean on their elbows, tell the housekeeper to make them
get up and clear the table.' At night the steward is to lock up and to see
that no tramp or robber is hidden in the cellars; and then all go off to bed,
each armed with a flat candlestick.

In the streets of Paris, far more than in the provincial cities, every class
in the nation was represented: the beggars who sat at the church doors
and by the bridges, the peasants who came in from the country to buy and
sell, the artisans and craftsmen in their open shops, the hawkers and
merchants; jongleurs and mountebanks, monks and friars, canons of the
cathedral and professors of the university, students and schoolboys;
couriers with their white wands, heralds in tabards, knights in armour;
nobles riding out to hawk or hunt outside the city, ladies taking the air in
litters, judges in their scarlet riding to the Law Courts, pilgrims going to
Ste. Geneviève, prisoners, gyved and bound, being driven to the Grand
Châtelet; and secure within his turreted fortifications, the King in the
Louvre. Paris was then, as now, an epitome of the life of France.

IV

Monastic Life

THE early ages of Christianity were haunted by the sense that the life of the world and the life of the spirit were antagonistic; and, impelled by this instinct, many renounced the world and retired to a desert place to lead a hermit life. Ascetic mortification was their only employment; mystic ecstasy their only joy.

But in France religion is always the concern not only of the individual but also of the community, and the mystic sense is usually accompanied by a power of organization in practical affairs. Long before Benedict had imposed monasticism on Europe, those who renounced the world were there living in communities under a Rule. About 360 St. Martin founded a monastery at Ligugé,[1] near Poitiers. The Rule was one of life in common, but the activities of the monastery were self-contained: it was not a centre of religious life for any but its own monks. However its ascetic severities may compare with those of the ordered monasticism of later times, they were not blind imitations of Eastern austerities. When a visitor from the East spoke of the cooked herbs and barley bread which formed the diet of the African hermits, the brethren replied: 'Let a Cyrenean endure it if he will, necessity and nature have accustomed him to eating nothing; but we Gauls cannot live after the manner of angels.' None the less, all early monasticism in France received its inspiration from the East; by 410 St. Cassian, a Provençal who had visited Egypt, had established his Rule at Marseilles, and it is after a pilgrimage in the East that St. Honorat founds the famous monastery in the Île de Lérins. By 530 Caesarius of Arles, a monk of Lérins, had compiled a Rule for his monks and another for his nuns. The tale of monasteries rapidly increased; in the fifth century those of Marmoutier, La Morinie, St. Martin near Tours, and St. Victor of Marseilles were established. They were followed by monasteries of royal foundation; Childebert I founded the abbey of St. Vincent—afterwards Saint Germain des Prés—outside the gates of Paris; Chlotor I endowed Saint Médard at Soissons, Radegund Sainte Croix at Poitiers. But as yet the monastic rule was subject to considerable variation, from the excesses of Oriental asceticism to the disorders of relaxation; and

---

[1]The first monasteries in Rome are little earlier.

(53)

monastic life was hardly developed enough to influence the nation as a whole.

The first attempt to strengthen its force came with the reform of the monastery of Luxeuil by Colombanus at the end of the sixth century. In his attempt to introduce a more homogeneous and severe organization he borrowed something from the contemporary system of law; his penitential code, with its classification of sin and crime, gives clear evidence of this. Indeed, the evolution of Christian discipline throughout the Middle Ages runs parallel with that of national discipline—witness the gradual substitution in both of the money payment for any expiatory act.

But French monasticism only really became national when the centre of its spiritual life shifted from Provence to Burgundy. From the ninth century until the end of the Middle Ages, Burgundy was the source of the monastic inspiration of France. It is there, after the reforms of Colombanus had been effected, that the Rule of Benedict of Nursia was first practised in France; and it is thence that the French form of Benedictinism spread through the land. Benedict of Aniane, who took the monastic vow and remained for some time in the monastery of Saint Seine near Dijon, was the instrument of the reform. As 'rector et doctor' of the Church of Christ, Charlemagne, on the advice of Alcuin, gave him the task of reforming the monasteries of Aquitaine. In 817 he presided over a reforming synod at Aix, and by royal authority all Frankish monasteries were ordered to accept his reformed Benedictine Rule. It is characteristic of the age that this Rule lays great emphasis on the saying of the Office and on devotion, and shows great contempt for profane learning. But, like the earlier Benedictinism, it involved three main principles. First, obedience to the abbot, as to a father. The Benedictine monastery is thus always a family under its abbot, and the Benedictine is always a member of it. Thus, too, the Benedictine monastery was and is an autonomous body: all abbeys followed the same Rule, but each was self-governing and not subject to any central authority within the Order.[1] Second, *conversio morum*; every member of the Order took vows of poverty and celibacy. Third, *stabilitas loci*; the Benedictine was as definitely attached to a community and a place as the serf to the manor and the glebe. Hildebert of Le Mans, in the eleventh century, describes the typical monastic building:

Quadratam speciem structura domestica praefert
Atria bis binis inclyta porticibus.

[1] It was, however, subject, unless the abbot was a mitred abbot, to episcopal visitation and control; and of course to the Papacy.

Quae tribus inclusae domibus, quas corporis usus
Postulat, et quarta quae domus est Domini,
Discursum monachis, vitam dant, et stationem,
Qua velut in caulis contineantur oves.
Quarum prima domus servat potumque cibumque,
Ex quibus hos reficit juncta secunda domus.
Tertia membra fovet lassata labore diurno;
Quarta Dei laudes assidue resonat.[1]

The clergy were divided into two classes: *clerici saeculares*, living in the world, administering the sacraments, and concerned with the cure of souls; and *clerici regulares* or *religiosi*, following a monastic Rule (*regula*) and belonging to an Order (*religio*) that they might better follow the counsels of perfection of the Christian faith.[2] They had abandoned the world, not in the sense that they had ceased to work in it or for it, but that they had put aside its passions and vowed themselves to poverty and celibacy. Their life differed fundamentally from that of the hermits, for it was as a community—an Order—that they existed, and not as individuals; they lived as a cohort of the Church militant. The prologue to the Order of St. Benedict expresses this: 'To thee are my words directed, whosoever thou mayest be, who, renouncing thine own self-will, and assuming the strong and splendid arms of submission, art ready to fight for the Lord Christ, the True King.' Further, monasticism differed from anchoretism in the part played in it by mysticism and asceticism; true to the spirit of the Latin Church it did not renounce practical activity, but endeavoured to keep the balance between the *vita activa* and the *vita contemplativa*.

After the reform of Benedict of Aniane the Order was devoted primarily to prayer and the faithful saying of the Office, and secondarily to labour. Benedictine labour was largely physical; the agriculture of the monks brought waste land under cultivation and their industries did as much for the development of material civilization as did their intellectual efforts in the propagation of learning. The Benedictine worked for the world and in the world.

'If the monk said his Office regularly, it was not for his own sake only or primarily, but for the sake of all Christ's Church of which he was himself one member among many, but one whose especial function it was to pray.

[1] The house presents a four-square shape; the cloister-court is adorned with four open walks, which, enclosed by three buildings required for bodily needs and a fourth which is the church, provide the monks with exercise, food and repose, so that here the sheep are kept as in a fold. The first of these buildings stores their bread and meat, and the second, counting next, feeds them therewith. The third provides rest for their limbs wearied by the day's labour, and the fourth for ever rings with the praises of God.

[2] There was always some rivalry between seculars and regulars. Theobald of Étampes, speaking in Oxford in the early twelfth century, described convents as prisons of the damned. The monks retaliated by calling him a wandering chaplain in effeminate dress.

If he sought perfection and followed its counsels it was not in order to get a certain salvation for himself in which others did not share; it was in order to show the world that the perfect law of Christ could be followed, and to stimulate others to follow it by showing a way. This was one reason why the monks were the apostles of England in the seventh century, and of Germany in the eighth, for they preached no more than they obviously practised.'[1]

Further, they worked in the world; the duty was laid upon them when Gregory the Great instituted a monastic apostolate and sent monks to convert the heathen. This function may be said to have ended when England and Germany became christianized, but the work went on in other forms. In the Dark Ages it was Benedictinism that kept the flame of learning tended; it is to its scriptoria that we owe our manuscripts as well of classical authors as of the Fathers of the Church. The styles of French Carolingian illumination all have their centres in the monasteries—the Palace style, at Paris and Soissons; the style of the Loire valley, at Tours and Fleury; and the styles of Rheims and Corbie. By the ninth century Saint Wandrille, Saint Germer de Fly, Saint Riquier, Saint Armand, Corbie, Charroux, and Aniane all have fine collections of books. Abbot Loup of Ferrières gets books from Fulda, Tours, Rome, and York to be copied by his schools of scribes at Ferrières and at Saint Josse-sur-Mer, and the scriptorium of the Abbot of Saint Bénigne at Dijon is equally active.

Beyond the finely decorated books produced within the cloister, Benedictine monasticism fostered and developed the arts in an age when the outside world was distraught with warfare and struggle—music for its services, architecture, sculpture and glass for its buildings, frescoes and work in gold, bronze, and ivory for their adornment.

The social work—road building, road repair, and poor relief—which the Carolingian Capitularies specifically assign to the monasteries, shows their importance in the economic system. Indeed it may be said that until the development of the towns in the eleventh century it is the monasteries who are the pioneers of industry and commerce. The best French vineyards are all of monastic planting, and many monasteries, like the abbey of La Chaise Dieu in the Auvergne, became important agricultural trading centres.

But the most fruitful of their fields of labour, and that which they made most peculiarly their own, was that of education. Every monastery had its school, primarily for its own novices, secondarily and more rarely for external pupils. It is to monks such as Gerbert of Aurillac and Fulbert of

[1] E. Barker, Oxford Lectures on Principles of Medieval History (1916). (Unpublished.)

Chartres that the foundation of learned education in France is due. Such schools as theirs were the universities of their age: and the life of a university is not one of complete seclusion and selfish isolation from the world.

On the side of politics and administration such seclusion soon became equally impossible. A monk as an individual held no property, but the existence of his community involved at least the existence of monastic buildings held by the community, and the lands attached to these buildings tended to increase. Kings in particular gave land cheerfully to churchmen, for they were exempt from the feudal vice of heredity and the appointment of worthy and loyal successors might be secured. One of the functions of the monk was to pray, and much land was given to the monasteries from the motive of assuring the good of the souls of the donor's family through their prayers. A typical deed of gift is one made in favour of the abbey of Gomerfontaine in 1207: 'I, Hugh of Chaumont, with the consent of my wife Petronilla, of my sons John and James, and of my other sons, for the salvation of my soul, of the soul of my wife, the soul of my father Galon, and of my mother Matilda, for the salvation of the souls of all my predecessors and of all my heirs, I make and concede in pure and perpetual alms the following donation. . . .' When lands were not ceded by gift, they were often bequeathed as a legacy. The poem *Hervis de Metz* (written in the time of Philip Augustus) begins, 'Today when a man falls ill, and lies down to die, he does not think of his sons or his nephews or his cousins; he summons the Black Monks of St. Benedict, and gives them all his lands, his revenues, his ovens, and his mills. The men of this age are impoverished and the clerks are daily becoming richer.' Further, many a man, whether knight or secular priest, joined the monastic Orders towards the end of life, 'ad succurrendum', as a last hope of salvation, and endowed the monastery with 'all his inheritance, whether of lands or of bondsmen and bondswomen or of woods and meadows'. These lands, revenues, ovens, and mills involved the exercise of seigneurial rights, and by their acquisition the monasteries strengthened their link with the world by their relation with feudalism. Moreover they acquired not only land but men: a serf flying from his master could take refuge in a monastery, and ask either to live there as a monk or to work there as a labourer. When once the abbot had declared him the monastery's man and had put the monastery bell rope round his neck to signalize his new servitude, his old master could not regain him.

Such relations with the world greatly modified the plan of the monastery itself. As early as the end of the ninth century the abbey of Corbie in Picardy was in the middle of a considerable space of ground, enclosed and fortified by a wall. Within the enclosure were three basilicas and four oratories; a monastery to hold between three and four hundred monks and a hundred and fifty lay brethren, with refectories, kitchens, cellars, dormitories, and chapter house; a guest house with quarters for bishops, lords, monks, clerks, and beggars, each with its separate oratory; a school; outbuildings to shelter the abbey's vassals in troubled times; and homes and workshops for forty workmen—cobblers, smiths, coopers, parchment-makers, founders, masons, carpenters, wood-carvers, brewers, and gardeners. Even the troubled years of the 'dark centuries' made little change to monastic life, and the remains of such an abbey as Fontenay in Burgundy are much like what Corbie must have been. Feudal lands and feudal dependents made the abbot's life very different from that originally contemplated by the founder of the Order. A record exists, for example,[1] of the activities of the Abbot of Mont Saint Michel, Robert de Torigni, in relation to the abbey's property from 1155 to 1159. In these five years he goes to England and the Channel Islands, to the King's Assizes at Gavrai, Domfront, Caen, and Carentan, to the courts of the Bishops of Avranches, Coutances, and Bayeux, and to that of the Archbishop of Rouen; proving his rights, exchanging, purchasing, receiving by gift or royal charter; acquiring here a piece of land, there a mill, a vineyard, a tithe, a church to add to the lands and rents, mills and forests, markets and churches, and feudal rights which the abbey already possessed. There are in these five years several instances of loans on mortgage, for the monasteries were the chief source of rural credit in this period, and as the land with its revenues passed at once into the possession of the mortgagee, the security was absolute, the annual return sure, and the chances of ultimate acquisition of the property considerable. With the resources of the monastery during his administration of thirty-two years this abbot was able to increase the number of monks from forty to sixty, to enlarge the conventual buildings, and to add a great façade to the abbey church. He also restored the library and added some 120 volumes to it, besides himself composing a variety of historical works which make him the chief authority for half a century of Norman history. Abelard laments that

'we, who ought to live by the labour of our own hands (which alone, as St. Benedict saith, maketh us truly monks) do now follow after idleness, that enemy of the soul, and seek our livelihood from the labours of other men. . . . So that, entangling our-selves in worldly business, and striving, under the sway of earthly covetousness, to be richer in the cloister than we had been in the world, we have subjected ourselves to

[1]See Haskins, *Normans in European History*, p. 172.

earthly lords rather than to God. We take from the great men of this world in the guise of alms, manors and tenants and bondsmen and bondswomen . . . and to defend these possessions we are compelled to appear in outside courts and before worldly judges, before whom we contend so shamelessly that we compel our own men not only to swear for us, but even to fight for us in single combat, to the extreme peril of their lives. . . . Who doth not know that we exercise heavier exactions upon those subject unto us, and oppress them with more grievous tyranny, than worldly potentates?"

So even monasticism, the first medieval counterbalance to feudalism, had become tainted by it. But if the monastic ideal suffered, the country gained, since the abbot was the head of a corporation that like a lay foundation owed both *auxilium* and *concilium*. An able churchman, though a monk, might, like Anselm and Lanfranc, rise high in the civil service of the country. The effect of all this was not only to secularize the monastic vocation, but also to make the monastery a local institution rather than a part of a Universal Church. Further, under its influence the observance of the Rule decayed, and monasteries tended to become comfortable residential communities.

The need for reform was felt as early as the tenth century, and resulted in the institution of a new Order, following the Benedictine Rule, but with *Consuetudines* of its own—the Order of Cluny. The monastery of Cluny had been endowed and founded by William Duke of Aquitaine in 910 in that Burgundian country where the monastic impulse was still strongest. Its first abbot, Berno, of noble Burgundian birth, had already founded a model monastery on his own land at Gigny, and had reformed the community of Baume, also in Burgundy, before he came to Cluny. The Burgundian tradition remained strong in the abbey; Odo, its second abbot, belonged to Semur, as did its greatest abbot, Hugh. Many abbeys were reformed by the abbots of Cluny, and many small priories were founded and given to the Abbey. By the beginning of the eleventh century an order of Cluny was in process of formation, and under Hugh it was fully established. Though the Benedictine principle of autonomy was renounced, and all the houses in the Order were directly subject to the Abbot of Cluny, the Benedictine Rule was strictly maintained.

The Cluniac interpretation of the Benedictine Rule followed that of Benedict of Aniane, but there was less of *labor* and more of *oratio*. Cluny remained the home of liturgical prayer, and the singing of the psalter took up much of the time that Benedict had allotted to manual labour. Indeed, Cluniac attachment to work in the fields was always half-hearted;

even when, about 1140, Peter the Venerable contemplated reform, he only decreed, 'We have ordained that the holy and ancient custom of manual work should be restored, at least in some degree, either within the monastic buildings, or wheresoever it may be carried on decently, far from the gaze of secular folk'. In other respects the Rule was strict enough; the *Consuetudines Cluniacenses* of 930 insist on black robes, silence, and downcast eyes.

Its central organization had important effects on Cluniac policy, which was anti-episcopal and pro-papal. The control of the Abbot of Cluny over his congregation could not co-exist with the control of the bishop; and Cluny, thus interested in evading the episcopate, turned to the Papacy, claiming to be subject to it and to it alone. The founder put it under the jurisdiction and protection of St. Peter, and Cluny was thus impelled to preach the universal power of Rome as the cover and shield of all its houses in Western Europe. On the other hand the Cluniacs were ready to buttress their Order with the aid of the secular power, and Odilo, the fourth abbot, was closely connected with the monarchy. Moreover, the Cluniac communities played an important part in bringing certain aspects of monastic learning, experience, and enthusiasm into relation with the life of the laity. Every Cluniac monk, whatever his monastery, had to come to the mother-abbey to make his profession, so that Cluny became as it were, a centre of monastic pilgrimage. To Cluny, too, was due the first French missionary impulse; it was with a missionary purpose that Peter of Cluny had the Koran translated in 1141.

Cluniac reforms, moreover, had a favourable influence in establishing a firmer discipline and a better moral order in the monasteries. In the strange picture of monastic life in the early thirteenth century afforded by the *Bible Guiot* the strictness of the Rule is insisted on. Guiot does not wish to join the Order, for

> *Trop tiennent bien leur convenanz*
> *Que il prometent la dedenz.*
> *Il me promistrent, sans mentir,*
> *Que quant je voldroie dormir*
> *Que il me convenroit veillier,*
> *Et quant je voldroie mengier*
> *Qu'il me feroient geüner.*[1]

Yet even the Cluniac Rule implied an insufficient degree of renunciation for some spirits, and Burgundy witnessed yet another attempt to

[1]'They keep too closely the vows which they make in there. They would insist, in truth, that when I wished to sleep I should have to keep awake, and when I wished to eat they would make me fast.'

return to the strictness of the Benedictine Rule. St. Robert, Abbot of Molesme, after seeking monastic perfection in several monasteries of Champagne and Burgundy, instituted the monastery of Cîteaux on the Feast of St. Benedict in the year 1098. Raymond Vicomte de Beaune gave the land; Eudes Duke of Burgundy, the endowment. Under the English abbot Stephen Harding of Sherborne the abbey reached a standard of almost puritanical simplicity; but its real force came when in 1112 Bernard, himself descended on the mother's side from the ducal house of Burgundy, retired there with his brothers to renounce the world. He came of that mixed Burgundian race that has produced so many men of spiritual and intellectual eminence; and he brought greatness to Cîteaux. The letter and spirit of Benedict's Rule continued to be rigorously kept. They had but one meal a day, and had done twelve hours' work to earn it; they never tasted meat, fish, fat, or eggs, and had milk but rarely. Their day began with matins at two in the morning, lasting till four. Next came the service of lauds at dawn. The interval between the two must have been the most precious time of the day, for the monk was free to spend it as he chose, whether in study in the cloister or in meditation. After lauds the celebration of Mass kept him in the chapel till nine, when he worked in the fields till two, and vespers and compline ended the day.

> *Omnem horam occupabis*
> *Hymnis, psalmis, et amabis*
> *   Tenere silentium.*
> *Super hoc orationem*
> *Diliges et lectionem,*
> *   Nutricem claustralium.*

The constitution of the Order was not monarchical like that of Cluny, for the daughter-houses, as they arose—and sixty-five of them were founded in the lifetime of Bernard—were subordinated on the feudal plan of subinfeudation, the right of visitation being vested in the immediate mother-abbey and not in Cîteaux herself. The Order was in fact a federation, governed by an aristocracy of abbots assembled in council. All were to follow the same Rule, the same customs, the same forms of chant, prayer, and service, 'ut una caritate, una regula, similibusque vivamus moribus'.

In interests, as in constitution, Cîteaux was opposed to Cluny. One of the clauses of the *Carta Caritatis* decrees that no Cistercian should compose verse; in none of the abbey churches of the Cistercian Order was it permitted to represent a human head or figure carved in stone. It is against

Cluny that Bernard's strictures on the beautification of monasteries are directed:

"What do you suppose is the object of all this?" he asks. *"Is it the repentance of the contrite, or the admiration of the beholders? Oh! vanity of vanities! but not more vain than foolish. The church's walls are resplendent, but the poor are not there . . . the curious find wherewith to amuse themselves, the wretched find in them no stay for their misery. What has all this imagery to do with monks, with professors of poverty, with men of spiritual minds? I will not speak of the immense height of the churches, of their immoderate length, of their superfluous breadth, costly polishing, and strange designs, which while they attract the eyes of the worshipper hinder the soul's devotion, and somehow remind me of the ancient Jewish ritual. Let all this pass. We will suppose that it is done, as we are told, for the glory of God. But, as a monk myself, I ask other monks: 'Tell me, O ye Professors of Poverty, what does gold in a holy place?'. . . Again, in the cloisters, what is the meaning of those ridiculous monsters, of that deformed beauty, that beautiful deformity, before the very eyes of the brethren reading there? . . . In fact, such an endless variety of forms appears everywhere that it is more pleasant to read in the stonework than in books, and to spend the day in admiring these oddities than in meditating on the Law of God. Before God, if they blush not at the impropriety, why do not they flinch before the expense?"*

Cîteaux, on the other hand, laboured in a field which Cluny hardly touched. Stephen Harding devoted profound study to producing a better edition of the Biblical text, and established standard versions of the missal, epistolary, collects, gradual, antiphonal, hymnal, psalter, lectionary, and calendar which had to be used in all Cistercian houses. Bernard's own great learning made him not only the opponent of Abelard, but also the arbiter in many disputes and the director of such work as the institution of the Rule of the Templars. He followed dialectic less than rhetoric; coming from the 'pays des orateurs', it is by the natural bent of his mind that he fights against the application of strict logical methods to revealed religion, even in its support.

Bernard kept Cîteaux from pursuing the arts of decoration, but he led them to the study of the art of music. He encourages his disciple Guy de Cherlieu to write a treatise *de Cantu* for the use of his Order; he tells his monks to sing 'Pure et strenue . . . non parcentes vocibus . . . sed virili, ut dignum est, et sonitu et affectu', and, with the help of his brethren, he reforms the music of the antiphonal.

Cistercian foundations were always made in solitary places; close touch with the world was avoided. Manual and not intellectual labour was to be the monk's portion, and teaching was forbidden to him. He might only read Gratian's *Decretals* at need; and in 1198 the chapter took action against a brother convicted of learning Hebrew. The only literary activities of the Order were in the field of ascetic oratory and allegorical comment.[1]

It is in the Cistercian convent of Clairvaux that the thirteenth-century story of the *Tombeur Notre Dame* is laid. The ignorant acrobat became a monk, but acquired no monkish learning in the cloister:

> *Car n'ot vescu fors de tumer*
> *Et d'espringer et de baler.*
> *Treper, saillir, ice savoit;*
> *Ne d'autre rien il ne savoit.*

So he secretly performed his best somersaults before the altar of the Virgin, since that was the only service he could render.

> *Hé! fait il, très douce roine*
> *Par vo pitié, par vo francise,*
> *Ne despisiés pas mon servise!*

And the monks who came to spy upon him saw the Virgin descend from her altar to fan his brow with the corner of her mantle.

Bernard himself had some of the simplicity of St. Francis. Jacques de Vitry tells us that 'when he rode abroad in the morning and saw boys keeping their flocks in the fields, he would say to his monks: 'Let us salute these boys, that they may answer to bless us; and thus, armed with the prayers of the innocent, we shall be able to ride on with an easy mind.' As a true follower of Stephen Harding, he found real literary force in his knowledge of the text of the Bible. In spite of his mystic and ascetic piety, he kept the saving common sense of the Frenchman,[2] and defined a wise man as 'one to whom all things taste even as they really are'. He had a true sense of the social side of religion, and a corresponding love of the word 'ordo', and so his passionate *vita contemplativa* seems only to have added new power to his active life. For a quarter of a century he dominated the religious life of France, giving new life to monasticism; reforming the secular clergy, warring against heresy, dogmatic, intellectual, and superstitious, ending the papal schism, and preaching the Crusade. Even

[1] The most far-fetched interpretations of the Song of Solomon are Cistercian in origin.
[2] In spite of his devotion to the Virgin, he firmly withstood the attempt to popularize the idea of the Immaculate Conception; and in spite of his views on crusading he took a stand against the persecution of the Jews.

the great Suger did not escape his criticism: 'At Saint Denis,' he said, 'they certainly render justly into Caesar those things which are Caesar's; but do they render unto God those things which are God's?' Bernard was the greatest monk of the Middle Ages, but there was no monk who lived oftener and for longer periods outside his abbey. He found it grievous and monstrous; but circumstances were too strong for him, and he could not fail to answer the call of a world which needed him.

Perhaps because the Cistercian Order depended too personally and directly upon him, perhaps because their inspiration to follow the austerities of his life was derived too immediately from his personal example, after his death the Order fell upon evil days. It was primarily a Burgundian Order, and Burgundy was commercially rich because of the traffic on the Brenner route to Italy. Trade gradually crept within the cloister, brought by the concourse of 'frères convers' who lived there without taking monastic vows.

A hundred years after its institution the corruption was admitted by the Order itself; the Chapter General of 1191 says, 'the congregation does not cease from acquisition, and the love of property has become a scourge'. Similarly the *Bible Guiot* states:

> *Provendes, Eglises achatent,*
> *En maintes manieres baratent;*
> *Acheter savent et revendre*
> *Et le terme molt bien atendre*
> *Et la bone vente dou blé.*
> *Et s'ai bien oï et taasté*
> *Qu'as Juis prestent lor deniers.*[1]

Any attempt at internal reform proved ineffectual; the Cistercians continued in commerce, selling their corn, retailing their wine, and even owning their own mercantile marine for sea and river traffic.

The development of monasticism gradually influenced the anchoretic life of the hermit. In 1084 St. Bruno first established the Carthusian Order in Savoy in which the hermit leads a solitary life as a member of a community, working, praying, cooking, eating, and sleeping alone, and only seeing his brethren at the morning mass and at meals in the refectory on the great feast days of the Church. The Order made some headway in France, and in sympathy with it the Limousin Étienne de

---

[1]'They buy livings and churches, and cheat in many ways. They know how to buy and re-sell, how to wait for settling day and the best sale of their corn, and I have certainly heard and proved that they lend their money to the Jews.'

Muret founded the contemplative Order of Grandmont, and another Frenchman, Aimeric Malefaye, Patriarch of Antioch, reformed the hermits of Mount Carmel; but it was long before the Carmelites became naturalized in France. Guiot de Provins condemned the Carthusians out of hand: they live in solitude and are no better than murderers, for they do not give their monks better food when they are ill.

These, then, are the chief Orders of the regular clergy. Between the regular and the secular clergy come the canons or *canonici*, following not *regula* but *canones*. Like a monk, the canon lived a corporate life attached to a cathedral or a collegiate church in a cloister or close. The monk was a member of an Order, but he was not necessarily 'in orders', though a certain number of monks in every monastery were ordained so that they might perform the sacraments for the community. The canon, on the other hand, was ordained, and, like a secular priest, might have a cure of souls and take the services of a church. As a member of a cathedral chapter or of a collegiate church he had two functions to perform. First, he and his colleagues were the officers of public prayer, and were responsible for the proper celebration of the Christian feasts. An ordinary week-day had five offices or 'canonical hours': matins, lauds, mass, vespers, and compline. On Sundays there were nine; and others were added for the greater feasts. Second, he and his colleagues formed the council of the bishop and were with him the administrators of the diocese. They therefore were monks, in so far as they led a corporate life, and secular priests, in so far as they had cure of souls. Their position was consequently anomalous, and about 750 St. Chrodegang of Metz attempted to bring them under a Rule—to make them *regular* clergy. Thus in time a distinction came to be drawn between canons secular—that is a community of secular priests—and canons regular, primarily monastic but also able to take charge of parishes. The common element in their rule of life was based on the writings of St. Augustine, and the first canons regular were black Austin Canons, who devoted themselves, among other works of piety, to the maintenance of hospitals. Such service, however, did not compare in hardness with the rigours of the Benedictine Rule. Their intercourse with the world was necessarily not limited, since they were also parish priests, and as such they received considerable dues. Peter, Precentor of Notre Dame de Paris about 1190, is bitterly eloquent on the part money played in their lives. Where the chapter deducts a certain sum for the canon's non-attendance at service, you may see them running up at the last moment 'like old women after a greased pig; some bent forward, others leaping over the bar to enter, others pressing in disorderly fashion through the open door'. It is to the Austin Canons that Guiot de Provins would belong:

> Benoeiz soit sainz Augustins!
> Des bons morsiaux et des bons vins
> Ont li chanoine a grant plenté.
> Molt sont gentilment atorné.
> Ici pourroie-je bien souffrir,
> Que j'aim miex vivre que morir.[1]

However, a stricter rule was followed by the white canons, the Premonstratensians, founded by St. Norbert at Prémontré in Champagne in 1119.

Benedictinism was the source of the monasticism of the early Middle Ages, and its activities justify their description as the Benedictine Age. In the course of the twelfth century the leadership passed from the Order: the monastic schools declined before such cathedral schools as those of Laon, Tours, Chartres, Orléans, and Paris, and the source of new developments in the history of the Religious Orders is to be found in the communities of canons who served the cathedrals. It is in a sense the reflection of the growing importance of the cities: the cathedral city is the capital of a province, but the monastery is apt to be hidden in some remote rural solitude—Clara Vallis, Fontenay, or Vaucler. So it is in connexion with the cathedrals that learned and didactic literature comes into close touch with vernacular literature through the *Miracles* and *Mystères*; that Latin hymns remain in relation with lay lyrics; and that the classical cycle—*Romans de Thèbes, de Troie, d'Enée, d'Alexandre*—passes from the scriptoria into French narrative verse, and that the foundations of the lay culture of the later Middle Ages are laid.

When monasticism was established idealism was impracticable in the world outside, and the cloister was the only place where a holy life could be led. But as the Church gradually influenced the national life the need of the nation for the wisdom and knowledge of the monks increased, and the division between the cloister and the world grew less marked. The greatest monks, such as Bernard, were driven by force of circumstance to spend much of their lives outside the cloister; and if for them this relaxation of the vow of *stabilitas loci* was a penance, for many it was a pleasure. By the time of Philip Augustus we find Philippe d'Harvengt, Abbot of Bonne Éspérance, asking, 'Where is the street, the square, the cross-roads where one does not see monks on horseback? Is there a feast, a fair, or a

---

[1]'Blessed be the holy Augustine! The canons have great plenty of fat morsels and good wine, and are very well provided for. Here I could very well endure, for I had rather live than die.'

market where they do not appear? They are seen at every tournament and every battle.' Clearly *stabilitas loci* was not congenial to the age; and the accounts of the corruption of the monasteries, to be found alike in the visitation-books of the bishops and in popular literature, show that the concomitant *conversio morum* was rare.

The Church, too, was developing an aristocratic standpoint in an age of democracy. The philosophical activities of the twelfth century had led to a theology of speculative subtleties which could only be comprehended by trained minds. The later developments of the Gregorian movement engrossed the Papacy in a policy devoted to the establishment of papal supremacy in temporal as in spiritual things. But if the Church was monarchical at its summit, it was democratic at its base, and in the thirteenth century this lay democracy became conscious of its individual and collective power. To many the spheres of dominion, judicature, and administration were closed, but every man had a sphere of expression in his spiritual life. Laymen became conscious of the power of judging their priests by standards which were Christian and which should have been priestly. St. Bernard expresses his sense of the corruption of the hierarchy of the church: 'The cardinals are full of avarice and evil living; without faith or religion they sell God and his Mother, and betray us and their fathers. Rome sucks and devours us, Rome kills and destroys all.' Almost for the first time men ventured to hold the opinion that the man may pollute the office rather than that the office must inevitably ennoble the man. The majority of men were filled with a profound conviction of the emptiness of sacerdotal Christianity and were ready to cry with Guiot de Provins: 'A congregation is made by charity, and should be full of charity. A monk may suffer much, read, chant, work, and fast; unless he has charity, in my opinion it counts for nothing. He is like an empty house in which spiders spin their webs, but quickly destroy what they have spun. To chant and to fast does not save souls: only faith and charity.' Hugues de Saint Cher preaches that 'this pompous religion shall be reduced to great need, so that the monks shall sometimes be compelled to beg their kinsfolk for food and raiment, to disperse their communities, to pawn their croziers and crosses, and to sell their books'.

The earlier institutions of the Church no longer fulfilled the needs they had once served; a new task called for workers of another kind. If the earlier centuries are the age of the Benedictines, and the twelfth century of the secular priests, the thirteenth century, in many ways the culmination of the Middle Ages, is the age of the friars.

Mystics such as Joachim of Flores, awaiting the coming of the Gospel of the Spirit; thinkers such as Arnold of Brescia, wishing either so to spiritualize the Church as to make it worthy of its Master or else to transfer the sacerdotal power into the hands of those prepared to follow Him; Amaury of Chartres, declaring, 'Now the sacraments of the New Testament are at an end, and the reign of the Holy Spirit becomes each day incarnate in each of us'; the Lombard Humiliati, penitents who went about the world preaching repentance and lowliness of spirit, crying *Pax et bonum* as they went—these are all precursors of Francis and Dominic. There grew up an ideal of individual striving for perfection, which is the common note of Franciscan and Dominican, of Albigensian and Vaudois; but it was recognized that such perfection lay not in cloistered seclusion but in leading a life at once pure and fruitful in the crowded highways of the world.

The French spirit of Crusade and chivalry had so beautified the lives of ordinary men that it was felt to be possible for those under vows to seek perfection even while working in the world. Francis, who knew the poetry and chivalry of Provence, thus dedicated his troubadour's spirit in the service of Christ, and so brought the glamour and romance of Provençal *courtoisie* into an ascetic Order in setting before the world the example of the *Joculatores Dei*.[1] Love and peace were their watchwords; courtesy and forgiveness their duties; absolute poverty and chastity their vows. But so far his Order was nothing but a chance confraternity, offering dangerous similarities with such heretics as the Pauvres de Lyon.[2] Before it could work in a Christian community it must be taken into the Church and be, as it were, ordained. The Roman Curia saw in its rules a dangerous resemblance to the innovations of the reformers, but Cardinal John of St. Paul overruled their prejudices. 'If we reject the petition of this poor man as something novel and too hard to fulfil', he declared, 'when all he asks is that the Law of Life of the Gospel be confirmed to him, let us beware lest we offend against the Gospel of Christ. For if any one shall say that in the observance of evangelical perfection and the vow to observe it, there is anything new or irrational or impossible of observance, such a one is convicted of blasphemy.' Recognition by the Church was thus secured in 1217; organization within the Church had then to be achieved. First, the friar's vows of chastity and poverty were confirmed. Next, the second monastic duty—obedience—was expressed in the image of parenthood, and all idea of lordship one over another was disclaimed. Then—and it is here that a great difference is apparent between the Benedictine and the

---

[1] He had a habit of singing French songs which he composed himself in the langue d'oil, and knew and loved the *Chanson de Roland*.
[2] In Germany, Hungary, and France the first Franciscans were taken for *Cathari*.

Franciscan Rules—instead of being bound to a communal life within the walls of his monastery, the friar was allotted to his province, Spain, Portugal, France, Germany, Hungary, England, Italy, or Syria. The government of the Order lay with a general chapter of the whole confraternity; the whole organization of the society was designed to weaken neither its democratic basis nor its ideal of the nomadic life. Though affairs in Italy prevented Francis himself from heading the French mission, as he had wished, by 1219 the Order was established at Paris, and by 1233 it had branches all over France. But as the reins of government ceased to be held by Francis alone, a tendency away from poverty and simplicity began to make itself felt, and in spite of opposition from one party in the Order, the conventual gradually superseded the nomadic life.

St. Dominic unconsciously began the foundation of his Order when, as a canon of the French Order of Prémontré at the cathedral of Osma in Spain, he undertook the mission of preaching to the heretics of Languedoc. Spain, like France and Italy, had felt the stirrings of the movement towards a return to simple Christianity, and the *Pauperes Catholici*—a sect which managed to remain orthodox though having a distinct affinity with the Vaudois of Aragon—are the precursors of the Dominicans. It was through their example that Dominic set out to destroy heresy, following the apostolic example as a pilgrim with wallet and staff, preaching the Gospel. Gradually a confraternity developed from his work, offering close parallels with the Franciscan Order. It was formally incorporated at Prouille in Languedoc. The first Friars Preachers numbered six Spaniards, one Englishman, and seven men from the provinces of France: the Île de France, Provence, Toulouse, Navarre, Lorraine, and Normandy.[1] Its rule was that of Dominic's own Order of Prémontré, without the obligation to lead a cloistered life. Dominic and Francis became friends; and Dominic, who had not originally intended the vow of poverty to extend to the Order as well as to the individuals composing it, was persuaded by Francis to adopt the Franciscan principle of communal renunciation of property. But in spite of their general similarity in aim and constitution, the two Orders preserved in a remarkable degree the stamp impressed upon them by the personality of their founders. The Dominican and the Franciscan mind are to this day marked and distinguishable. The Dominican love of souls accompanies a fiery zeal for conservative orthodoxy, which the more emotional temper and more democratic sympathies of the Franciscan have constantly threatened. It has been the maxim of

[1] It was decided as early as 1220 that the general assembly should be held alternately in the University centres of Paris and Bologna. The Order was established in Lyons 1218, Rheims and Limoges 1219, Poitiers 1220, Metz and Montpellier 1221, Bayonne 1222.

the Dominican *Ordo Predicatorum* to preach the Gospel by word and example—*verbo pariter et exemplo*, and the Franciscan to exhort *plus exemplo quam verbo*. Further, the Dominican trusts first to reason, and the Franciscan first to feeling; as St. Bonaventura says, 'Praedicatores principaliter intendunt speculationi . . . et postea unctioni; Minores vero principaliter unctioni et postea speculationi'. Each remained faithful to the spirit of their founder:

> *L'un fu tutto serafico in ardore,*
> *L'altro per sapienza in terra fue*
> *Di cherubica luce uno spendore.*

The specific function of both Orders was and is to preach the Gospel: every friar was a missionary to his province. Nor was this missionary effort confined to Christendom. Francis himself at the time of the Crusade went to Damietta and strove to prevent battle between the Christian and Paynim hosts. He went unarmed to the camp of the Sultan and explained his mission to convert the world, and as the Eastern mind always respects the religious fanatic, he was received and dismissed with courtesy. He then went to found a province of his Order in Syria. By 1245 missionaries of the Mendicant Orders had reached Persia, and in 1252 St. Louis sent the Franciscan Guillaume de Rubriquis to the Great Khan, at whose court he held disputations with Nestorian Christians, Moslems, and Buddhists. In 1253, at the request of St. Louis, Innocent IV founded the Society of *Peregrinantes propter Christum*, recruited from the Franciscans and Dominicans. By 1276 the Dominican mission to Bagdad under Ricold de Montecroix had reached considerable proportions; a bishopric was founded there in 1318, embracing twenty-five churches in the new capital of Sultaniyeh. Meanwhile a Franciscan mission under John of Montecorvino had penetrated to India, and thence reached China in 1298. They were well received by the Khan, and were allowed to preach and build a church. Learning the Tartar language, they translated the Psalms and the New Testament, founded a missionary college, and by 1304 had secured more than five thousand converts. In the early fourteenth century Pope John XXII corresponded with missions in Georgia, Persia, China, Tartary, and Turkestan, and in 1329 founded the bishoprics of Lesser Armenia, Tauris, and India.

Thus the Mendicant Orders became to the Papacy of the later thirteenth century what the Jesuits were to be to that of the sixteenth. Further, they helped the Papacy to combat heresy at home. The Mendicant Orders themselves had in their origin something in common with the heretical sects they were to combat, in their desire to return to a simpler Christianity. The Vaudois, or Poor of Lyons, show the most obvious parallel. About 1170 a rich merchant of Lyons, Pierre Valdo, had certain books of the Bible and of the Fathers translated into the vulgar tongue,[1] and basing his teaching upon them strove to return to the conditions of the primitive Church. But it was a lay reform that never received ecclesiastical sanction: he was excommunicated and the *Pauvres de Lyon* were denounced as heretics by Lucius III. More definitely heretical were two sects of the South of France: the Petrobrusians, founded by Pierre de Bruis in the early twelfth century, as a sect opposed to infant baptism, worship in churches, reverence for the Cross, the doctrine of the Real Presence, and the saying of masses for the dead; and the Cathari or Albigensians, who inherited from the Eastern Manichaeans a dualistic religion steeped in morbid and fanatical asceticism. Theirs was a definite schism from the Church; for them the God of the Old Testament was the devil, the Roman Church 'the Synagogue of Satan'. Such sects threatened the Church, and though the Papacy resisted the appeal to force again them until 1207, even before then conversion had passed into persecution. With papal and popular support the Albigensian Crusade of 1209 was carried out with almost incredible cruelty. Provençal civilization, already weakened, received its death-blow. The *Besant de Dieu*, written about 1230, says,

> *Quant Franceis vont sor Tolosans*
> *Qu'il tienent a popelicans*
> *E la legacie romaine*
> *Les i conduit et les i maine,*
> *N'est mie bien, ceo m'est avis.*
> *Bons e mals sont en toz pais.*[2]

All this was secular action, but the Church preached that mercy to those who rejected the true faith could be nothing but disobedience to God. The Mendicants very gradually made the Inquisition their own. They were bound by no ties of locality, they were free from episcopal dominion, and were directly dependent on the Holy See. Consequently some of the functions of the papal courts were delegated to them. The Inquisition was never formally founded and never formally vested in the friars, but its

---

[1] It is interesting to note how many of the 'heresies' within the medieval Church were based on a Biblical version in the vernacular.

[2] 'When men of France attack the men of Toulouse, whom they consider heretics, and the Roman Legate leads them and drives them on, in my opinion it is not at all a good thing. There are good and bad men in every country.'

powers gradually passed into their hands, and by 1258 two Dominicans held commissions as Papal Inquisitors of Albi, while others were working in France and Aragon in a similar capacity.

By the later thirteenth century the living force in the Church was a didactic force. The canons of the cathedrals, the doctors of the universities, the Friars Preachers, the Mendicant missionaries, even the Inquisitors were all there to teach men the truths of the Gospel. In face of the opposition of his chapter the then Abbot of Cîteaux opened a Cistercian college in Paris in 1227, and by the end of the century there were Cistercian houses at all the great universities. By knowledge shall men reach salvation, and on the portal of the thirteenth-century cathedral Christ stands as the Teacher of the world.

V

Pilgrimage and Crusade

MEN can never altogether forget their nomadic past; even when necessity no longer drives the tribe, they do not rest quietly for all their lives in the corner of the earth they have made their own. Beyond the next hill lies always a new Jerusalem: such is the romance of life.

Christian Rome turned to Asia to find in Jerusalem itself the sanctity of a vision. Constantine excavated to find the grotto of the Holy Sepulchre and the site of Calvary; the piety of Helena was rewarded by the Invention of the True Cross. Pilgrims came to the basilicas of the Sepulchre, the Mount of Olives, and Bethlehem from all the Christian countries of the West. Devout men desired, as Paula wrote to St. Jerome: 'To put the finishing touch to virtue by adoring Christ in the very place where the Gospel first shone forth from the Cross.' As early as 333 a native of Bordeaux made the pilgrimage and wrote an account of all the stages of the journey from Bordeaux by way of Constantinople to Jerusalem.[1] Some fifty years later St. Jerome founded a convent and monastery on the Egyptian model with a dependent hospice for pilgrims, and the first settlement of Western Christians in the Holy Land was established. Not even the barbarian invasions of the fifth century could put an end to pilgrimage; the attraction of the Holy Land had grown strong enough to survive the strain and stress of the most troubled years of the Dark Ages. Even after the establishment of Arab power in Syria after 633, the pilgrimage was occasionally undertaken as a penance, though it sometimes took as much as seven years to perform.

As the imperial power weakened, so did the glamour of Rome's past glories strengthen. To go *ad limina sancti apostoli* was to go to the chief city of the world:

> *Roma nobilis, orbis et domina*
> *Cunctarum urbium excellentissima,*
> *Roseo martyrum sanguine rubea . . .*

When Charlemagne went to Rome for the first time in 773, he got down from his horse on Monte Mario, the Mount of Joy, from which the

---

[1]Other early pilgrims are: Silvia of Aquitaine, *c.* 380; the Frankish Bishop Arculf, *c.* 680; Prince Willibald of Kent, *c.* 730; Bernard of Mont St. Michel, *c.* 870.

city first appears, and entered it on foot as a humble pilgrim.[1] In his day the way thither came to be marked by hostels for pilgrims, and the *via Cornelia* from the Tiber to St. Peter's was lined by *Scholae peregrinorum*.

Charlemagne was himself not only a pilgrim, but a defender of pilgrims. With him the Frankish Emperor became in the eyes of the world the champion of Christendom. The Arab invasion had been checked at Constantinople in 718 and at Poitiers in 732, and a certain balance of power between East and West had been attained. Charlemagne was therefore able to employ the diplomatic relations with Bagdad established by Pepin the Short for the confirmation of the Western Emperor's right of protectorate over Christians in the Holy Land.[2] Since it involved no diminution of his political power, Haroun-el-Raschid confirmed Charlemagne in this privilege, and further made him an absolute gift of the Holy Sepulchre. As early as 870 the square in front of St. Mary Latina at Jerusalem was known as the Frankish Market.

So to the pilgrimage to Rome in a friendly country was added the pilgrimage to Jerusalem in a neutral country under friendly protection; and to these was later added a third pilgrimage, this time under arms. The Arabs of Spain were beaten at Poitiers, but through the centuries that followed they remained a perpetual menace to France. The struggle to keep them back had been the effort that helped to make France a nation; there is political truth behind the cry of Charlemagne in *Aymeri de Narbone*:

> *Ralez vos en, Borguignon et François,*
> *Et Hennuier, Flamenc et Avalois,*
> *Et Angevin, Poitevin et Mansois,*
> *Et Loherain, Breton et Herupois.*
> *Je remendrai ici en Nerbonois,*
> *Si garderai Nerbone et le defois!*

In 1015 the Norman Roger I de Toéni, Seigneur de Castillon, led the first French expedition against the Moors since the time of Charlemagne,[3]

---

[1]M. Bédier has ably shown (*Légendes Épiques*, vol. ii), how far the later Carolingian epic cycle is linked up with the stages of the pilgrimage to Rome.

[2]To the conservative Orient Europeans are still *Franks* in the Levant.

[3]There were no less than thirty-four such expeditions. Among the most important are:

> 1033.   Odilo of Cluny enrols Burgundian army.
> 1063.   Expedition from Aquitaine.
> 1065.   Expedition under Thibaut de Semur.
> 1073.   Eble de Rouci, with support of the Pope.
> 1078.   Hugues de Bourgogne.
> 1085.   Eudes de Bourgogne, Raimond de Bourgogne, Raimond de St. Gilles, Robert de Bourgogne, Savaric de Donzy, Humbert de Joinville.

On the whole question see Boissonnade, *Du nouveau sur la Chanson de Roland*, pp. 3–68.

and this was quickly followed by other hosts from Burgundy and the south. It is a Burgundian who becomes King of Portugal after seventeen victories against the Moors; and another mounts the throne of Castille.

For them the shrine of St. James at Compostella, which at first had been of merely local importance,[1] became the goal of a pilgrimage under arms. This, the first Crusade, undertaken by Frenchmen of the north, the east, and the south, brought a new element into Christian life; for the early Church, unlike Islam, had no tradition of Holy War. The Church of France by the land-peace and the *Truga Dei* had sought to check the abuse of war in feudal society; in the Crusade the fighting instincts of Christian feudalism were directed to a Christian end. With Turpin before Ronces-vaux, the Church 'par penitence les cumandet a ferir'. With Roland she said to those who died fighting:

> *Seignors barons, de vos ait Deus mercit!*
> *Tutes vos anmes otreit il pareïs!*
> *En seintes flurs il les facet gesir!*
> *Meillors vassels de vos unkes ne vi.*[2]

The crusading spirit is a French impulse, and only keeps its vitality so long as it is in close touch with France. There is little doubt that its first inspiration came from the Burgundian monastery of Cluny and its daughter-houses; by 1015, Raoul Glaber tells us, Cluniac minds were already haunted by the idea of leading men to seek glory and martyrdom in Saracen lands. Pilgrim and crusader were one and the same; the one defended himself, the other attacked his enemies in order to reach his goal. They had the same rallying cries:

> *Cunctae gentes, linguae, tribus,*
> *Illuc vunt clamantes*
> *Sus eja! Ultreja!*

And the crusaders set out on the first stage of the journey unarmed and in pilgrim's garb. So Joinville begins his journey: 'Then I departed from Joinville on foot barefoot in my shirt, not to re-enter the castle till my return; and thus I went to Blécourt, and Saint Urbain, and to other places thereabouts where there are holy relics. And never while I went to Blécourt and Saint Urbain would I turn my eyes towards Joinville for fear my heart should melt within me at the thought of the fair castle I was leaving behind, and my two children.' So Fra Salimbene meets St. Louis at Sens

---

[1]The tomb called that of St. James was only discovered about 830.
[2]'Lord Barons, may God have mercy on you! May he grant all your souls rest in Paradise! May he set them amidst the Holy flowers! Never have I seen better vassals than you.'

'in a pilgrim's habit, with the staff and scrip of his pilgrimage hanging about his neck'.

With the establishment of feudal order after the tenth century pilgrimages became more and more frequent, whether undertaken in expiation of sin, in fulfilment of a vow, or as a holy end to life. Peter, Abbot of Josselin, says there are three sorts of pilgrims: 'the first is of those who seek the holy places for the sake of piety; the second of penitents, on whom a pilgrimage has been imposed as a penance, or who undertake it of their own free will; the third of those near death, who desire sepulture in holy ground'. In the sculpture of the Last Judgement at Autun all the dead are naked except two who have died on pilgrimage, who still have their wallets, one with the cross of Jerusalem and the other with the shell of St. James.

Pilgrimage first appears as a penalty in the legislation by which the Church strove to modify feudal warfare; any one who killed a man during the *Truga Dei* was to be exiled from his province and to go on pilgrimage to Jerusalem. Later it became a punishment that was also decreed by the civil authority; a royal ordinance of 1371 decrees, 'we will that our said échevins shall be able to enforce and commit those who by them shall be condemned for their offences to make any journeys or pilgrimages by penalty of fixed sums of money'. Such a punishment might even be imposed on a community through its representatives. A treaty signed at Arcques near Saint Omer on Christmas Eve 1356, between the King of France, Count Louis of Flanders, and the Flemish cities, stipulates that 300 men of Bruges and Cambrai must go on pilgrimage, a hundred to St. James at Compostella, a hundred to Saint Gilles in Provence, and a hundred to Rocamadour.

By the end of the eleventh century pilgrimages were divided into two categories: the greater pilgrimages to Rome, Compostella, and Jerusalem, and the lesser pilgrimages within a man's own country. The departure for each was hallowed by the Church; the *Coutume de Normandie* describes the ceremony, which usually took place at nightfall. 'Then the pilgrim, having received his scrip with cross and holy water in the parish church, is conducted in procession outside the parish, to seek Jerusalem, Rome, or St. James, or to go on another pilgrimage "per cruce signationem".' The *Roman de Mont Saint Michel*, written between 1154 and 1186, describes the pilgrims two hundred years before Chaucer:

> *Li jorz iert clers e sanz grant vent.*
> *Les meschines e les vallez*
> *Chascuns d'els dist verz ou sonnez.*

Neis li viellart revunt chantant
De leece funt tuit semblant;
Qui plus ne seit si chante outree
E Dex aie *u* Asusee.
Cil jugleor la u il vunt
Tuit lor vieles traites unt
Laiz et sonnez vunt vielant.
Li tens est beals, la joie est grant.
Cil palefrei e cil destrier
E cil roncin e cil sommier
Qui errouent par le chemin
Que menouent cil pelerin,
De totes parz henissant vunt
Par la grant joie que il unit.
Neis par les bois chantonent tuit
Li oiselet grant et petit . . .
Entor le mont el bois follu
Cil travetier unt tres tendu
Rues unt fait par les chemins.
Plentei i ont de divers vins,
Pain e pastez, fruit e poissons,
Oisels, obleies, veneisons,
De totes parz avet a vendre
Assez en ont qui ad que tendre.[1]

Besides Mont Saint Michel there were innumerable pilgrimages within France itself: to Chartres, to see the Tunic of the Virgin; to Sainte Geneviève at Paris, to Saint Denis, to Notre Dame du Puy, to Saint Martial at Limoges, to Saint Martin at Tours, to Saint Sernin at Toulouse, to Sainte Marie Madeleine at Vézelay. The last named gained far more than local importance through its geographical position at the crossing of the route from Channel to Mediterranean and from Central France to Rome; thousands came to it three times a year, at Easter, Whitsun, and on July 22. But such pilgrimages, like that to Mont Saint Michel, were

[1]'The day was clear, without much wind. The maidens and the young men each of them said verse or song; even the old start singing again: all have a look of joy. Who knows no more sings 'Outree!' or 'God help!' or 'Asusee!' The minstrels there where they go have all brought their viols, and go playing lays and songs. The weather is fine and joy is great. The palfreys and the chargers, the hackneys and the packhorses which amble along the road that the pilgrims follow, go neighing on all sides for the great joy that they have. Even in the woods all the little birds sing, great and small. . . . About the mount, in the leafy wood, the victuallers have set up tents and turned the paths into streets. Plenty was there of divers wines, bread and pasties, fruit and fish, birds, cakes and venison; everywhere was there for sale enough for him who had the means to pay.'

easy and happy: 'Li tens est beals, la joie est grant': and they tended to degenerate into attendance at fairs in pilgrimage places, and to become one with travel that lacked a religious purpose.

Indeed, the spiritual value of a pilgrimage and the consequent strength of its tradition would seem to depend upon its difficulty. Thus the three major pilgrimages—to Rome, to Compostella, and to Jerusalem—had the greatest importance. To go to Rome was by custom the duty of a bishop upon his consecration, and many humbler pilgrims followed. The Pilgrims' Way from France lay over the St. Bernard or the Mont Cenis; the roads they used still bear in many places the name of 'via francesca'. They brought back to France a memory of the troubled greatness of Rome, though for them it was a city of ghosts speaking an unknown tongue. History might be lost in legend; the emperors and poets might figure as magicians; but it is none the less the Capitoline statue of Marcus Aurelius—whom they believed to be Constantine—which reappears upon the church façades of Southern France; and the French battle-cry 'Montjoie!' comes from the *Mons Gaudi* whence the pilgrims first saw Rome.

Yet, though from April to July the long files of 'romieux' and 'paumiers' might pass along the roads, the pilgrimage to Rome lacked the heroic tradition. Cluny, it is true, did its best to supply it; but even their stories of the pilgrimage of their Abbot Saint Maieul, of his being attacked by Saracens, and his miraculous escape, failed to do more than make his tomb at Souvigny a local centre of pilgrimage.

The pilgrimage to Compostella held the romance and purpose that were lacking from the pilgrimage to Rome: French monks of Cluny had inspired the knights of Burgundy and Aquitaine to conquer it from the Moors and had peopled Spain with Cluniac colonies.

Cluniac monasteries marked the stages of the four great roads to Compostella. From Tours, Vézelay, Le Puy, and Arles, Saint Gilles, Saint Pierre de Moissac, Saint Jean d'Angly, Saint Eutrope de Saintes offered hospitality and sanctity, and the chain of Cluniac monasteries was continued over the frontier into Spain along the 'Camino francés' to Compostella. In the twelfth century Cluniac monks inspired the compilation of a guide book for the journey, the *Liber Sancti Jacobi*. It gives the hymns to the saint, recounts his history and his miracles, and describes the roads and the stages. The 'Advice to the Traveller' includes a brief Basque vocabulary, a list of rivers of which the water is wholesome, and of relics that should be seen on the way. A Latin poem of the same date, composed by monks of the abbey of Roncesvalles, describes the hospitality it offered;

all who came were welcomed. At the door a man offered bread, and took no price; within, a barber and a cobbler were at the service of the pilgrims.

Si videres pauperum ibi sobtulares
Resarciri corio, tunc Deum laudares.

There were two hospices for the sick, with beds and baths; the cellars were reported to be full of almonds, pomegranates, and other fruit. Even if the pilgrim died there, his salvation was assured by sepulture in holy ground. In 1161 the Order of St. James of the Sword was founded—with the device *Rubet ensis sanguine Arabum*—in order to protect the pilgrims; and by its care, and that of the innumerable confraternities of St. James, hostels to give shelter for the night arose at all the stages of the road.

The eleventh-century French Crusade in Spain and the subsequent pilgrimages had a double influence on the art of France. When Raymond of Burgundy re-peopled Avila in 1090, he summoned not only ninety French knights, but also twenty-two masters of *piedras tallar*, and twelve of *jometria*. These built the walls and the churches, and left the stamp of France upon them. With more settled times the workmen came as pilgrims; men from the Île de France form the architectural style of Leon; men from Chartres leave their handiwork in passing on the door-jambs of Sangüesa. The monasteries on the *Camino francés*—such as those of Las Huelgas and Villa Sirga—show the influence of French workmen. Indeed, from the eleventh to the fourteenth century there was a wave of French architecture into Spain along the pilgrim's way; and if the French workmen gave much, they received something in return. In the eleventh century Moorish architecture was perhaps the most advanced in Europe; and the Romanesque style of Cluny and her daughter-churches on the roads to Spain show the lobes, the framing to the arches, and the parti-coloured stone of the Moorish style which is reflected in the eleventh-century architecture of the church of St. James at Compostella.

The pilgrims of France did more than this for art. All epics are at bottom journey-songs; and behind the measures of the *chansons de geste* sounds the rhythm of the pilgrims' march. Monsieur Bédier tried to prove that the whole cycle of Guillaume d'Orange owed its historic basis to documents of monasteries—Saint Julien de Brioude, Saint Honorat des Aliscamps, Saint Guilhem du Desert—on the *via Tolosana* to Compostella; and that the *Chanson de Roland* and others of the Carolingian cycle arise out of the Crusades of the men of Burgundy and Provence who followed in Charlemagne's footsteps to fight the Saracens. He pressed his theory too far, yet it is true that in the French epic cycle we have the immediate past of France as the inspiration of the first French classic, and the chivalry of France as the indirect creator of the first *style noble*.

Thus Roland and Oliver appear as Christian heroes on the sculptures of the twelfth-century cathedrals, and even the jongleurs who sing them find a place.[1] The jongleurs, indeed, were pilgrims for life,[2] and in their hands the traditions of the road were safe. Bertrand de Bar-sur-Aube tells how he got the story of his *Girard de Vienne* from such a pilgrim:

> *A un juedi, cant dou mustier issi,*
> *Ot escouté un gaillart pallerin*
> *Qui ot Saint Jacque aoré et servi*
> *Et par Saint Piere de Rome reverti.*
> *Cil li conta ce que il sot de fi,*
> *Les aventures que a repaire oï*
> *Et les grans poines que dans Girars soufri*
> *Ains qu'il eüst Viane.*[3]

The development of the pilgrimages to Rome and Compostella in no wise detracted from the importance of the pilgrimage to Jerusalem. All the medieval maps give the Holy City as the centre of the world; for all nations the difficulties of the journey and the glamour of the Holy Places made it the greatest pilgrimage of all. The conversion of the Hungarians to Christianity at the end of the tenth century made it possible to travel by land, by way of Constantinople and Asia Minor. At the end of the century the first band of pilgrims arrived from Iceland; the confines of Europe acknowledged the claims of the Holy Places. But at the beginning of the eleventh century the position of the Franks in the Holy Land was rudely changed. The Caliph Hakem, in a sudden attack of Shiite fanaticism, ordered the demolition of the Holy Sepulchre, the confiscation of its treasure, and the destruction of all Christian relics and symbols. The majority of the Christians were massacred, and the survivors heavily penalized: they were not only under legal disabilities, but had to wear a copper cross ten pounds in weight. Though this persecution came to a sudden end in 1020 it had destroyed the Frankish protectorate, which was succeeded by the Byzantine power. The basilicas were rebuilt and the

---

[1] Jongleurs appear on the sculptures of the churches of Ferrières, Souvigny, and Bourbon-l'Archambault; the jongleresse walking on her hands at Amboise; the acrobat with his head between his legs at Saint Martin de Tours.

[2] St. Julian, the traveller's saint, was their patron; witness the church of Saint Julien les Ménétriers at Paris.

[3] 'One Thursday, as he came out of church, he listened to a lusty pilgrim who had worshipped and served St. James and had come back by St. Peter's at Rome. He (the pilgrim) told him what he knew of a truth, namely the adventures he heard of on his way home, and the hardships which Giraud endured before he captured Vienne.'

Christian quarter was fortified, but though the position of Christians in Jerusalem might be more secure, the schism between Eastern and Western Churches involved the western pilgrim in difficulties under a Byzantine protectorate. Hence, though the number of pilgrims increased, they no longer came individually, but in armed and organized companies. In 1016 the company of Normans coming back from Syria was strong enough to help the Salernitans against the Saracens, and so to begin the Norman settlement of Southern Italy. In 1027, again, the Norman band that set out at the expense of Duke Richard II numbered seven hundred, and was followed the next year by another led by the Bishops of Poitiers and Limoges. With the progress of the century the difficulties increased. Gerbert, Pope under the name of Sylvester II, made the pilgrimage and returned to make an appeal to Christendom against pagan persecution. In 1064 the Seljuk Turks began to threaten both the Byzantine Empire and the Fatimite Caliphate, and by 1081 they held the East and had destroyed the churches of Asia Minor.

Already the crusading spirit was abroad in France; and when at the Council of Clermont in 1095 Pope Urban II—himself a Cluniac monk and a Frenchman from the diocese of Soissons—besought men to come to the deliverance of the Holy Sepulchre and the Christians of the East, the cry went up through France, 'Diex lo vot! Diex lo vot!' and many thousands took the cross. The vow was irrevocable; the Church, in the person of the local bishop, became responsible for the protection of the goods of those absent on Crusade. The *Chanson d'Antioche* pictures the return of a baron from the assembly at Clermont:

> *Li quens Robers de Flandres part de la baronie*
> *A Arras est venus a Climence sa mie,*
> *Souavet li conseille doucement en l'oïe:*
> *'Dame, jou ai la crois, ne vous en poise mie!*
> *De vous voel le congié; s'en irai en Surie*
> *Delivrer le sepulchre de la gent paienie.'*
> *Quant l'entent la contesse, s'a la colour noircie:*
> *'Sire,' ce dist la dame, 'pour moi, n'irés-vous mie;*
> *Vos avés dui biaus fis que Jhesus beneïe!*
> *Grant mestier ont de vous et de la vostre aïe.'*
> *Quant li quens l'entendi, si l'a estroit baisie:*
> *'Dame,' ce dist li quens, 'tenés, je vous afie,*
> *Si tost com au sepulcre iert m'ofrande coucie,*
> *Et je l'aurai baisié et m'orison fenie,*

Dedens les quinze jors vous afi, sans boisdie,
Me metrai al retour, se Diex me donne vie.'
La dame tent sa main et li quens li afie;
N'i a cel de plorer n'ait la face moillie.[1]

The wives had to accept their husbands' vows, and could only ask to be remembered oversea:

Lor seigneurs en apelent a cui sont espousées:
'Seigneur, a la foi Dieu somes-nous mariées,
Loiautés vous avons plevies et jurées;
Por Dieu! quand vous arés les terres conquestées,
Et vous verrés la vile ou Diex soufri colées,
Souveigne-vous de nous, n'i soions oubliées!'
Ha Diex! Adont i ot maintes larmes plorées.[2]

The Pope's appeal was repeated by many itinerant preachers, one of whom—Peter the Hermit, a native of Amiens—took in later legend the place of the Pope as the originator of the Crusade. These appeals were primarily directed to the feudal classes whose position and military training fitted them to become the defenders of Christendom, but the call to Crusade was unexpectedly answered by the organization among townsmen and peasants of contingents pledged to go to the deliverance of Jerusalem. They set out to fight the 'gent mescreue' as they might have set out on any other pilgrimage. The spirit of adventure was no longer the prerogative of the knightly class, but offered even to the villein an escape from the monotonous round of his existence. The appeal to Crusade had special force at a time when general scarcity encouraged emigration. Urban himself said: 'The land in which you dwell, shut in on all sides by mountain and sea, holds too straitly your over-great numbers; she is stripped of riches and barely yields nourishment to those who cultivate her soil. For this reason you hate and destroy one another in envy, and

[1]'The count Robert of Flanders left the assembly and is come to Arras, to his dear Clémence; gently he tells her in her ear, "Lady, I have taken the cross; do not let it make you sad! I bid you farewell, for I am going to Syria to deliver the Sepulchre from the pagan folk." When the countess heard him, her colour changed; "My lord," said she, "for my sake, do not go! You have two fair sons, whom may Jesus bless; they have great need of you and of your help." When the count heard her, he kissed her close; "Lady," said he, "Hold my hand, and I give you my troth, that as soon as my offering is laid on the Sepulchre, and I have kissed it and finished my prayer, within a fortnight, I swear to you without deceit, I will set out to return, if God gives me life." The lady held out her hand and the count gave his troth; no one was there but had his face wet with tears.'

[2]'They cry to their lords to whom they are wed: "My lord, we are married in the faith of God; we have engaged and sworn loyalty to you; for God's sake, when you have conquered the land, and you see the city where God suffered on the Cross, remember us, let us not there be forgotten!" By heaven, then were many tears shed.'

slay your brethren. Appease your hatred, and take the road to the Holy Sepulchre.'

The warlike spirit of feudalism was as yet in no wise subdued; Fulcher of Chartres, in his account of the First Crusade, *Gesta Dei per Francos*, says, 'Christianity was growing fearfully worse in both clergy and people; war was preferred before peace by all the Princes of the earth, who quarrelled ceaselessly.' Guibert de Nogent gives a vivid picture of the movement.

'The French at that time', he says, 'suffered from famine; bad harvests year after year had raised the price of corn to a great height, and avaricious merchants according to their wont took advantage of the general misery. There was little bread, and that was dear; the poor had to eke it out with roots and wild herbs. Suddenly, the cry of Crusade, sounding everywhere at once, broke the locks and bars that closed the granaries. Provisions that had been beyond price when every one stayed where they were, sold for nothing when every one was stirring and anxious to depart. Famine disappeared and was replaced by abundance. As every one hastened to take the road of God-each hurried to change into money everything that was not of use for the journey, and the price was fixed not by the seller but by the buyer. It was strange and marvellous to see every one buying dear and selling cheap: everything that was needed for the journey was very costly, but the rest was sold for nothing. . . . It touched the heart to see these poor crusaders shoeing their oxen as if they had been horses, and harnessing them to two-wheeled carts on which they put their small belongings and their little children. At each castle and each city they passed on the road they stretched out their hands and asked if they had not yet reached that Jerusalem which all were seeking. I have heard that men speaking an unknown tongue came to our seaports; they put their fingers together in the form of a cross, to show that they wished to be enrolled in the cause of the Faith.'

This crowd of peasants, ignorant and ill-organized, straggled across Bohemia and Hungary ravaging the country like an invading army. By the time they reached Hungary the inhabitants were up in arms against them, and many were slain. On August 1st, 1096, Peter the Hermit and a remnant of his followers reached Constantinople, and tried to plunder it, having lost all they had ever had. By the time they reached Asia they were demoralized and disbanded; the Crusade of the People had come to a miserable end.

But in the same month that Peter the Hermit reached Constantinople with the broken remnant of his followers the first armies of the real Crusade—the Crusade of Feudalism—set out for Constantinople on their way to the Holy Land. The army was divided into three hosts: the first, composed of men of Flanders and the Rhineland, subjects of the Emperor, under Godfrey of Bouillon, Duke of Lower Lorraine; the second of men of Normandy, the royal domain, and Burgundy, under the King's brother Hugh the Great of Vermandois, Robert of Normandy, Alan of Brittany, and Stephen of Blois; the third of men of Gascony, Aquitaine, and the Midi under Raymond of Toulouse. Unfortunately, on their arrival at Constantinople, the Emperor Alexis did not welcome them as deliverers of the Holy Sepulchre, but was not content until with much difficulty he had persuaded them to take an oath of allegiance to him and to make the reconquest of his Empire their first charge. Thus they embarked upon a perilous campaign in Asia Minor, culminating in the siege of Antioch. After three years they were in a position to lay siege to Jerusalem in June 1099. Many attacks were made in vain: finally a solemn procession all round the walls of the city was followed by a valiant and successful assault, and after an appalling massacre of its inhabitants Jerusalem was in Christian hands.

The dawn of the twelfth century saw the foundation of the Latin principalities of Jerusalem, Tripolis, Antioch, and Edessa. The story of the crusaders' success brought reinforcements from Europe, and helped to establish a European colony fed without intermission by new immigrants and visited by innumerable pilgrims and merchants. The foundation of this European settlement in the East is of importance for the social, political, and economic history of the West. It was definitely international in character: not only was it an expression of the Oriental idea of the 'Empire of the Franks', but the Eastern merchants of every race who thronged its bazaars made it a cosmopolis of the Middle Ages. The Italians were an important element in its sea-coast towns, as they still are in the Levantine ports; the Teutonic nations were represented; but the predominant national element was French. They furnished the largest contingent of the crusaders who captured it; they secured the election of Godfrey de Bouillon as King—or, since in humility he forswore the title, as 'Advocate of the Holy Sepulchre'—and theirs was the official language of a kingdom whose fiefs spread between Egypt and the Euphrates and from the Euphrates to the Peloponnese. So French rose above the rusticity and diversity of its dialects to the creation of a literary language; and so the rhythms of poets such as William of Poitiers, who went on Crusade in 1103, started a lyric tradition which was followed not only by the Latin countries, but also by Germany and Scandinavia and even by Iceland. So, too, did the French style in architecture become international: Jerusalem, Ramleh, Beirut and Tortosa still have churches that are evidently and entirely French; Jean Langlois, the architect of Troyes, went on pilgrimage to Jerusalem in 1267, and to his journey may be due the fact that the cathedral of Famagusta is in the style of Troyes.

The political and constitutional development of the Latin Kingdom is remarkable. The Emperor had neither part nor lot in it; since there was never any question of his suzerainty, the growth of public spirit and public power is witnessed here even earlier than it is in England and Sicily. The power lay less in the hands of the King than in the Court of Lieges or High Court established by Godfrey of Bouillon, which enabled vassals and even under-vassals to exercise a permanent control over the royal power, and even to determine the succession to the throne.

But this kingdom, outwardly prosperous and progressive, had one fatal weakness: political necessities, arising from lack of real political unity, weakened its military organization. The claims of merchants, burgesses, and settlers weakened one side of feudalism as an elected monarch with greatly limited powers weakened another. The recognition of the need for greater military strength in a kingdom so precariously situated led to the institution of Orders of Chivalry. The French Church of the eleventh century in its attempt to bring all classes of men and all branches of social activity into conformity with the *lex evangelica* had attempted the difficult task of the moralization of war. As early as 1100 a Church service at the initiation of young knights sought to impress on the feudal world the lesson that its weapons must be used in Christian ways and consecrated to Christian ends, such as the defence of the weak. At about the same time a band of French lords, led by the Provençal Pierre Gérard, founded the Order of Hospitallers by making themselves responsible for the Amalfitan Hospital at Jerusalem. By 1113 their military organization was developed; by 1118 all members took vows of obedience, chastity, and poverty: the fighting layman had become a *religiosus*. In this year Hugues de Payens and Geoffrey de Saint Aldemar came oversea with nine other Frenchmen, and obtained from Baldwin II the grant of a house near the Temple of Solomon. Thus the Order of Templars came into being, to receive its Rule, written under the inspiration of St. Bernard, in 1228.[1] Their life was to be one of perpetual exile and Holy War till death; they were never to refuse combat, even of one against three; they were never to ask quarter and never to give ransom. Besides these, they took the monastic vows of chastity, poverty, and obedience. The Prologue to their Rule states:

[1]The Spanish knights of Calatrava were also under Cistercian influence; founded by Raymond, Abbot of Cîteaux, they simply added military duties to the Cistercian Rule.

'Our word is primarily directed to all those who despise their own will, and with purity of mind desire to serve under the one true King; and with minds intent choose the noble warfare of obedience and persevere therein. We therefore exhort you who until now have embraced secular knighthood in which Christ was not the cause, you whom God in his mercy has chosen out of the mass of perdition for the defence of Holy Church, to hasten to associate yourselves perpetually together.'

At the first chapter-general, held about 1160, there were already three hundred knights and as many serving-brethren, nearly all French. The first chivalry, the result of the clerical consecration of war—clearly to be distinguished from the thirteenth- and fourteenth-century lay chivalry—had reached its zenith.

The Orders rapidly acquired by papal and royal gifts great riches and power, all dedicated to the service of the Cross. Their military strength brought real support to the Kingdom of Jerusalem, but their power only intensified its lack of political unity, since their Grand Masters were not under the King, but acknowledged obedience only to the Pope. Thus the middle years of the twelfth century witnessed a time of internal strife and disorganization, which once more permitted Saracen inroads into Christian territory. So serious was the situation after the fall of Edessa in 1144 that St. Bernard preached a new Crusade at Vézelay, at Easter, when pilgrims from every part of France were assembled there. The immediate response was enthusiastic: all the crosses provided were not sufficient, and he had to cut up his own vestments to furnish enough.

The jongleurs seconded his sermons with their *chansons de croisade:*

> *Pris est Rohais,*[1] *ben le savez,*
> *Dunt crestiens sunt esmaiez,*
> *Les mustiers ars e desertez:*
> *Deus n'i est mais sacrifiez.*
> *Chivalers, cher vus purpensez,*
> *Vus ki d'armes estes preisez;*
> *A celui voz cors presentez*
> *Ki pur vus fut en cruz drecez.*
> > *Ki ore irat od Loovis*
> > *Ja mar d'enfern avrat pouur,*
> > *Char s'alme en iert en pareïs*
> > *Od les angles nostre segnor.*[2]

[1]Er-roha, Edessa.

[2]'Edessa is taken, you know it well, at which Christians are dismayed; the churches are burnt and desolate, and God is no more sacrificed therein. Knights, think well of it, you who are prized for arms, give your hearts to Him who was lifted up upon the Cross for you. He that shall now go with Louis, shall nevermore have fear of Hell, for his soul shall go to Paradise with the Angels of Our Lord.'

But the ultimate response proved unexpectedly limited, and the armies were accompanied by bands of non-combatant pilgrims. St. Bernard's grandiose scheme of attacking Islam simultaneously in Portugal, in Syria, and on the coasts of Elba fell before the political ill-feeling existing in Europe, notably between Byzantium and the Normans in Sicily, and his Crusade came to nothing.

The second half of the twelfth century saw the gradual decline of the Latin Kingdom of Jerusalem, in spite of a close alliance with Byzantium, before the growing power of Saladin. By 1179 he had made serious inroads, gradually surrounding the Christian territory. In 1187 Jerusalem and the Holy Places fell into his hands, and the Christians held only Tyre, Antioch, and Tripolis of all their former possessions. A new army of crusaders had to be found to step into the breach.

To preach this Crusade was the first act of Gregory VIII (1187); but hardly had he proclaimed a Truce of God to last for seven years before he died, leaving the organization of the Crusade to his successor, Clement III. The news of the loss of Jerusalem stirred Europe to real emotion. The Pope's adversary, Barbarossa, acknowledged his duty to the Church and joined the Crusade; Philip Augustus and Henry II were reconciled and took the cross; Pisa made peace with Genoa, Venice with Hungary, William of Sicily with the Byzantine Emperor. All the countries of Europe played their part; at the Diet of Mainz alone thirteen thousand Germans took the vow of Crusade, while twelve thousand crusaders came from Scandinavia. The crusading spirit had passed beyond France into Christendom. There was real enthusiasm for the defence of Christianity in the East and the recovery of the Holy City, but the century that had elapsed since the First Crusade had so added to the complexity of European politics that this enthusiasm was bound and limited by political interests. Christendom could still be conscious of itself as a united body face to face with a united Islam, but its unity was no more than the temporary federation of individual nations.

How little strain such a federation could stand soon became painfully evident, when all the crusading hosts were concentrated at their rallying-point to besiege the city of Saint Jean d'Acre. In the course of a two-year siege violent quarrels broke out between the crusaders of different nationalities, and loss of discipline among the troops made it difficult to face disasters of famine and flood. Such disasters and the length of the siege meant not only that each army felt a certain respect for its opponents but also that the siege was at moments relaxed and followed by a tacit truce. The crusaders recognized a kindred chivalry to their own in their heathen enemies, just as their ancestors had done in the *Chanson de Roland*. The author of *L'Estoire de la Guerre Sainte* wrote:

> *Fierre iert la gent et orgoillose*
> *En la cité e merveillose;*
> *Se ço ne fust gent mescreue,*
> *Onques mieldre ne fut veue.*[1]

The influence of *courtoisie* upon chivalry had begun. The other side of this influence is manifest in the lament of Conon de Béthune, starting upon the Third Crusade: 'Alas, love! What a cruel leave I must take from the best lady who was ever loved and served! May the good God restore me to her, as surely I leave her with sorrow. What have I said? If the body goes to serve the Lord the heart remains entirely in her power. On to Syria, sighing for her.'

Jerusalem might be lost, but the effects of intercourse between East and West in the territories of the Latin Kingdom had brought about a better understanding that in some sense could survive even open warfare. This feeling was shown in marked degree when Saint Jean d'Acre at last fell in 1191. On the departure of Philip Augustus, Coeur de Lion had become the leader of the crusaders, though his temperament ill fitted him to keep peace between them. When Acre had fallen, after much dissension in the crusading hosts, he arranged a truce of three years with Saladin. Ascalon was to be destroyed, and English crusaders were to be allowed to make pilgrimages to the Holy Sepulchre. Jerusalem remained in Moslem hands, but for the first time an attempt was made to regain it by negotiation when force had failed. European influence was modifying the French idea of a Holy War, and the conflict was now one between equals in civilization, terminable by honourable negotiation.

The death of Saladin in 1193 and the consequent division of his Empire plunged the East in civil war and altered the balance of power between Orient and Occident. At the same time the Emperor Henry VI, the one powerful sovereign in Europe, extended his ambitious schemes to include a project of Oriental sovereignty. The Holy Lands were no longer to be the patrimony of the Church but of the Empire; as Emperor he laid claim to the common conquests of the faithful in the East. The Crusade which he was to lead might well have permanently extended the frontiers of Christendom and of the Empire, had it not been stopped by

[1]'Brave and proud and wonderful were the folk in the city; if they were not unbelievers, better men would never have been seen.'

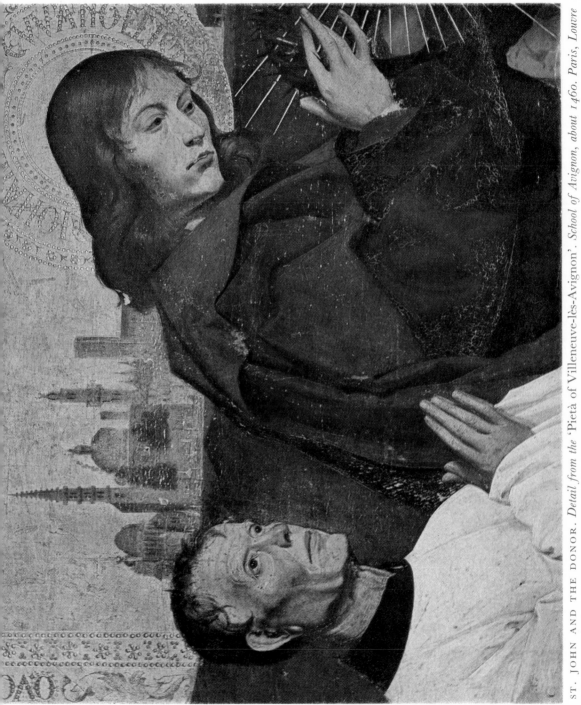

ST. JOHN AND THE DONOR. *Detail from the 'Pietà of Villeneuve-lès-Avignon'. School of Avignon, about 1460. Paris, Louvre*

his sudden death in 1197, at a time when his son was an infant and there was no monarch competent to succeed to his policy and his power.

The end of the twelfth century, then, marks a profound modification of the idea of Crusade. It was no longer a French, but a European idea. Its centre was no longer the Holy City, but the coast towns of Syria; once these were held, it was felt, Jerusalem could be negotiated for. The economic interests of the Italian cities had become one of the most important elements in Christian policy in the East, and had modified the French idea of a war of extermination. National pride and national piety played a lesser part, and the Christian princes received with indifference the appeals to Crusade circulated by Innocent III and his encyclicals after the death of Henry VI. A change of policy and of ideal is manifest in the story of the Crusade under Thibaut de Champagne made familiar by the narrative of Villehardouin. His account shows the extreme importance of political negotiation in the organization of the Crusade; the part played in it by the merchants of Venice, Pisa, and Genoa, and its divagation from its true purpose to the taking of Zara and Constantinople. The establishment of a Latin Kingdom in Constantinople and the Balkan peninsula at the expense of Byzantine power crowned the acropolises of Corinth, Mistra, Kalamata, and Athens with French feudal castles, and established Louis of Blois at Nicea, Hugues de Saint Pol at Demotica, Geoffroi de Villehardouin and Guillaume de Champlette in the Morea, and the Burgundian house of La Roche at Athens; but such successes are proof of the failure of a Crusade originally directed against the forces of Islam. Such an end to the enterprise did not satisfy Innocent III; he was steadfast in his aim of the restoration of the Christian States in Syria. In 1212 he therefore again preached a Crusade, but the state of Europe prevented the realization of his dream: instead, Christendom itself witnessed Crusades against the Albigensian heretics, the Moors in Spain, the excommunicate John of England, the heathen in Prussia, and the Greeks of Constantinople. Yet still Innocent persevered. The Emperor Frederick II took vows of Crusade after his coronation 'to show his gratitude to God for all the benefits he had received'; a general peace was proclaimed for four years, to be kept under penalty of excommunication; every one was to help either in service or in money. Everything was prepared and on the point of fruition when Innocent died in 1216. Without his master-hand to steer it, the project failed through lack of unity of leadership or plan. Frederick II refused to join in the Crusade of 1218, remarkable only for its aim—Egypt, not Syria—and for its complete failure. But with his coronation at Rome in 1220 he renewed his vows, to fulfil them in a spirit strangely different from that of the earlier crusaders. When he finally set out in 1228 the purely political character of the expedition was sufficiently evident; Saracen soldiers were included in his army; he himself was excommunicate and brought every place to which he went under an interdict: the Military Orders were expressly forbidden to obey him. Yet he did not underrate the knowledge of Eastern diplomacy he had gained in his half-Eastern kingdom of Sicily, and by playing off one Eastern power against another he found himself, without serious warfare, in possession of Jerusalem, Bethlehem, Nazareth, and the road to Jaffa. No better contrast between the earlier and later Crusades can be found than that between Godfrey of Bouillon refusing to wear a temporal crown in the city where his Master had worn a crown of thorns, and Frederick II, excommunicate from the Church, himself taking the crown from the altar of the Holy Sepulchre, and with no religious ceremony crowning himself King of Jerusalem.

The death of Frederick II changed the political balance of Europe; and in the middle of the thirteenth century the rise to power of a nomadic Mongol tribe under Jenghiz Khan upset the stability of Asia. By 1216 he held Pekin; by 1219 the road to the West lay open. By 1223 he was in Armenia, having destroyed the Seljuk power. His death failed to put an end to the Mongol invasion, for his admirable organization survived; by 1237 they held Moscow and Kieff, and by 1240 they reached the borders of Hungary. Such a menace completely over-shadowed the Moslem domination of Syria, though fugitives from the Mongol inroads strengthened the armies of the Sultan of Egypt and enabled him to recapture Jerusalem in 1244.

The loss of Jerusalem, the Tartar menace to Europe, and the imminent peril of the Byzantine Empire made some action inevitable. Baldwin II of Constantinople and the Patriarchs of Constantinople and Antioch came to the Council of Lyons in 1245, and a Crusade was preached. But the conflict between Guelf and Ghibeline was at its height, and popular feeling was against the Crusade. England resisted the imposition of forced levies, and the burgesses of Ratisbon showed their imperial sympathies by a decision to punish by death any who took the cross. The only king in Europe whose piety and whose position was sufficiently strong to make it possible for him to lead it was St. Louis, and it remained a purely French Crusade. Like the Franciscan and Dominican missions into Asia, the Crusade of 1248 is the expression of an age of idealism. Like the first French Crusades in Spain, it brought new life to French literature. Who can forget Joinville's account of the departure?

'*In the month of August we entered into our ship at the Roche-de-Marseille. . . . When the horses were in the ship, our master mariner called to his seamen, who stood at the prow, and said, "Are you ready?" and they answered, "Aye, sir; let the clerks and priests come forward." As soon as these had come forward, he called to them, "Sing for God's sake!" and they all, with one voice, chanted: "Veni Creator Spiritus." Then he cried to his seamen, "Unfurl the sails for God's sake!" And they did so.*

'*In a short space the wind filled our sail and had borne us out of sight of land, so that we saw naught save sky and water, and every day the wind carried us farther from the land where we were born. And these things I tell you, that you may understand how foolhardy is that man who dares, having other's chattels in his possession, or being in mortal sin, to place himself in such peril, seeing that, when you lie down to sleep at night on shipboard, you lie down not knowing whether, in the morning, you may find yourself at the bottom of the sea.*'

Who can forget the gallantry of the landing at Damietta? They found

'*all the power of the Soldan—a host fair to look upon, for the Soldan's arms are of gold, and when the sun struck upon them they were resplendent. The noise they made with their cymbals and horns was fearful to listen to. . . . But I caused my people to land in front of a great body of Turks, at a place where there were full six thousand men on horseback. So soon as these saw us land, they came towards us, hotly spurring. We, when we saw them coming, fixed the points of our shields into the sand and the handles of our lances in the sand with the points set towards them. But when they were so near that they saw the lances about to enter into their bellies, they turned about and fled. . . . At our left landed the Count of Jaffa, who was cousin-german to the Count of Montbéliard, and of the lineage of Joinville. It was he who landed in greatest pride, for his galley came all painted, within and without, with escutcheons of his arms, which arms are* Or, a cross patée gules. *He had at least three hundred rowers in his galley, and for each rower there was a targe with the count's arms thereon, and to each targe was a pennon attached with his arms wrought in gold. While he was coming it seemed as if his galley flew, so did the rowers urge it forward with their sweep; and it seemed as if the lightning were falling from the skies at the sound that the pennants made, and the cymbals, and the drums, and the Saracenic horns that were in his galley.*'

But neither the faith of St. Louis nor the honourable chivalry that followed him sufficed to bring success to the Crusade; after the fall of Damietta disaster followed disaster. St. Louis himself suffered imprisonment in Moslem hands, and the Crusade ended in retreat to Syria after the Christian prisoners had been ransomed at great cost. Joinville, who had seen and survived the Egyptian *débâcle*, had yet enough faith and courage left to support St. Louis in his desire for a fresh campaign, but there was no response from Europe, and soon after the death of Blanche of Castille in 1252 the crusading host left Syria and the remains of the Christian power there to a time of conflict and insecurity. The second Crusade of St. Louis was more disastrous than the first, and in it he met his death at Tunis. As he died his pilgrim thoughts turned back to Compostella, and he said St. James's prayer: 'Keep, Lord, Thy people, and sanctify them, that fortified by the help of Thine Apostle St. James, they may please Thee in their works and serve Thee with a quiet heart. Amen.'

The crusading enthusiasm died with St. Louis; there was no response to an appeal from Syria in face of fresh Mameluke inroads in 1290. Finally, Saint Jean d'Acre, the last remaining Christian possession in the East, was taken in 1291 after a gallant resistance from its garrison of military knights; of the Latin Kingdom of Jerusalem nothing but the memory lived on into the fourteenth century.[1] It is significant of the changed spirit of feudalism that the loss of Acre, instead of impelling men to undertake a fresh Crusade, caused nothing but discouragement, in spite of the efforts of the Church. It is perfectly true that hardly a year passed without some prince taking vows of Crusade, but nothing came of the proposed expedition beyond taxation to pay for it and occasional diplomatic negotiation. To Philippe le Bel, indeed, taxation for the purpose proved a regular source of revenue. War in their own country monopolized men's energies, and the idea of re-establishing the Latin Empire of Constantinople was politically more important than the deliverance of the Holy Sepulchre.

The crusading spirit was dead, but a fresh movement turned men's spiritual forces into a new channel. The idea of the *conversion* of the heathen began to supersede that of their *extermination*: the conquest was to be not of territory but of souls. It was as natural a reflection of the age of Dominic and Francis as the initiation of the Crusade was of the age of Cluny, but it involved a real change of attitude toward the East. This was made possible by the fact that the Mongol hordes included followers not only of their national religion, but also of all the religions of the East, including Nestorian Christians. When the Venetian merchants of the Crimea made this known to Europe, Innocent IV sent Franciscan and Dominican envoys to the Great Khan, and an interview took place at Karakorum in the presence of Yaroslav, Grand Duke of Russia, the

---

[1] The Christian kingdoms of Cyprus and Armenia survived.

vassals of Georgia and the Caucasus, the Seljuk Sultan of Asia Minor, Mongol generals, Chinese men of learning, and lamas from Tibet.

St. Louis in 1253 sent Rubriquis to the Khan of Tartary, at whose court he found not only a Parisian goldsmith, but also a Nestorian monk who spoke of setting out on pilgrimage to St. James of Galicia. The pioneers were such Mendicants as these, but the man who gave real force to the movement was a man who came from the *Camino francés* that leads to Compostella: Raymond Lull, the son of a Catalan lord who had helped to conquer Majorca from the Moslems. After a stormy youth he handed over his property to his wife and went to the sanctuary of St. James, where he bought a slave from whom he learnt Arabic. Then he persuaded the King of Majorca to found a monastery at Miramar where thirteen friars Minor were to learn Arabic. In 1285 he began his voyages: to Rome, Paris, Tartary, Armenia, Ethiopia, Africa, and Tunis, everywhere disputing with the Moslems in their own tongue, until he was eventually martyred in North Africa. It was through him that the Council of Vienna in 1311 decided to found six schools of Oriental languages in Europe. The Crusades had been the Christian policy of the past, but Raymond Lull formulated the policy of the future. 'I see the knights going overseas to the Holy Land thinking to take it by force of arms, and in the end exhausting themselves without achieving their aim. Then I think that this conquest should be made as Thou madest it, Lord, with Thine apostles: that is by love, by prayer, and by shedding of tears. Then let the holy knights of religion set forth, let them arm themselves with the sign of the cross, let them be filled with the grace of the Holy Ghost, let them preach to the heathen the truths of the Passion.' *Peregrinantes propter Christum* were to take the place of crusaders on 'the road of God'.[1]

The early fourteenth century found Europe, and particularly France, so bound and limited by constraint of circumstances that men's mental activities found an outlet not in action but in theory. No Crusade was undertaken, but many treatises were addressed to the Pope and to the monarchs of Europe on the best way of delivering the Holy Land from the Moslem yoke. Some of these treatises were the work of visionaries; others, of which the best known is Marino Sanudo's *Secreta Fidelium Crucis*, were written by men with real experience of the Levant gained in missionary or commercial enterprise. All kinds of views were current; in 1303 an ecclesiastical judge of Aquitaine suggested besides the more usual

---

[1]Lull was a Majorcan, and it is the Aragonese Popes who did much for Christian missions. Christianity, much of it the Nestorianism indigenous to India, was more widely spread in Asia in the fourteenth than in any other century.

preparations for Crusade, that a certain number of girls should be taught the practice of medicine and surgery, grammar, logic, and the elements of mathematics, in order to make good wives for the princes of the East. The Armenian Prince Haiton, who had taken monastic vows at Poitiers, two years later expounded a plan of which the basis was the recovery of his own country.

The French theorists of the time of Philippe le Bel—notably Pierre du Bois and Guillaume de Nogaret—continued to put forward Ghibeline views: the conquest was to be monarchical and not papal. The Empire was to be hereditary in the French dynasty; the Pope was to live in France; Papacy and Church alike were to give up their temporal possessions to furnish funds for the Holy War. All the theorists recognized that the greatest difficulty lay in the political disunion of Christendom and many proposed the establishment of an international board of arbitration of which half the members should be laymen and half ecclesiastics. A further difficulty was recognized in the rivalry between the Templars and Hospitallers, and various plans were put forward by which they and the other Orders of Chivalry were to be united under a single head, the King of Jerusalem.

The basis of all the plans of action was a commercial blockade of Egypt, and an alliance with the Mongols, but nothing was done to put them into execution. The Military Orders were not united; commerce with Egypt did not cease; no lasting alliance was formed with the Mongols; and the princes who took the cross made no effort to fulfil their vows.

Meanwhile the Holy Land lapsed into a state comparable with that of the century before the Crusades. The Ottoman invasions of the early fourteenth century added a new element to the complex of Eastern politics, and the only Christian settlements in the Levant were those of the Hospitallers at Rhodes and in the Sporades and of the French dynasty of Lusignan in Cyprus. Pierre de Lusignan was conscious of his position as defender of an outpost of Christendom, but his romantic journey across Europe in search of aid failed to stir men to action, and the taking of Alexandria was the only success—and that a passing one—of his expedition. His was the last serious effort at Crusade, yet the idea of the deliverance of the Holy Sepulchre was not quite dead: we find it haunting the minds of Henry V and Joan of Arc. Rutebeuf wrote:

> *Tornoieor, vous que direz*
> *Qui au jor du juyse irez?*
> *Devant Dieu que porrez respondre?*

Quar lors ne se porront repondre
Ne gent clergies, ne gent laies,
Et Diex vous monstrera ses plaies!
Se il vous demande la terre
Ou por vous la mort soufferre,
Que direz vous? . . .
Ha! Antioche, terre sainte,
Com ci a dolereuse plainte
Quant tu n'as més nus Godefroiz!
Li feus de charité est froiz
En chascun cuer de crestien.[1]

But the age was too troubled for any such enterprise; from East to West the balance of empire was shaken. The Mongol dynasty fell in China, and with it the Christian missions;[2] Islam triumphed in Central Asia under Tamerlane, and by 1390 Bajazet was master of the Balkans and the Byzantine Empire was in dire peril, while Serbian independence lay dead upon the field of Kossovo. An attempt to check the Turkish advance ended in the disastrous defeat of Nicopolis; and in spite of the journey of the Emperor Manuel to Venice, Paris, and London beseeching help, nothing could have saved Constantinople had not Tamerlane invaded the territory of Bajazet and defeated him at Ancyra. This defeat prolonged the existence of Christian power in the East into the fifteenth century, but the crusading spirit was dead. French power in the East had fallen to the commercial cities of Italy, and the question of commercial advantage had become more important than that of religious conquest, whether territorial or spiritual. In 1415 Mahomet I entered into alliance with the Grand Master of the Knights Hospitallers of Rhodes. The fall of Constantinople in 1453 is the last episode of the relations of medieval Christendom with the East. It was made possible by the inability of the sovereigns of the fifteenth century to take common action and by their indifference to everything not tangible and immediate. It marks the beginning of that Eastern question which still awaits solution.

The relations of France and the Moslem peoples of Spain and the East fill six hundred years of the Middle Ages: what effects did they have upon French civilization? Few aspects of medieval life—political, artistic, intellectual, commercial, or domestic—escaped their influence.

[1]'Jousters, what will you say who will come to the Day of Judgement? What will you answer before God? For then neither clerk nor layman will be able to conceal himself, and God will show you his wounds. If He asks of you the land where for you He was willing to suffer death, what will you say? Oh, Antioch, holy land, what sad complaining is there when thou no longer hast a Godfrey! The fire of love is cold in the heart of every Christian.'
[2]Bishops of Pekin are heard of till 1456, but were non-resident.

Indeed, the dominating fact of French medieval history—the gradual centralization of power in the hands of the monarchy—owed something to the Crusades. The prestige of the King spread beyond his own domain, and the absence of his barons, and their death by mischance of war, famine, pestilence, or the hardships of the journey, did much to increase the power of the royal officers who were in the meantime entrusted with the administration of his kingdom. Moreover, when the lords returned, not only were their sympathies insensibly democratized by their absence from feudal conditions, but they were also financially poorer, and therefore willing to sell much of their land and many of their rights. Thus service was commuted for a money payment, and another step was taken towards the emancipation of the rural classes and the enfranchisement of the bourgeoisie. Indeed, even lords such as Joinville began to enrol themselves in service in return for a money payment and not for a fief; the land-basis of feudal society was seriously shaken.

So, too, the Crusades affected the basis of men's dreams. A new life, a new country, new contact with other races, provided a stimulus to their imagination that is reflected in their literature: it is no mere coincidence that vernacular epic and vernacular history appear simultaneously with the Crusades, nor is it accident that makes the *Chansons d'Antioche* and *de Jerusalem* unique as epic histories written by a contemporary.[1] Contact with the East gave the medieval poet many traditional themes—stories of Solomon, of the Trojan war, of Alexander the Great;[2] but it was the inevitable shock of romance in the strangeness of the Crusades themselves that made him realize that he was living in an epic world. For the first time men felt that their own *mémoires* were worth writing; and Villehardouin is one of the first chroniclers and Joinville the first autobiographer to write in French. Further, the Crusades—*Gesta Dei per Francos*—helped to make French a universal language, spoken at the courts of England, Portugal, Sicily, Constantinople, Athens, Cyprus, Antioch, and Jerusalem; so that French songs spread through Christendom and became a part of the literary heritage of all nations. With her poetry spread French lay music, a monody in strict time accompanied on instruments of many countries, Northern, Byzantine, Latin, and Arab. Guillaume de Machaut's list of musical instruments shows how varied is the list:

[1]It is not till later that such cycles as the *Chevalier du Cygne* are fathered on Godfrey de Bouillon and spangled with irrelevant marvels and incongruous romantic episodes under the influence of *courtoisie*.
[2]Aimon de Varenne in 1188 got the story of his *Florimont* from a Greek source; the *Eracle* of Gautier d'Arras, the *Athis et Porphirias* of Alexandre de Bernai, and the *Empereur Constant*, all come from Oriental or Byzantine sources.

Orgues, vielles, micanons,
Rubebes et psalterions,
Leus, moraches et guiternes
Dont on joue par ces tavernes,
Cymbales, citoles, naquaires,
Et de flaios plus de dix paires . . .
Cors sarrasinois et doussaines,
Demi-doussaines et flaüstes
Dont droit joue quand tu flaüstes,
Trompes, buisines et trompettes,
Guigues, rotes, harpes, chevrettes,
Cornemuses et chalemielles.

To take but one, and that the most familiar, *lute* is derived from the Arabic *al'ud*, and is a legacy of the Crusades. Heraldry, again, that seems to us the typical accompaniment of European chivalry, is an Eastern institution. The Arab Emirs used heraldic bearings before the eleventh century, and it is from them that European knighthood took the custom.[1] The thirteenth-century 'roman d'aventure' of *Galeran* describes the knights arming themselves before a tournament:

Chascun de soy armer se peine
D'armeures neufves et fresches.
Li un y porte unes bretesches
En son escu reluisant cler,
Cil un lyon, cil un cengler,
Cil un liepart, cil un poisson.
Cil porte son heaulme en son
Beste ou oisel ou flour aucune.
Cil porte une baniere brune,
Cil blanche, cil ynde, cil vert.
L'autre y poez veoir couvert
D'armes vermeilles foillollées.[2]

Such a description is true of the court of Philip Augustus, but it would have been equally true of the court of any Sultan of Bagdad. Not only did the knights of Europe adopt the heraldry of the East, but they also wore

---

[1]Raymond of St. Gilles, Count of Toulouse, was the first to bear blazon; he bore the cross of Constantine, 'croix clichée, vuidée et pommettée'.

[2]'Each strives to arm himself with new clean coat-armour. One has a tower shining brightly on his shield, one a lion, one a boar, this man a leopard, and the other a fish. One has a beast or bird or flower on the peak of his helmet. This man bears a sable banner, another white, another azure, and another green. You can see another blazoned with a red coat covered with leaves.

its dress: the Arab *kouffieh* round the helmet (the origin of heraldic mantling) and the flowing robe. Saladin in 1192 sent Henry of Champagne an Arab tunic and turban, and Henry in his reply wrote: 'You know that your robes and turbans are far from being held in scorn among us. I will certainly wear your gifts.' In *Galeran* the hero, after being dubbed knight, puts on a robe of silk and gold 'qui sont faites en la terre aux Maures'. The only place where the shoes with turned-up points of the noble of thirteenth- and fourteenth-century France are still in use is the East, and it was from the East that France borrowed them. The knights thence brought back the custom of bathing in tubs, and a liking for enclosed gardens; medieval castle architecture owed its curtain walls to the East. The leper-houses of the Orient are the ancestors of the hospitals of Europe. The breed of horses was improved; silkworms and dyeing became French industries, and windmills (in Normandy called *turquois* or Turkish) came to the help of the miller.

The *Assizes of Jerusalem*, drawn up in Cyprus, the legal focus of the Latin kingdoms, with their numerous clauses on the regulation of industry and commerce, attest the importance of Levantine trade. This trade was far earlier than the Crusades; as early as the fourth century colonies of Eastern merchants, generically called Syrians, were established in Gaul, Italy, Africa, and even Britain. In France their chief settlements were at Bordeaux, Lyons, and Narbonne, always important commercial centres. The establishment of Latin settlements in the East in the tenth and twelfth centuries made their position more secure, and the establishment of the Kingdom of Cyprus and the taking of Constantinople in 1204 made the commerce of the Eastern Mediterranean of great importance in the thirteenth century. Narbonne, Montpellier, Arles, and Marseilles had their consulates and agencies in the Levant as well as the merchants of Genoa, Pisa, Venice, and Amalfi. Marseilles, indeed, as the centre of transport from France to the Holy Land, had in 1253 and 1255 to pass statutes to regulate the traffic. Not more than fifteen hundred pilgrims were to be taken in any one ship. First-class passengers, with deck cabins, were to pay 60 sous; second-class, between decks, 40; third-class, on the lowest deck, 35; and fourth-class, in the hold, 25. Each pilgrim received a numbered ticket, after inscribing his name and that of his guarantor in a register. This was kept in duplicate, one copy being preserved in the communal archives of Marseilles.

In the Souks of Jerusalem, and at the great annual fair outside the walls, every kind of Eastern merchandise was sold either for use in the Latin Kingdom or to export to Europe; cotton, linen, and silk (*taffetas*, and *muslin* are both of Arabic origin, muslin from Mosul); dyes, indigo, madder, saffron, and the blue we still call ultramarine, from *oultremer*; spices from the Far East; sugar, rice, and all kinds of produce. From Damascus, always important commercially as the starting-point of the caravan routes to the Holy Places of the Mahommedan world, came pottery of all kinds, much glass—the Venetian glass factories were founded by workers from Syria—damask silks, Damascus swords, damson plums, damascened metal work of all kinds, as well as furs from the Caspian ports of the Volga and ostrich feathers from the East. For such Levantine trade, nineteen centuries earlier, money had first been coined in Ionia; in the Latin Kingdom the Lombard system of banking was elaborated and an international system of exchange revived. Such a trade called for a more highly developed organization than did the local markets of France: commercial treaties were drawn up, a court to regulate the mercantile marine was instituted; and those 'merchant's marks' that take the place of the knight's armorial bearings among the merchants of the cities were instituted to serve as trade-marks among people who could not read a European script.

The main current of Eastern learning reached Europe not through the Crusades and the Latin Kingdom, but from Sicily and Spain. Yet one of the most important branches of Arab learning was the science of geography, and it is through the commercial activities of the Latin Kingdom that this was shared by Europe. The studies of Arab scholars of the eighth century in geometry, in astronomy in the ninth, in trigonometry in the tenth, had given a great impetus to Arab navigation. The use of the sextant and the astrolabe supplemented that of the compass, itself an Eastern discovery, and from an Arab table of longitudes drawn up in 1230 we find they had a very exact idea of Mediterranean distance. More than this, since the eleventh century thay had known the coasts of India, Ceylon, Indo-China, and the islands of Java, Sumatra, and Borneo, and it is thanks to them that the Eastern half of a medieval map of the world is not wholly blank.

Moreover, it was the Sultan's part to encourage learning among his subjects. While on Crusade St. Louis heard that a Saracen Sultan had collected the books of Moslem philosophy at his own expense, and had formed a library for his subjects' use. St. Louis was inspired to follow his example on his return to Paris by 'diligently and generously' giving money for the copying of the works of Doctors of the Christian Church; and the library thus formed is the direct ancestor of the Bibliothèque Nationale.

VI

Learning

ALL knowledge is based on tradition; we inherit not only a mass of received opinion that it is easy to accept, but also a mass of refuted hypotheses which it is easy to set aside. Neither empiricism nor experiment can be independent of this tradition, even when their relation to it is contradictory. The more we are conscious of the historic past, the more are we indebted to our heritage of knowledge; the more the past transcends the present in congruity, in splendour, or in force, the blinder is our faith in its doctrines and its beliefs.

Thus medieval thought is based on a classical heritage, and its history is the story of the acceptance, the comprehension, and the transmutation of that tradition. Latin was its vernacular: in that language alone could the seven liberal Arts be studied—the Trivium, the study of speech, in Grammar, Logic, and Rhetoric, and the Quadrivium, the study of number, in Arithmetic, Geometry, Music, and Astronomy. It is only through Latin paraphrase and Latin transmutations that Greek thought was known in medieval Europe until the Renaissance.[1]

Thus freed from the boundaries of language, medieval learning was international; to distinguish the *nuances* of nationality in the learned literature of the Middle Ages is one of the most delicate tasks that the critic can set himself, for not only must he consider the nationality that men inherit, but the modifications that they acquire through education and work in a foreign land. French thought and learning have their beginnings in the scholars whom Charlemagne called to his court in 781, and yet not one of them was French; Alcuin was English, Leutrad Norman, Peter Pisan, Agobard Spanish, and Theodulf an Italian Goth. Throughout the Middle Ages the learning of France was an integral part of the learning of Europe, and the rise of Paris to be the intellectual centre of Christendom only served to raise French learning still further above the limits of nationality.

The Dark Ages were inevitably conscious of the overwhelming greatness of the past. Men approached the classics not as critics, but as docile

---

[1] For instance the logic of Aristotle was taught at Rheims about 980 from translations made by Boethius at Rome about 510. Certain exceptional men like Grosseteste and John of Salisbury may have known some Greek, but it was not a common instrument of knowledge until the sixteenth century.

pupils. For them they were the only storehouses of knowledge; poetry, eloquence, history, philosophy, natural science, law and polity were to be found therein. As Richard de Fournival writes in his *Bestiaire d'Amour*, 'cil qui ont esté cha en arrière ont seu tel chose que nus qui soit orendroit ne le conquerroit de son sens, ne ne seroit seu, s'on ne le savoit par les anciens'.[1] Century by century medieval learning not only added to its independent store but also drew more deeply from classical sources. It is convenient to speak of the Renaissance of classical learning as coming at the end of the Middle Ages, but the phrase is false in its assumption that classical learning had ever died. There is a continuous and steadily growing tradition; the new birth is rather one of freedom of thought at a time when the classics had at last become thoroughly assimilated.

But if the Middle Ages inherited the lore of Greece and Rome, they turned it to fresh ends. Every medieval book that is more than a translation is inspired by the idea of man's salvation. The desire of the medieval scholar was not only a desire to know, for the sake of knowledge, but a desire to be saved, and to that end to possess knowledge in its saving forms. This purpose, early made clear in Ambrose's *Hexaëmeron*, is again evident in Charlemagne's open letters of general admonition, *de litteris colendis* and *de emendatione librorum*: it is to advance the easy and true understanding of the mysteries of Scripture that learning is to be cultivated and encouraged. Even the sources of ancient history were apologetic, and not written for history's sake alone: the *Civitas Dei* was written to refute those who laid Alaric's sack of Rome in 410 at the Church's door, and Orosius's *Seven Books of Histories* are *adversus paganos*. The Scriptures rightly interpreted held the sum of saving knowledge, and therefore there was no question with a valid claim to human curiosity which the Scriptures, through their interpreters, could not be called upon to answer.

It is because of this primary importance of scriptural interpretation that the Fathers of the Church are so important an element in medieval thought. St. Augustine permeates the Middle Ages. The Christianized Platonism which they owed to him exercised an even stronger influence than the Aristoteleanism they gained from Latin translations and commentaries. The idea of the seven Arts (on which Augustine began a treatise) is itself Platonic. With him Christian learning reached a compass which it was not to pass for a thousand years. It has been said that he 'brought all intellectual interests into the closure of the Christian faith, or discredited whatever stubbornly remained without'. He catholicized the

[1]'Those who have already lived before us have known certain things of which no man who lives now could acquire knowledge by his own intellect, nor would they be known did we not know them from the men of old.'

pagan virtues, which Ambrose had borrowed from Plato's *Republic*. With him the substance of Christian doctrine was defined; the principles of symbolism and allegory were set; the part to be played in man's salvation by the human will was reasoned out; and the great truths of man's dependence on God were uttered in words which men still use. Succeeding generations had not to add to his work, but to learn to comprehend it and to make it a part of their own thought. Classical learning and the memory of the Empire might play an important part in the Middle Ages, but they were dominated by patristic learning and the vision of the *Civitas Dei*. It is the Augustinian tradition which is handed on, with little change but reclassification, by Isidore of Seville; and there are few learned books of the Middle Ages that do not owe some of their material to his *Etymologiae*.

But if classical and patristic learning form a part of the intellectual heritage of France, they were not the only element in its tradition. An examination of the literary art of the Dark Ages reveals an element that is definitely not classical: a heroic treatment of national history, in which Teuton, Scandinavian, and Celt alike find an expression of their peculiar heritage; systems of mystic thought, ways of imagination, tunes of poetry, that are alien to the Latin mind; just as an examination of the art of the same period reveals motives of ornament, fantastic creations of the imagination, and a balance and proportion that utterly changes the whole, though it be made of material that dates from Rome itself. It is this elusive element of nationality which in combination with the traditional classical element bears fruit in medieval France; it is through its action that there is a truly medieval literature and not merely a decadence of classicism.

The first phase of medieval learning is one of mystical allegory, but these elaborations of Augustinian exposition are not primarily a French but a German development. The first allegorical work of any importance is that of Hrabanus Maurus (d. 857), a native of Mainz, and his contemporaries and compatriots Honorius of Autun and Walafrid Strabo.

Gradually, as this mass of material was acquired, construction of a kind arose, that attempted to classify and to systematize even though it did not question. In this development France played a part, and the impress of French thought was set upon a formless tradition. The most important of these systematic expositions of a symbolical or sacramental plan of the universe is the *Rationale of the Visible World* written in the first half of the twelfth century by a Saxon Monk of a convent near Paris, Hugh of St. Victor. He argues that the world is made for man, and that to understand man the world must be understood; but man's body exists for his spirit's sake, and thus the material creation has a spiritual meaning. Symbolism is then rooted in the character and purpose of material creation; and therefore the allegorical interpretation of the Scriptures can alone reveal their true meaning. A sacrament is *sacrae rei signum*, and so the whole world has a sacramental significance. The sacraments of natural law are *umbra veritatis*, those of written law *imago vel figura veritatis*, and those under grace *corpus veritatis*. He begins with an exposition of the six days of Creation, corresponding to the six ages of restoration; for a more minute treatment his *De Arca Noë morale* and *De Arca Noë mystica* must be studied. There every detail of the Ark, typifying the Church, is allegorically applied to the Christian scheme of life and salvation. For instance, he considered the dove as the symbol of the Church. 'It has two wings, since there are for the Christian two kinds of life, the active and the contemplative. The grey-blue feathers of its wings show heavenly thoughts. The changing colours of the rest of its body, like a troubled sea, symbolize the sea of human passion on which floats the Church. Why are a dove's eyes golden-yellow? Because yellow, the colour of ripe fruit, is the colour of experience and maturity. The yellow eyes of the dove symbolize the glance of wisdom which the Church casts on the future. Finally, the dove has red feet, for the Church progresses through the world, her feet reddened by the blood of martyrs.' To his work much of the allegorical inspiration of medieval literature is due: Dante gratefully gives him a lofty seat in Paradise.

Hugh of St. Victor, though he wrote in France and bears the stamp of French training, was not French by birth. The next great medieval symbolists, Guillaume Durand and Adam of St. Victor, belong altogether to France; they naturalize Hugh of St. Victor's symbolism by transmuting it into terms of art. The *Rationale divinorum officiorum* of Durand takes the office of the mass as containing the greater part of what was fulfilled by and in Christ from His descent to earth to His Ascension, and all the sacrifices of the ancient law, and then explains every part of the edifice of the church in which mass is performed as typifying one or another of these aspects of it. Here it is that symbolism is accepted by art, for the *Rationale divinorum officiorum* is mirrored in the sculpture and architecture of the French cathedrals, for instance at Chartres and Bourges.

The second great French symbolist was a pupil of Hugh of St. Victor, but was a Breton by birth. Adam of St. Victor received the symbolism of Hugh, but embodied it in sequences of hymns for church use; in his turn he transmuted it to imagery. His work can only be appreciated in its Latin form, but it is purely French in the vividness and clarity of its style.

With him, as with the French cathedral builders, symbolism serves a true artistic purpose:

> *O Maria! Stella maris!*
> *Dignitate singularis,*
> *Super omnes ordinaris*
>   *Ordines coelestium!*
> *In supremo sita poli*
> *Nos commenda tuae proli,*
> *Ne terrores sive doli*
>   *Nos supplantent hostium!*

Yet artistic symbolism is not the most important intellectual activity of medieval France. Its fundamental interest was the study of logic: that reasoning science by which men can proceed from fact to abstraction, from abstraction to principle, from principle to law. In this sphere not only did France recreate medieval science, but she also gave new life to its language. Latin was of necessity the language of learning, which cannot be trammelled by the bonds of dialect; and Latin in French hands was given a new subtlety, a new flexibility, and a new power of dealing with the matter of abstract thought. Scholastic Latin is a living language that owes its vitality to France.

The process of civilization often consists in substituting a conscious method for a half-conscious process, and this is what the dialectic of Paris did for European thought in the Middle Ages. It is no doubt true that method was in some sense developed at the expense of content; we find Robert de Sorbon asking, 'Does not he who day and night practises the tortures of dialectic walk in the way of vanity and darkness of the mind? Is not the labourer mad who is for ever sharpening his ploughshare without ever ploughing the field? The art of dialectic should sharpen the mind, but in order to prepare it for greater things.' Yet even if medieval logicians were not in a position to use their dialectic so fruitfully as later ages have done, they built up a system of clear thinking that has ever since been the foundation of science not only in France but also in Europe.

The central problem of medieval thought was the problem of the priority of the universal over the particular. Two schools of thought endeavoured to answer it; the Realists believed universals—let us say the Church, Humanity, Divinity—to be prior to the particular—the churchman, the individual man, the Persons of the Trinity—and held that the universal must first be comprehended in order to comprehend the particular. Further, the universal had existence as a thing, *res*: the Church is an

THE MASS OF ST. GILES
Painting by the Master of St. Giles, about 1480.
London, National Gallery

entity; humanity exists; the Unity of the Deity is: hence came their name of Realists. The most complete Realist is Anselm. He held with Plato that universals exist eternally in God, and are the interior discourse of His mind: models and types after which particulars are created. Anselm used Realism as the servant of the orthodox faith: his motto was the Augustinian *credo ut intelligam*: I believe in the God of Revelation, in order that in the light of that belief I may understand the world. His most famous thesis was the ontological argument in proof of the existence of God: God is the highest being of which the human mind can conceive; and the mere fact that such a conception is attainable and permanent is the proof of the existence of a Being corresponding to such a conception.[1]

The second answer was given by the Nominalists, who upheld the importance of the particular: *post rem universalia*. What had to be comprehended was the concrete uniqueness of the particular: the universal to them was *nomen*; it had a grammatical existence only. Their inspiration was ultimately Aristotelean; but they exaggerated the Aristotelean view that universals were concepts of reason predicable about particulars, and instead of emphasizing the importance of such concepts, and of reason in furnishing them, reduced them to what their leader Roscellinus called *flatus vocis*. Like all Aristoteleans they ended by paying attention to the particular itself and thus furthered the progress of scientific observation.

The typical French medieval logician is Abelard. He began as a student of logic, and remained a logician pure and simple up to 1113. He inclined to Nominalism; he started from the individual, and believed that by the effort of thought we rise from it to the universal. But he approximated to the Realists in his belief that universals are not merely names, but are creations of the mind, necessary in the sense that thought is impossible without them, and real in virtue of their necessity. This conceptualism combines the analytic and the synthetic points of view, and is remarkable in two ways: that it approximates to the doctrine of Aristotle in the Posterior Analytics, which were not known in Paris till twenty years after Abelard's death,[2] and that it emphasizes the creative power of reason. The reasoning mind arrives at universals, and thus constitutes the universe as thought.

Abelard not only created a fresh philosophical point of view, but extended philosophy's sphere of vision. France is never content to let discovery in one province of knowledge be without influence upon other

---

[1] Cf. Descartes' ontological argument in proof of the existence of God.
[2] In his *Theologia* he declares he has gathered his citations of pagan authors from the Fathers, and not from the books of the philosophers 'quorum pauca novi'.

kinds of learning. Even in the eleventh century Berengar of Tours had argued that 'true courage lies in flying to dialectic in all things, since to fly to it is to fly to reason'; and had accordingly treated the doctrine of Transubstantiation in logical fashion. But with Abelard the fusion of the reasoning methods of dialectic with theology is more complete; he sought to rationalize in categories of formal logic every matter apprehended by his mind, and when he went to become Anselm of Laon's pupil in theology he crossed a dangerous threshold. He rapidly passed from pupil to master; as he tells us in his *apologia pro vita sua*, fitly called *Historia Calamitatum*:

'*Then it came about that I was brought to expound the very foundation of our faith by applying the analogies of human reason, and was led to compose for my pupils a theological treatise on the Divine Unity and Trinity. They were calling for human and philosophical arguments and insisting upon something intelligible, rather than mere words, saying that there had been more than enough of talk which the mind could not follow; that it was impossible to believe what was not in the first place understood, and that it was ridiculous for any one to set forth to others what neither he nor they could rationally conceive* (intellectu capere).'

It was impossible to believe what was not in the first place understood: Abelard reversed the Augustinian motto, and made *intelligo ut credam* his starting-point. 'By doubting we are led to inquire: by inquiry we perceive the truth.' It is impossible to rely entirely upon tradition, for tradition has inconsistent elements; two inconsistent things cannot be believed simultaneously, for it is the mark of truth that it is self-consistent. Reason and intelligence must do the preparatory work of solving or reconciling inconsistencies before faith can have a consistent body of belief which alone is credible. This is the fundamental idea of Abelard's method of marshalling his theological arguments: the method of *Sic et non*, by which he clarified the inconsistencies of Church tradition by opposing contradictory statements of the Fathers on a hundred and fifty-eight theological questions. His purpose is thus constructive and not destructive; it is to point beyond the inconsistencies of tradition to a reconciliation, and not to destroy faith by a mere exposure of inconsistencies. Yet this was the light in which his work struck traditionalists and mystics like Bernard and Norbert; not only could they point to single sentences, like that famous one in Abelard's lost *De Trinitate*, 'that a thing is not believed because God said it, but received as true because proved to be so', but they could and did object to the whole tone, spirit, and method of his theological teaching. He had presumed to try to understand and to explain the mystery of the Trinity, and had dared to bring all things in heaven and earth to the test of reason.

The proof of the constructive character of Abelard's method is the influence it exerted in the succeeding generation. The disciple of Abelard was Peter Lombard, Bishop of Paris in 1159, the *Magister Sententiarum*, whose *Sentences* were the received text-book of theology for the later Middle Ages.[1] Here was carried on the positive work made possible by the negative criticism of Abelard: Peter followed his master in stating the *pro* and *contra*, and then harmonized them by distinctions or inferences. His work is not so much original in itself as progressive in its systematization.

This systematization was due to Abelard, but as a logician Abelard died thirty years too soon. Of the treatises of the Aristotelean *Organon* he only knew the first two, the *De Interpretatione* and the *Categories*, the first treating of the constituent parts and kinds of sentences and the second of the classes of logical propositions. Not until the latter half of the twelfth century was the whole *Organon* known to the West; the introduction is probably due to another Frenchman, Thierry of Chartres.[2] The discovery of the laws of the syllogism, of logical demonstration, and of the refutation of false conclusions enlarged the intellectual horizon and advanced the method of scholastic thought. The centre of study was still Paris; the Parisian doctor Gilbert de la Porrée is for the generation of Dante the master of the Six Principles of Logic for Christendom as a whole.

But if the scholars of the thirteenth century recovered the ancient principles of logical reasoning, they also discovered fresh material on which to exercise them. Greek mathematics, medicine, and science came back to Europe, both from Moslem Spain and from the Byzantine East. Knowledge once more took an encyclopaedic turn; but the pioneers were not Frenchmen, but foreign doctors of Paris—the English Alexander of Hales and the Swabian Albertus. Albertus, an active Dominican, vowed to strict poverty and unable to own even his own manuscripts, fulfilling his duty as Provincial of Germany by walking barefoot through the province under his supervision, yet found time and energy to serve science. At the beginning of his exposition of Aristotle's *Physics* he says that substantial philosophy has three parts, physics, mathematics, and metaphysics, and 'it is our intention to make all the said parts intelligible to the Latins'. The marvellous thing is that he accomplished it, and that he lived in an age

---

[1] In the thirteenth century Dominican convents always had a *Sententiarius* to lecture on the Sentences as well as a *Biblicus* to lecture on the Bible.
[2] By the eighth century Aristotle and his Greek commentators had been translated from Syriac into Arabic and with the growth of learning in Spain this was translated by the Spanish Jews into Hebrew and thence in 1128 into Latin.

that could understand his work. He took and made his own the Aristotelean view that the love of knowledge is natural to man, and though he is medieval in his reliance on his sources, he yet recognizes that even Aristotle may be fallible. He is the link between Abelard and Roger Bacon, for he says, 'experiments should be made not in one way only, but according to all the circumstances'. Moreover, for him the compass of knowledge was not yet complete: 'It must be stated that not all the demonstrative sciences have been established, but that many still remain to be discovered.' He does not test the opinions of others by experiment, but he does observe natural phenomena and incorporate his observations in his work.[1] The twenty-one books of his work cover Logic, Physics, Metaphysics, Ethics, Politics, and the main branches of natural science—Botany, Mineralogy, Zoology, and so forth.

The new body of learning thus began to be systematized, and as this happened it had simultaneously to be incorporated in the Christian scheme of the universe. St. Louis, who had been impelled by the example of the Sultan to collect a library, furthered this incorporation by lending Vincent of Beauvais twelve hundred manuscripts, from which he and his staff compiled an encyclopaedia.[2] This was composed of four parts—three, the *Speculum Naturale*, the *Speculum Doctrinale*, and the *Speculum Historiale*, forming the *Imago Mundi*, and the fourth, the *Speculum Morale*—a later work—dealing with the spiritual world. The *Imago Mundi* is arranged in scriptural order: it treats first of the Creator, next of the creation, then of man's fall and reparation, and then of events—*rebus gestis*—chronologically. The history, however, is still that of the *City of God*, of saints of the old and the new law. Ancient history is 'historia filiorum Cain'; but Vincent none the less shows a sound knowledge of Virgil, Horace, Ovid, Lucan, Cicero, and other authors in the episodes he admits. There are three evils in the world; ignorance, sin, and mortality, for which there are three remedies; wisdom, represented by *philosophia theorica*, virtue, represented by *philosophia practica*, and action, by *philosophia mechanica*. 'Theorica,' he says, 'driving out ignorance, illuminates wisdom; Practica, shutting out vice, strengthens virtue; and Mechanica, providing against penury, tempers the infirmities of the present life. Theorica, in all that is and that is not, chooses to investigate the true; Practica determines the right way of living and the form of discipline, according to the institution of the virtues; Mechanica, occupied with fleeting things,

[1] His book *De mineralibus*, for instance, contains a number of first-hand observations, and is the first medieval lapidary to do so.
[2] He was thus the first man to earn the right to be called a bookworm: *librorum helluo*.

strives to provide for the needs of the body. For the end and aim of all human actions and studies, which reason regulates, ought to concern either the reparation of the integrity of our nature or the alleviation of the needs to which life is subjected. The integrity of our nature is repaired by wisdom, to which Theorica relates, and by Virtue, which Practica cultivates. Need is alleviated by the administration of temporalities, to which Mechanica attends. Last found of all is Logic, source of eloquence, through which the wise who understand the aforesaid principal sciences and disciplines may discourse upon them more correctly, truly, and elegantly; more correctly through Grammar; more truly through Dialectic; more elegantly through Rhetoric.' Medieval philosophy still keeps the liberal arts within its synthesis: education is still based on the Trivium and still lies within the province of religion. On tombs of the thirteenth century no one is represented in pursuit of his calling but the priest with the chalice, since the Church says 'tu es sacerdos in aeternum', and the professor seated teaching from his chair, for he teaches the truth which is also eternal.

It remained for one not a Frenchman, but a doctor and teacher at Paris, to wed the whole of the recovered Aristotle to the teaching of the Fathers and the traditions of the Church, as Abelard had wedded Aristotelean logic to theology. Aquinas strictly follows the scholastic method of *Sic et non*, and never forgets to consider any side of the question; he expounds syllogistic argument within syllogistic argument with unfailing lucidity; he, the Angelic Doctor, constructs an ideal universe that by reason springs from the Christian faith. A true syllogistic structure supersedes the plan of the *Sentences* in setting one excerpted opinion against another, to the end of arriving at an adjustment. His conclusion is that final and perfect beatitude can only be in the vision of the Divine essence. 'For perfect beatitude it is necessary that the intellect should attain to the very essence of the first cause. And thus it will have its perfection through union with God as its object.'

Thus philosophy and theology were made one in the dialectical processes of the Aristotelean syllogism. It remained for Dante to show the congruity of medieval humanity and medieval Christianity in his symbolic transmutation of material to spiritual, mortal to eternal. His is the true ability to *reducere ad unum*, for he makes his *Divina Commedia* not only a *summa salvationis* but also a poem.[1]

All the learned books so far described were clerical, professional, and for the ordinary man, abstruse. Written in Latin, they were intended for

[1] The way was paved for it by Raóul de Houdan's *Voie d'enfer* (a vision of Hell) and *Voie de Paradis*.

the clerk and not for the layman. But since learning was a part of religion, the friars helped to bring it as part of religion down to the popular level. It is true that St. Francis was on the whole opposed to learning and that the Dominican constitutions of 1228 forbade the brethren to study 'books of the Gentiles and secular sciences'. But the new religious movement attracted men of intellectual energy, who, leading an uncloistered life, could not escape the influence of the new learning. We have seen the importance of the encyclopaedic work of the great Dominican Doctors Albertus and Aquinas, and in the same century we find the facts, if not the philosophical structure, of these Latin works reproduced in *oeuvres de vulgarisation* in the vernacular. Such works were in real demand; even a German Franciscan with a strong dislike of France confesses in his *Notitia Seculi* of 1288 that the French are filled with the 'amor sciendi', and Etienne de Bourbon records that Robert d'Auvergne, who died in 1234, made out of historical curiosity so large a collection of books 'concerning heresy and heretics', to which he devoted forty years of his life, that his own orthodoxy became suspect. The thirteenth century witnessed a considerable production of quasi-scientific treatises in French, usually translated from Latin: books on astronomy and astrology, on animals (*bestiaires*), birds (*volucraires*), stones (*lapidaires*), and plants (*herbiers*), on weather, on medicine, on physiognomy, and on world history. Some are merely descriptions of the 'proprietez des choses'; some cater for the romantic with 'merveilles', and some for the pious with allegorical 'senefiances'.

The most interesting are the treatises with an encyclopaedic scope, and of these the *Image du Monde*, written by a friar of Metz in 1247, is one of the earliest. It is based on Honorius's *Imago Mundi*, Cardinal Jacques de Vitry's *Historia Hierosolymitana*, and the *Anticlaudianus* of Alain de Lille, and is divided into three books; the first concerned with God, with human intelligence, and the cosmogony of the universe; the second with earth and the four elements that compose it; and the third with the Heavens, and a good many discursions which found no other place.

The friar begins by describing the ancients, who

> *Ne penserent pas comme bestes*
> *Qui ne quierent fors la pasture . . .*
> *Ainz veillierent par mainte nuit . . .*
> *N'orent de nul autre avoir cure*
> *Fors d'aprendre science pure.*[1]

[1]'They did not think like the beasts, who only seek for food, but watched through many a night, nor had heed of anything but to learn pure knowledge.'

'By their efforts the seven Arts were established, and many were martyred in the cause of knowledge. We shall only make like progress in our time if we are equally disinterested. In these days men think only of riches, and only at Paris does learning survive. There, thank God, the Mendicants have lately come and "retiennent or la flour de clergie".'

The author proceeds to describe a globular, geocentric universe. Earth is the heaviest of the four elements, and so our world is at the centre,

> *Quer qui pluz poise plus bas tret*
> *Et quanque poise a lui atret.*[1]

Men should remember that as the earth is tiny in relation to the heavens, so is earthly life petty in comparison with the heavenly. The earth is divided into four parts. Asia is the earthly paradise where is the tree of life and the fountain whence rise the four great rivers: the Indian Phison, the Egyptian Nile, the Tigris, and the Euphrates. India is surrounded by the great sea, where is the Isle Taprobane (Ceylon). There summer and winter come twice in the year, but so mildly that the trees are always green. There are found gold and precious stones guarded by dragons and griffins; there too are cannibals. India is divided into four and twenty provinces, all very populous. There are pygmies, who live in tribes; 'brahmanes', who throw themselves into the fire; and others who worship the sun. There are hairy people who eat raw fish and drink salt water, as well as hordes of monstrous creatures. In India are serpents that can eat deer, and many terrible beasts. The Indians and Persians are used to fighting on elephants, seated in little towers.

Europe can be dismissed in a string of names, since all men know them. Africa is a dark continent. Then come the islands—Colchis, where Jason went for the Golden Fleece; the island where St. Denis was born; Delos, that first appeared above the waters of the Flood; Paros, with its white marble; Samos, whence came the Sibyl who prophesied the coming of Christ; Sicily, where Pythagoras was born, and where pottery was first made; Sardinia, the Balearics, Meroes, where there is no shade, and the lost land that Plato knew that sank beneath the sea.

Then to the north, Ireland where there are no snakes, and Thule with its evergreen trees, and its division of the year into one long day and one long night.

Then follows a long description of the marvels of nature; every-day things that none the less cannot be explained.

---

[1]'For that which is heaviest falls lowest, and draws to it all things which have weight.'

> *Quar il n'est si petite chose*
> *Dont nus hom puist savoir la glose*
> *Veraiement por coi ele est*
> *Fors si com a Damnedieu plest.*[1]

From the exterior of the earth the author passes to a vivid description of hell. This concludes the section on earth, and the author proceeds to deal with the other elements: water, with a consideration of mineral springs; the air, with a description of the reasons why the weather changes; and fire, which is a kind of air, noble, subtle, and shining, with no trace of humidity. Thence the author passes to astronomy: day and night, the phases of the moon, and the hidden forces of the heavens on earthly things. Ptolemy of Egypt was the first to make great progress in the study of the planets, and he invented clocks. These are a great help to man, since God loves order and regularity.

> *Si sont ore maintes gens mors*
> *Qui, se lor afferes eüssent*
> *Ordenez si com il deüssent*
> *Chascun jor a heure establie,*
> *Qui encore fussent en vie.*[2]

It is to Ptolemy that we owe the calendar, revised by Caesar, the next great astronomer. So we come to a general consideration of Philosophy. What is it?

> *Philosophie est connoissance*
> *Et fine amour de sapience . . .*
> *Dont Platon respondi aucun*
> *Qui li demanda en commun:*
> *'Sire Platon, avez apris*
> *Qui tant avez vostre tans mis*
> *Et estudié por aprendre? . . .*
> *Quar nous dites aucun bon mot.'*
> *Et Platons, qui plus que nus sot,*
> *Lor dist, si comme a cuer dolant,*
> *Qu'il n'avoit rien apris fors tant*
> *Qu'il se sentoit et jour et nuit*

---

[1]'For there is no thing so small that man can know the meaning of it truly for what it is unless it pleases God.'
[2]'How many men are dead, who if they had ordered their business as they ought, each day at a fixed hour, might still be alive?'

Ausi com un vaissel tout vuit;
Tant leur en respondit Platons.[1]

There also exists a second version of the *Image du Monde*, written a few years later. To this the author has added a certain amount of information drawn from personal experience, including an account of the ascent of Etna:

Je, qui cest livre fis ici,
Celes .ii. monteignes je vi
Et montai en son la plus grans
Pour veïr ce qu'ist de leans.
La bouche vi de la fumée
Qu'adès fume sanz reposée . . .
U feu ting ma main nuement:
Suer la me fist doucement . . .
Grans esté fu; si oi grant soif,
Si bui de l'engelee noif . . .
Au descendre oï la tonnierre
Plus bas de moi desouz mon erre
Pour la nue en quoi il tonnoit,
Qui plus basse de moi estoit.[2]

It is evident that writing in the vernacular makes the book more personal and in closer touch with common life. This directness may have influenced Brunetto Latino, who, while passing three or four years in French lands after 1263, wrote his encyclopaedic *Livre du Trésor* in French 'porce que la parleure et plus delitable et plus commune a toutes gens'. His book, too, makes no claim to originality, it is 'compilés seulement de mervilus diz des autors qui devant nostre tens ont traitié de philosophie'. Its philosophic aim is to show that the function of nature is to accord the discordant principles—hot and cold, wet and dry—so that 'totes diversités retornent en unité'.

The next encyclopaedia was written in Latin by an Englishman, Bartholomew Glanville, who is said by Salimbene to have first delivered its substance as a course of lectures at the University of Paris. It was, at all

[1] 'Philosophy is knowledge and a noble love of wisdom. About which Plato answered one who asked him in company: "Sir Plato, what have you learnt, who have studied and spent so much time in learning? Pray tell us something witty." And Plato, who knew more than anyone, said to him as if his heart was heavy, that he had learnt nothing but that he felt night and day like an empty vessel. That is what Plato answered.'
[2] 'I who have made this book have seen these two mountains, and have climbed the larger to the top, to see what comes forth there. I saw the mouth of the smoke that always smokes without ceasing. . . . I held my naked hand near the fire, and it made it sweat gently. . . . It was high summer, and I was very thirsty, and drank from the frozen snow. Coming down I heard the thunder, beneath my path lower down, out of the cloud in which it thundered, which was lower than I.'

events, popular there; not only was it on the official list of books on hire from the university booksellers to the students, but it was also owned in duplicate by the Sorbonne. It is intended for the use of preachers who need illustrations for their sermons, and lacks the philosophic scope of the earlier encyclopaedias. It is significant that it was almost immediately translated into French by Jean Corbichon, and that it is in the translated form that it was most used.

The very popularity of Bartholomew's book shows a certain decline. The *Summa Theologiae* of Aquinas is the true crown of French scholastic thought. The aim of such thought, both in detail of method and in breadth of aim, was *reducere ad unum*; with the next generation the aim was changed, and the French systematization of thought went to pieces in English hands. The aim of Roger Bacon and Duns Scotus was not to lead thought back to unity but to find out new truths. Yet Gerson could still call the University of Paris 'the Paradise of this world, where is the tree of knowledge of good and evil', and for the later Middle Ages she was still the fountain to which all streams of knowledge could eventually be traced.

The work of the Frenchmen of the later Middle Ages was less to increase the sum of learning than to make that sum more generally profitable. The gradual assimilation of learned and popular writings, no longer definitely divided by the test of the language in which they were written, marks the growth of a class of enlightened laics, and the transformation of learning from the prerogative of the Church into a national possession. A leading part in this transformation was taken by Charles V, who was, like the rich amateur Philippe le Bon of Burgundy, the elegant René of Anjou, and the poet Charles d'Orléans, both a student and a collector of books. Christine de Pisan is a witness to his learning: 'Shall we not also speak of the wisdom of King Charles, of the great love he had for study and knowledge? He clearly showed it by his fair array of notable books, and his fair library of all the most notable volumes which had been compiled by sovereign authors, whether of Holy Scripture, theology, philosophy, or the sciences, all well written and richly adorned; and the best scribes who could be found ever employed by him in such work; and whether his study was well ordered and well planned, since he wished all his possessions fair and clean, well kept and well ordered, it behoves not to ask: for a better could not be.'

Nor was it only by the collection and study of books that Charles forwarded the growth of a learned literature in French; it was due to his patronage that Pierre Bersuire translated Livy into French, Nicholas d'Oresme Aristotle, and Raoul de Presle Augustine's *City of God*, 'for the public utility of the realm and of all Christendom'. His library contained a considerable number of French translations of the classics of the two preceding centuries, such as the *Rationale* of Guillaume Durand and the works of Hugh of St. Victor. He possessed remarkably few works of scholastic theology, and among the legal books only one Latin text of the Institutes of Justinian as compared with numerous—and often duplicated—French works: translations of the Institutes, the Digest, the Code, and commentaries on them; the *Coutumier de Normandie* (three copies), Pierre de Fontaines, and French translations of six works on Canon Law. In science, besides the library of a specialist in astrology, we again find a marked preponderance of French works—the encyclopaedias are all French translations from Latin, Aristotle appears in French translation, and all the rest but a few old texts are in that language. In history there was not a single Latin book without a translation appended, and not a single example of a history of France written in Latin is mentioned in an inventory of very considerable length, including a large number of rhymed chronicles. The library of Charles V was not confined to learned literature,[1] but was rather a collection of the literary work of the French nation among which works of erudition took their place. Even at the university heavy punishments were being decreed in vain against the students who spoke French; and with a generation accustomed to think in French, succeeded by a generation that read from printed books, a new chapter in the history of learning began.

[1] It also included twenty-four romances of the Carolingian cycle, seventeen *Romans de la Table Ronde*, fifteen romances of classical subjects, seven *Romans d'aventures*, several collections of satirical compositions, and fifteen of lyrics.

VII

Education

THE medieval view of man set his function and end before any other aspect of his being: 'the proper function does not come into existence for the sake of the being, but the latter for the sake of the former'. Consequently it was natural that medieval education should be definitely fitted to the function that the child was eventually to perform, whether as noble, as cleric, or as artisan. So it can be divided into three kinds—the practical, the speculative, and the technical—each of which was so to prepare the child to do his duty in his station that his existence might be justified and his function fulfilled.

The training of the noble child was rather *éducation* in the French sense than instruction of an academic kind. He had to carry on the practical work of feudal government: to fight, to be a courtier, to learn the self-control and the decision that befit a member of the governing class. A thirteenth-century sermon tells us: 'Peasants spoil their children and make them little red frocks, and then, when they are a little older, they put them to the plough. On the other hand, the nobles first set their children beneath them and make them eat with the serving lads; and then, when they are grown up, set them on high.' All the writers of the Middle Ages agree that to spare the rod is to spoil the child. It is a mistake, also, to begin too late—the bough should be bent while it is still green. Philippe de Novare in his *Quatre Ages de l'homme* explains that after the age of ten, children have the 'franc arbitre' between good and evil, and too much allowance must not be made for them. Rather are they to be corrected when young: 'N'avient pas sovent que anfant facent bien se ce n'est par doute ou par ansaignement.'[1] Punish them first with words, then with rods, then, if you must, with imprisonment. Make them learn the Credo, Pater Noster, and Ave Maria; then the two first commandments of the law: 'Aimme ton Seigneur ton Dieu de tout ton cuer et de toute ta pensée et de toute ta langue et de touz tes manbres et de toute t'ame', and 'Aimme ton proïme si comme toi meïsme'.

Such religious education seems usually to have been the parent's prerogative; we have still the psalter from which Blanche of Castille

---

[1]'It does not often happen that a child does right unless it be from fear or from teaching.'

taught St. Louis his letters, and Joinville describes St. Louis teaching his own children in his turn: 'Before he lay down in his bed he would cause his children to come to him, and bring to their minds the deeds of good kings and good emperors, telling them that it was of such men they should take example. And he could bring to their minds also the deeds of great men who were wicked, and by their ill-doing, and their rapine, and their avarice, had brought their kingdoms to ruin. . . . He made them learn the Hours of Our Lady, and say before him the Hours of the Day, so as to accustom them to hear the Hours when they ruled over their own lands.' Much of the moral training thus received rested upon the idea that the man of noble birth should in every thought and deed set a good example to others. So we find St. Louis reminding Joinville that if he would be honoured in this world and go to Paradise in the next, he should keep himself from knowingly doing or saying anything which, if the whole world knew of it, he would be ashamed to acknowledge. So, too, good manners were a duty. The romance of *Urbain le Courtois* tells us:

> *Li bon enfant deit ester*
> *Devant son seigneur a manger.*
> *Il ne se doit apouuer*
> *Ne nul membre de doit grater . . .*
> *Si homme vous doigne petit u grant*
> *Tant com vous este joesne enfant*
> *En genouillant le recevez*
> *Et doucement lui merciez.*[1]

and the child was brought up to speak politely to clerks and not to make a noise in church.[2] France was early aware—and has never forgotten— that good manners are based on consideration for others, and are thus a part of morality. By 1247 the author of *Sidrach* teaches that you should listen, even if you are bored; 'car si est un grand sens de courtoisie de regarder a celui qui parle, car il li fait plaisir.' You must show neither haughtiness nor shyness; every one has a right to play a part in society, and if from either of these reasons a man is silent, 'il pert sa raison et son droit'. It is selfish to show your feelings: when Galeran is in love he is reproved by his chaplain-tutor for looking miserable:

> *Tout le monde blasme et reprent*
> *Jeune varlet et riche et hault*

---

[1]'The good child ought to stand upright before his lord at meals, and not lean against anything or scratch his limbs with his finger. . . . If any one gives you anything, great or small, while you are still a young child, receive it kneeling and thank him nicely.'
[2]*Doon de Mayence*, thirteenth century.

> *Qu'en ne voit envoisié et baut . . .*
> *S'en vous voy faire chiere mate*
> *En vo pays repris serez.*[1]

And in another romance Joufroi has to hide his feelings when he hears of his father's death:

> *Car n'avient pas a nul baron*
> *Qui face dueil outre raison.*[2]

Even St. Louis had occasionally to be reminded of this duty of self-control. Joinville tells us that when he lost his mother he 'made such lamentation that, for two days, no one could speak to him. After that he sent one of the varlets of his chamber to summon me. When I came before him in his chamber, where he was alone, and he saw me, he stretched out his arms, and said: "Ah, Seneschal, I have lost my mother!" "Sir," said I, "I do not marvel at that, since she had to die; but I do marvel that you, who are a wise man, should have made such great mourning; for you know what the sage says: that whatever grief a man may have in his heart, none should appear in his countenance, because he who shows his grief causes his enemies to rejoice and afflicts his friends." '

There was much for the child to learn besides religion and good manners. *Les Quatre Ages de l'Homme* expounds the typically French view that the whole function of life is to be able to follow one's profession well; to do this the child must next learn its 'métier'. 'Clergie et chevalerie' are the most honourable callings, and both must be learnt young. 'A poines puet estre bon clers qui ne commance dès anfance, ne ja bien ne chevauchera qui ne l'aprent jones.'[3] The thirteenth-century romance of *Aiol* describes the ideal education for a boy of noble birth:

> *Il n'ot valet en France mieus dotriné(s),*
> *Ne mieus a .i. preudome seust parler.*
> *Del ceval et des armes seut il assés,*
> *Si vos dirai comment, se vous volés:*
> *Car ses peres l'ot fait sovent monter*
> *Par la dedens le bos ens en .i. pré*
> *Et le boin ceval core et trestorner,*
> *De dit et de parolle l'en a moustré,*
> *Aiols le retient bien comme senés;*

[1]'Every one blames and rebukes a young man, rich and well born, who does not look gay and gallant. . . If they see you looking sad you will be rebuked in your own country.'
[2]'For it befits not a baron to mourn beyond reason.'
[3]'A man may rarely be a good clerk who does not begin in childhood, any more than he may be a good rider if he does not learn young'.

Et des cours des estoiles, del remuer,
Del refait de la lune, del rafermer,
De chou par savoit il quant qu'il en ert:
Avise la ducoise l'en ot moustré;
Il no't plus sage feme en .x. chités.
Et Moisès l'ermite l'ot doctriné
De letres de gramaire l'ot escolé:
Bien savoit Aiols lire et enbriever,
Et latin et romans savoit parler.[1]

In the early fourteenth-century romance of *Sone de Nansai* the hero learns to read and write, to play chess and backgammon, to hawk, hunt, and fence; to study geometry, 'magic', and law; and has as many as four masters.[2] Fencing was learnt not so much for its own sake as to develop the lungs; in *L'Escoufle* Guillaume studies it:

Por combatre nel fait il mie,
Mais por avoir grignor alaine.
Et c'est une chose certaine
Que hom va plus bel et plus droit
Et si en est on mout plus droit:
To cis biens vient de l'escremie.[3]

Of his other studies, chess and backgammon, hawking and hunting, were knightly occupations: law befitted one who had judicial powers; and fair speech was a necessity. Writing was less important, and went more against the grain. *Sidrach* describes how difficult it is: the man who writes labours with his body and his eyes and his brain, and dare neither think nor look nor laugh nor speak nor listen while he is writing. Only the scribe knows what an art it is.

Yet reading, writing, and a little Latin were useful for a man of high birth, and by 1454 we find Charles, Duke of Berry, aged eight, owning five school books—an ABC, a copy of the Seven Penitential Psalms,

[1]'There was no youth in France better brought up, nor who knew better how to speak to a gentleman. He knew enough about horses and arms, and if you like I will tell you how: for his father made him often ride through the woodland and in the meadow and learn how to trot and turn the horse, and showed him by word and deed, and Aiol remembered it well as a sensible youth. He knew all about the courses of the stars, the changes of the moon, . . . Avice the duchess had shown him; there was no wiser women in ten cities. And Moses the hermit had taught him, and schooled him in letters and grammar. Well did Aiol know how to read and write, how to speak in Latin and French . . .'
[2]A similar account is given in *Galeran.*
[3]'He does not do it for fighting, but to have deeper breath; and it is a certain thing that one is fitter and more erect and much straighter for it. . . . All these good things come from fencing.'

Donatus on the eight parts of speech, Cato's moral distichs with a French translation, and a rhymed abstract of Priscian's Latin Grammar.

On the other hand it was, generally speaking, better for womenfolk to be unlettered. *Urbain le Courtois* gives good advice.

> *Si femme volez esposer*
> *Pensez de tei, mon fils chier.*
> *Pernez nule por sa beauté*
> *Ni ki soit en livre lettrié;*
> *Car sovent sunt decevables.*[1]

What women must know is how to spin and sew, to embroider and sing; and above everything to acquire 'la bele contenance et simple'; to look straight in front of them, quietly and unaffectedly, and to learn to behave without either prudery or over-familiarity.

Social condition was the directive force in education among the lower classes as among the nobility. Children learnt their *métier*, most often from a parent or near relative; and they had other schooling, chiefly in learning to read in the Psalter, for which time is usually claimed in the indentures of their apprenticeship. Even girls got a certain amount of such teaching; the nunnery of Prouille, near Castelnaudary, was founded by St. Dominic for the special purpose of training nuns to act as village school-mistresses. A certain number of mistresses worked in Paris under the control of the Precentor of Notre Dame, who gave them the licence to teach in *litteris grammaticis.*

Yet since each exists to fulfil a specific function in society, men and women of noble or artisan birth had little concern with the sphere of learning. That sphere was the province of the clerk; it was his heritage as much as his land was the knight's or his trade the craftsman's; and, like them, he had to learn his *métier* young.

Medieval clerkly education in France begins with Charlemagne. Alcuin's school was migratory, and followed the court, but it did much to establish a tradition, which was strengthened by the enactments of 787 and 789 that every cathedral should have a school for young clerks. Down to the beginning of the eleventh century the chief educational centres were the monastic schools. Rheims was the most important; here Gerbert did much to found the French educational tradition. Towards the end of his life he wrote to the abbot of the monastery of Tours:

[1]'If you wish to marry a wife, dear son, consider your own good; take none for her beauty, nor any that have book learning, for they are often deceitful.' A similar view is expressed in *Les Quatres Âges de l'Homme.*

'*I am not one who . . . would sometimes separate the good from the useful, but rather . . . would mingle it with everything useful . . . And as morality and the art of speech are not to be severed from philosophy, I have always joined the study of speaking well with the study of living well. . . . In preparing for such a business (of establishing a school) I am eagerly collecting a library; and as formerly at Rome and elsewhere in Italy, so likewise in Germany and Belgium, I have obtained copyists and manuscripts with a mass of money and the help of friends in those parts. Permit me likewise to beg of you also to promote this end. I will append at the end of this letter a list of those writers whom I wish to have copied. I have sent for your disposal parchment for the scribes and money to defray the cost.*'

It is to Gerbert that we owe the musical stave and the scale that takes its notes from the hymn to St. John:

> Ut *queant laxis*
> Resonare *fibris*
> Mira *gestorum*
> Famuli *tuorum*
> Solve *polluti*
> Labii *reatum*
> Sancte *Johannes.*

At Rheims, as at most of the monastic schools, there were two departments, one for the monastery's own *oblati* and one for external pupils. The oblates—who were usually received into the community at about the age of seven—were under a strict discipline. The fourteenth-century custumal of Saint Bénigne at Dijon, for instance, decrees,

'*At Nocturns, and indeed at all the Hours, if the boys commit any fault in the Psalmody or other singing, either by sleeping or such like transgression, let there be no sort of delay, but let them be stripped forthwith of frock and cowl, and be beaten in their shirt only. . . . Let the masters sleep between every two boys in the dormitory, and sit between every two at other times. . . . When they lie down in bed, let a master always be among them with his rod and (if it be night) with a candle, holding the rod in one hand and the light in the other. If any chance to linger after the rest, he is forthwith to be smartly touched; for children everywhere need custody with discipline, and discipline with custody. . . . When they wash, let masters stand between each pair. . . . When they sit in cloister or chapter, let each have his own tree-trunk for a seat, and so far apart that none touch in any way even the skirt of the other's robe. . . . Let them wipe their hands as far as possible one from the other, that is at opposite corners of the towel. . . . Nor doth one ever speak to the other, except by his master's express leave, and in the hearing of all who are in the school. . . . One reporteth whatsoever he knoweth against the other; else, if he be found to have concealed aught of set purpose, both the concealer and the culprit are beaten.'*

But if the cloister had its terrors for the schoolboy destined for the Church, so had the alternative, the private tutor. Guibert de Nogent, who was born in 1053, has left a sad little picture of his childish education under a tutor at home:

'When I was set to learning, I had indeed already touched the rudiments, yet I could scarce put together the simplest elements when my loving mother, eager for my teaching, purposed to set me to grammar. . . . The man to whom my mother was purposed to give me over, had begun to learn grammar at an advanced age, and was so much the more rude in that art, that he had known so little thereof in his youth. Yet he was of so great modesty that his honesty supplied his lack of learning. . . . When therefore I was set under his care, he taught me with such purity and guarded me so sincerely . . . that he kept me altogether from the general games, never suffering me to go forth unaccompanied, nor to eat away from home, nor to accept any gift without his leave . . . whereas the others of my age wandered everywhere at their own will. . . . I for my part was shackled by constant restraints, sitting in my little clerical cloak and watching the bands of playing children like some tame animal. . . . But while he lay so hard upon me, and all who knew us thought that my little mind must be sharpened to its keenest edge by these incessant pains, all men's hopes were none the less frustrated. For he himself was utterly ignorant of the arts of composition, whether in verse or in prose; so that I was smitten with a grievous and almost daily hail of fierce words and blows, while he would have compelled me to learn that which he himself knew not. . . . Weary nature should sometimes find her remedy in some diversity of work. Let us bear in mind how God formed his world, not in uniformity, but with vicissitudes of day and night, of spring and summer and autumn and winter, thus refreshing us by the change of the seasons.'

To almost every boy the elements seem to have been hardly taught, and it is the hardship and not the method that is recorded for posterity. Only Anselm's voice is heard to remind the teacher that his boys are human like himself, and have need 'of loving kindness from others, of gentleness, mercy, cheerful address, charitable patience, and many such like comforts'.

School education developed slowly and gradually, changing not with any change of view but to meet the slow development of the national life. The oblate schools survived, but Bec was the last of any great importance, and in the eleventh century the control of education passed into the hands of the secular clergy in the cathedral schools. Of these, Chartres, Laon,

Auxerre, Sens, Rouen, and Clermont were the chief; and at all these cathedrals, as at Notre Dame de Paris, the sculptured figures of the Seven Liberal Arts appear on the façade: Grammar as an old woman with the rod of correction, Dialectic with the serpent of wisdom, Rhetoric with the tablets of the poet, Arithmetic counting on her fingers, Geometry with the compasses, Astronomy with the astrolabe, and Music striking a peal of bells with a hammer.

Grammar, the science of words, was followed by the sciences of thought: Logic, which Vincent de Beauvais says argues from theses, that is from abstractions, and Rhetoric, that argues from hypotheses, or circumstantial evidence. Rhetoric, indeed, covered both poetry and law; Brunetto Latino gives an account of all its 'couleurs': 'aornemens, tourn, comparaison, clamour, fainture, trespas, demonstrance, adoublement',[1] and the *Image du Monde* says that from Rhetoric

> *sont li Droit estrait*
> *Par coi li jugement sont fait*
> *Qui esgardé sont par raison*
> *En court de Roi et de Baron . . .*
> *Qui Retoricque bien sauroit*
> *Il connoistroit et tort et droit.*[2]

The cathedral schools rose to importance by virtue of the ability of the teachers who ruled them—Fulbert, Saint Ives, Gilbert de la Porrée, and their peers—and therefore it was natural that they should mark a real development of pedagogic method. The best teachers found themselves in a position to teach as they pleased, and to link their own learning more closely to the teaching of their scholars. Fulbert, appointed Bishop of Chartres in 1006, was the direct heir of Gerbert's learning and helped firmly to establish his educational system. Not only were pupils of all ages instructed in the Trivium—Grammar, Logic, and Rhetoric—but the higher faculties were also included. The improved methods of arithmetical computation which Gerbert had brought from Spain, including a use of Arabic numerals if not of the cipher; music; astronomy, with clear teaching on Greek lines on the horizon and the parallels; medicine—Fulbert himself cast the Hippocratic receipts into verse for memorizing; much theology of a traditional kind, based on the study of Augustine, and the study of some Canon and Roman Law and the Capitularies of Charlemagne,

[1] 'Paraphrase, form, comparison, apostrophe, imagination, metaphor, description, and repetition.'
[2] 'Does Law come forth, by which judgements are made which are rightly considered in King's and Baron's courts. . . . Who well knows Rhetoric knows both right and wrong.'

made Fulbert's school at Chartres representative of the extreme compass of learning in eleventh-century France.

At Chartres John of Salisbury, about 1140, received his classical training from William of Conches on the method invented by Bernard Sylvester—a method which is the direct ancestor of the *lecture expliquée* which still forms the basis of French teaching. Most of the available classical authors were studied in turn. After questioning his pupils on parsing, scansion, construction, grammatical figures, and 'oratorical tropes' in the passage read, the lecturer commented on the varieties of phraseology which there occurred, and pointed out possible alternatives. Then the subject-matter was analysed and annotated. The next morning the students, under threat of the severest penalties, had to repeat what they had been taught the previous day. Such study of texts was supplemented by teaching in verse and prose composition in imitation of the authors read, and by frequent discussions on set themes. It is obvious that teaching such as this inevitably leads to more advanced work; it is thus that the transition from school to university teaching was insensibly effected.

It is almost accidental that a succession of great teachers of law—Irnerius for Roman Law and Gratian for Canon Law—at Bologna, and a succession of philosophers, William of Champeaux, Hugh of St. Victor, and Abelard at Paris, should have given Bologna and Paris permanent importance as the two great seats of medieval learning. But though the University of Paris, even in its most rudimentary state, did not exist until a generation after Abelard, and there was nothing in Abelard's schools to distinguish them from any cathedral school made famous by a single master, it must not be forgotten that he helped to inaugurate the intellectual movement out of which the University of Paris sprang. His career at Paris exactly coincided with the first steps of its rapid rise to commercial and political importance; his renown drew thither crowds of students from the remotest parts of Europe. For a century and a half his method of teaching and inquiry was the method that essentially characterized the university, and for the same length of time the stream of students contributed to make Paris the Mistress City of Transalpine Europe, and enabled Eudes de Chateauroux to declare that France was the oven where the intellectual bread of the whole world was baked.

Constitutionally speaking, the university was an outgrowth of the cathedral school, administered by the bishop and canons. Gradually the right of granting the licence to teach was transferred from the bishop to the chancellor of the cathedral. The need of organization among those thus licensed led to the formation of a guild of masters, and thus the university itself arose.

A university is far more closely allied to a guild than we usually remember. *Universitas vestra* is the polite form of address to any corporate body, whether it be a corporation of teachers or of cobblers, and in the Middle Ages *universitas* is therefore never used absolutely, but is always qualified: 'The University of Paris' is a convenient abbreviation for the University of the Chancellor, Masters and Scholars of Paris. The medieval phrase for the place where higher studies are pursued was *studium generale*, but this did not mean a place where all subjects were studied, but a place where students from all parts could pursue their studies.

The University of Paris first came into being about 1160.[1] By the thirteenth century is was full-grown; it was no longer a question of chapter-schools and wandering teachers, but of an organized university with regular doctors teaching permanently, where the student could proceed to the higher faculties of theology, law, and medicine after taking his degree in arts. Their guild of masters had taken its place in the city.

The earliest written statutes—which arose, like so many university regulations, out of a town and gown row—date from about 1208 and are guild regulations of the simplest kind. Members of the university are to wear a plain round black cloak, reaching to the heels, 'saltem dum nova est'; they are to follow the 'accustomed order' in lectures and disputations, and are to attend the funerals of deceased masters. The first statutes confirmed by the Pope, dating from 1215, lay down regulations for the actual teaching; Grammar and Logic are to be studied on ordinary days, and Rhetoric and Philosophy reserved as a treat for festivals. The next versions of the statutes—those of 1228 and 1244—give the university the legal right of suspending lectures as a protest against any injustice done to its corporation or to any of its members.

Since all lectures were in Latin, the student had to be able to read, write, and understand it, and necessity took the place of an entrance examination. A Statute of Paris makes the ability of a petitioner to state his case before the rector in Latin, without any 'interposition of French words', a test of his *bona fide* studentship. The university curriculum was in its turn inherited from the cathedral school. The Seven Liberal Arts— the more advanced of which hardly formed part of school training—comprised the whole sphere of education, not only in France, but in every

[1] The author desires to express her indebtedness to Rashdall's account of the University of Paris in his *Universities of the Middle Ages*.

civilized country. But then, as now, each university tended to focus its efforts on a single aspect of knowledge; in Italy Grammar and Rhetoric received much attention, and Logic was studied with them for its importance on the legal side: Canon Law, indeed, came to be the aim of much Italian education. In Paris the goal proved to be Theology, and this is the dominating interest towards which all other studies, notably the study of Dialectic, were consciously or unconsciously bent. Further, the sphere of intellectual interests was extended through the re-discovery of Greek thought through Arabic translations. Aristotelean logic is the basis of the structure of scholastic thought as Aristotelean science is of the content of its *Summae*; and, in addition, the mathematical sciences also received a new impetus from the same source. The Elements of Euclid were translated from Arabic into Latin by Adelard of Bath after a voyage in the East about 1130, and in 1202 Leonard of Pisa published his *Liber Abaci*, giving not only the Arabic numerals, but also the use of the cipher in a decimal notation. At the same time the great teachers come from a new source. Just as about 1100 the monks were displaced in education by the secular clergy, so in the thirteenth century the seculars began to be supplanted by the friars.

The older monastic orders did not produce a single great theologian after St. Bernard until scholastic theology was superseded by learned 'professional' theology. Monasteries only needed a few members able to preach an occasional sermon and to instruct the novices in elementary theology, and a few canonists to transact their legal business. The real services of the monks to literature in the later Middle Ages lie in the production of histories, a field quite alien to the studies of the universities.

All the great doctors belonged to the Mendicant Orders. The Dominicans were the first to reach the universities; as Friars Preachers their function was to combat heresy, and to this a course of study was a necessary preliminary. Thus they were drawn to the universities, where they gained two ends—the training of those who were already in the Order, and the opportunity of recruiting into it students and even teachers of the university. The Dominican centre in each country was at the seat of its chief university: Bologna, Paris, and Oxford.

Francis in the beginning had been opposed to learning. 'These brethren of mine', he declared, 'who are led away by curiosity of knowledge, in the day of tribulation shall find their hands empty. . . . Books are a temptation; the brethren who cannot read shall not seek to learn.' The Franciscans, however, like the Dominicans, had to be competent to combat heresy, and thus had to have some intellectual training, though for some time their studies were confined to the Bible and its commentaries, and did not include the Sentences or philosophy. But while the university was still a scattered community of seculars, without colleges or community life outside the lecture-room, the convents or halls of the Mendicants, communities within the community, inevitably acquired considerable importance. Further, the dispersion of the university of Paris by its masters in 1229, as a protest against the action taken by the provost in a town and gown quarrel, not only drove many of the secular masters to the rising universities of Oxford and Cambridge and to the smaller *studia generalia* of France—Toulouse, Orléans, Rheims, and Angers—but also changed the relations of the Mendicants and the university. They did not migrate, but established schools of theology of their own. On the re-opening of the university these were brought under its control, but a struggle was inevitable between the university as a guild of secular clergy and the corporate Orders of the friars. It began, as might be expected, with the Orders' claim to immunity from the rules of the guild, that is from the statutes of the university. The friars of Paris decided it was inconsistent with their profession of humility to supplicate for the Doctorate, yet they wanted the degree. Therefore in 1250 they procured a Papal Bull declaring that they should be admitted to the degree without supplicating. The struggle lasted for eight years. With the support of the Papacy the friars gained their point, but while the university was able to insist that no friar should be a member of the faculty of arts leading to the M.A., and that secular doctors should have a monopoly of teaching secular students theology, the university had to give in to the papal view of its work, and to discourage as heretical those wider studies which the increasing knowledge of Greek thought was reviving. So the struggle had certain ill effects. In the first place the intellectual activities of the Orders came to be to a great extent self-contained; there was little outside contact to check the Dominicans in their tendency to be inflexible adherents of their doctor Aquinas, and the Franciscans were divided between their own doctors, the mystic Bonaventura and the realist Alexander of Hales. Further, the support given by the Papacy to the friars against the guild of secular masters tended to make the university as a whole anti-papal. Finally, the university was no longer free to develop humanistic studies to their full extent. The exclusion of Civil Law from its curriculum by Honorius III in 1219 made it less truly a *studium generale*, though it did much to develop the legal universities of the southern provinces where the tradition of Roman Law was always strongest. The important school of Orléans, where the classical traditions of Chartres had been perpetuated, even in an age of dialectic, developed into such a university at a convenient distance from the capital.

But the Papacy did more than this; it is through its intervention that a French university was first formally founded. Toulouse was the centre of the religious and intellectual ferment of the Albigensian heresy, and therefore the Pope decided that it should be the home of a great school of orthodoxy. On Maundy Thursday 1229–30, the final treaty between the conquered Count Raymond of Toulouse and St. Louis was signed before the great door of Notre Dame de Paris. By an article of that treaty it was provided that for ten years Raymond should pay the salaries of fourteen professors: four Masters of Theology with fifty marks a year, two Decretalists with thirty, six Artists with twenty, and two Grammarians with ten. The theological faculty was to be in the hands of the friars—a *Propaganda Fide*—and the masters of the other faculties were to come from Paris.

Students flocked to every university in France, but most of all to Paris. About 1210: 'Never before in any time or in any part of the world, whether in Athens or in Egypt, had there been such a multitude of students. The reason for this must be sought not only in the admirable beauty of Paris, but also in the special privileges which King Philip and his father before him conferred upon the scholars.'[1] Seventy-five years later we are told:

> *Clerc vienent as estudes de toutes nations*
> *Et en yvier s'asanlent par plusuers legions:*
> *On leur lit et il oient pour leur instructions;*
> *En esté s'en retraient moult en leurs regions.*[2]

Soon after 1219 the students of the university had to be divided into four nations: France, England, Picardy, and Normandy. The French nation was further subdivided into five 'tribes', corresponding with the five ecclesiastical provinces of France. When the English Wars made the name of England too hateful for use, her 'nation' was re-christened *Nation d'Allemagne*, but the title was never really accepted.

Since there was a total absence of organized amusement—to play 'ad pilam vel ad crossiam vel ad alios ludos insultuosos' is forbidden by the 1379 statutes of the Collège de Narbonne—the students were apt to take their exercise not only in studious walks in the Pré aux Clercs but also in fighting the men of other nations. Jacques de Vitry tells us:

[1]Guillaume le Breton.
[2]'Clerks of all nations come to study, and in winter assemble in their legions; they are lectured to and listen for instruction, and then in summer many go back to their homes.'

'Because of the differences of their homes they disagree, are envious and insulting, and without shame offer each other much insult and contumely, saying that the English are drunkards and have tails; that the French are proud, soft and womanish; the Germans mad and indecent in their feasting; the Normans stupid and boastful; the Picards traitors and fair-weather friends. Those who come from Burgundy they hold to be brutish and slow, and thinking the Bretons fickle and unstable, they often throw the death of Arthur in their faces. The Lombards they call avaricious, full of malice, and unwarlike; the Romans given to sedition, violent people who bite their nails; the Sicilians tyrannical and cruel; the men of Brabant men of blood, incendiaries, freebooters, and robbers; the Flemings wasteful, prodigal, given over to feasting, and soft as butter. And because of such wrangling they often proceed from words to blows.'

The student was under little restraint; coming into residence about the age of sixteen or rather later, he was free to arrange most of the conditions of his life as he liked. Unless his parents had settled it beforehand, he chose the master whose lectures he was to attend, and the hall or hostel to which he was to be attached. By 1290 statutes had to be passed forbidding masters to tout for work among the freshmen. Jacques de Vitry warns them against the young professors, 'who draw their teaching not from memory and experience, but from notebooks and cupboards'.

No freshman escaped some kind of initiation ceremony that varied with the university. At the logical university of Paris the *bejaunus* or *bec-jaune* seems to have been treated as a fool, and hoaxed; in the legal universities of the south he was treated as a criminal and given a mock trial. At Paris he was finally driven through the streets on a donkey, and then 'purged' by a bath. History is silent as to the details of the ceremony. Once made free of the community, the freshman had still to submit to the yoke of student etiquette. At Avignon the seniors held a court twice a week under their 'abbot' to enforce their regulations. The freshmen were to serve them at table, not to stand between them and the fire in Hall, to give place to them on all occasions, not to sit at the first table in Hall, and not to call one another 'Sir'. The decisions of the Court were enforced by a certain number of blows with a wooden spoon; in addition the freshmen had one blow each all round whenever the Court met. In the early years of the university such student rule was the more important as there was no proper residential organization. The principal of a hall was often a student himself, and held an office like that of the president of a modern Junior Common Room. Not until the fifteenth century were the halls organized under a master, with doors locked at night, and formal requirements for residence; it was only after the endowment of colleges had made student-ship a privilege that discipline could be enforced.

The colleges of Paris were initiated by the charity of a burgess of London, who on his return from Jerusalem bought a room in the Hôtel-Dieu and endowed it to be a dormitory for eighteen students, who in return were to watch by the dead of the hospital and assist at their funerals. This Collège des Dix-huit was followed by those of the Bons-Enfants Saint Honoré in 1208, of Sainte Catherine du Val des Écoliers in 1229, of the Bons-Enfants Saint Victor in 1248, of the Collège de Prémontré in 1252, the College du Trésorier in 1268, and the Collège de Navarre in 1304. In all, sixty colleges were founded at Paris between 1137 and 1360.

Robert de Sorbon, who founded his great college in 1250, with the help of St. Louis, was indebted for some details of his organization to the Mendicant Orders; his 'pauvres maîtres' have something of their discipline as of their nomenclature. But his advice to his scholars is full of inspired common sense based on the views of St. Bernard. The scholar, he says, who wishes to profit by his studies must observe six essential rules: first, to dedicate a fixed hour to each kind of reading, as St. Bernard advises in his letter to the brothers of Mont Dieu. Second, to concentrate his attention on what he is reading, and not merely to skim over it. 'There is as much difference between reading and study, says St. Bernard, as there is between an acquaintance and a friend, between bows exchanged in the street and an unchanging affection.' Third, to extract from his daily reading some thought or saying of truth, and to store it in his memory with especial care. Seneca has said, 'Cum multa percurreris in die, unum tibi elige, quod illa die excoquas'. Fourth, to write an abstract of everything he reads, since words which are not committed to writing vanish like dust in the wind. Fifth, to discuss his work with his fellow students, whether in formal disputation or in friendly talk. This is even more important than reading, for it leaves no loop-hole of uncertainty or misunderstanding. 'Nihil perfecte scitur, nisi dente disputationis feriatur.' Sixth, to pray, for prayer is the true road to understanding. St. Bernard teaches that reading should stir the soul, and that then, without ceasing from study, the heart should be lifted up to God. Robert de Sorbon at the same time condemns those scholars who, 'so as not to seem to have wasted their time, bind up many sheets of parchment into thick volumes, full of blank pages inside, but bound in fine red leather; and so go home with a little bag stuffed with a learning that rats and bookworms may eat, and that fire and water may destroy'.

The student, indeed, was not always a deep scholar. Even by the end of the thirteenth century his critics were singing:

> *Iam fit magister artium*
> *qui nescit quotas partium*
>   *de vero fundamento;*
> *habere nomen appetit,*
> *rem vero nec curat nec scit,*
>   *examine contento.*
> *Iam fiant baccalaurei*
> *pro munere denarii*
>   *quam plures idiotae;*
> *in artibus, et aliis*
> *egregiis scientiis*
>   *sunt bestiae promotae.*

Yet Paris had already become a paradise of books for the scholar. The *Stationarii* who employed the writers, and the *Librarii* who sold their productions,[1] were both under the control of the university, which appointed a joint board of four masters and four chief booksellers to supervise them. No book might be sold or, as was more usual, hired out, until the board had tested its correctness and fixed its price or rate of hire. A book might not be sold to a stranger until he had informed the Congregation of the University of his purpose, so that they might, if they wished, take measures to prevent its going out of their reach.

To those who could not afford to buy or hire, the library of Notre Dame was always open, while the Sorbonne soon acquired an excellent library, since from its earliest days its doctors, at their death, left their books for the common use. It is not surprising that Richard de Bury should write,

'O Holy God of Gods in Sion, what a mighty stream of pleasure made glad our hearts whenever we had leisure to visit Paris, the paradise of the world! . . . There are delightful libraries, more aromatic than stores of spice; there abundant orchards of all manner of books . . . there, indeed, opening our treasures and unfastening our purse strings we scattered money with joyful heart and bought books without price.'

It is, perhaps, harder to recover a clear idea of the life of the student than of the doctor; undergraduates' letters rarely say much about their curriculum. Rather, like the student who writes to Christian of Stommeln about 1280, do they tell us that they have not been well for the whole of

[1]By 1323 there were twenty-eight booksellers besides keepers of open-air bookstalls. When the Rector of the University attended the Foire du Lendit in state it was officially to buy parchment for university use.

Hilary Term, but, now that Easter is come, they are so far recovered that they can eat even College eggs; or else they write in the strain immortalized by Eustache Deschamps some hundred and twenty years later:

Lettres des escoliers d'Orliens:
Treschiers peres, je n'ay denier,
Ne sanz vous ne puis avoir riens;
Et si fait a l'estude chier,
Ne je ne puis estudier
En mon Code n'en ma Digeste:
Caduque sont. Je doy de reste
De ma prevosté dix escus,
Et ne treuve homme qui me preste:
Je vous mande argent et salus!

Trop fault, qui est estudiens;
Se son fait veult bien advancier,
Il fault que son pere et les siens
Lui baillent argent sanz dangier,
Par quoy cause n'ait d'engagier
Ses livres, ait finance preste,
Robes, pannes, vesteure honneste,
Ou il sera un malostrus;
Et qu'om ne me tiengne pour beste,
Je vous mande argente et salus.

Vins sont chiers, hostelz, autres biens;
Je doy partout; s'ay grant mestier
D'estre mis hors de tels liens:
Chiers peres, vueillez moy aidier.
Je doubte l'excommunier,
Cité suy; cy n'a n'os n'areste:
S'argent n'ay devant cette feste
De Pasques, du moustier exclus
Seray. Ottroiez ma requeste
Je vous mande argent et salus.

L'Envoy

Treschiers peres, pour m'alegier
En la taverne, au boulengier,
Aux docteurs, aux bediaux, conclus,

Et pour mes colectes payer
A la burresse et au barbier,
Je vous mande argent et salus.[1]

Numbers rose and fell; in 1350 Gilles le Muisis complains that once the schools of Paris were full of scholars, 'gens de plusieurs estats', who were sure of an honourable career. Now the benefices go to hunting parsons and except among the Mendicants there are fewer scholars. Among the seculars only lawyers and doctors can be sure of a livelihood, and then, when they have saved money enough, of securing a benefice. Yet Dr. Rashdall made a calculation to show that the numbers a hundred years later were very considerable. About 1450 there were, he thought, at least 2,500 members in residence at Paris, of whom about 800 were graduates; and in 1464 a record of dues paid shows that there were at least 3,000 members in residence.

Jean de Jandun, writing in 1320, said that to be in Paris was to exist in the absolute sense, *simpliciter*, but to be anywhere else was to exist relatively, *secundum quid*. Yet the intellectual life of Paris gradually weakened, in spite of a temporary revival which owed its impulse to Oxford, and in 1452 the university had to have its curriculum reformed. Earlier statutes had required masters to lecture *extempore* instead of dictating; they had even gone so far as to prescribe the exact pace at which he was to speak; not drawlingly, *tractim*, but rapidly, *raptim*, 'bringing out the words as rapidly as if no one was writing before him'. Indeed penalties were prescribed for students who by hissing, groaning, or throwing stones tried to make him go slower. But by 1452 the lecturing tradition had greatly changed; the new statutes of that year only prescribe that the master should read the lecture himself, and not hand its manuscript to a student for him to dictate it to the rest. Similarly, though the regulations for undergraduates of the Sorbonne were strict—they had to ask leave to go

---

[1]"Thus runs the Orléans scholar's letter: "Well beloved father, I have not a penny, nor can I get any save through you, for all things at the University are so dear; nor can I study in my Code or my Digest, for their leaves have the falling sickness. Moreover, I owe ten crowns in dues to the provost, and can find no man to lend them to me; I ask of you greetings and gold.

"The student has need of many things if he will profit here; his father and his kin must needs supply him freely, that he be not compelled to pawn his books, but have ready money in his purse, with gowns and furs and decent clothing; or he will be damned for a beggar; wherefore, that men may not take me for a beast, I ask of you greetings and gold.

"Wines are dear, and hostels and other good things; I owe in every street, and am hard bested to free myself from such snares. Dear father, deign to help me! I fear to be excommunicated; already I have been cited, and there is not even a dry bone in my larder. If I find not the money before this feast of Easter, the church door will be shut in my face; wherefore grant my supplication. I ask of you greetings and gold.

Envoi.

"Well beloved father, to ease my debts contracted at the tavern, at the baker's, with the professors and the bedels, to pay my subscriptions to the laundress and the barber, I ask of you greetings and gold." '

out, and might only walk the streets in couples—the fifteenth-century register of the College suggests that discipline was not much above its usual level. Clerks are sconced a pint for 'very inordinately' knocking at the door during dinner; for being very drunk, for 'confabulating' in the quad late at night, and refusing to go to their chambers when ordered, and for asking for wine at the buttery in the name of a master and drinking it themselves.[1]

The University of Paris gradually lost its international character with the growth of the English, Italian, and German universities, and in France itself Montpellier, Toulouse, Orléans, and Angers flourished in spite of war. It is true that on the side of scholastic theology Paris was the theological arbiter of Europe, 'ratio dictans in ecclesia'; and it is largely due to her performance of this function that Northern Europe was spared the horrors of the Inquisition. But so far as real intellectual activity was concerned Oxford was in the fourteenth century more important than Paris. The University of Paris, however, in losing her international character gained national importance. She was the only great medieval university in a capital city, and that city was more like a modern capital than any in Europe. Thus in that city she came to play a political part not unlike that of the Corporation in London. She was immune from secular justice: in France all students were assumed as matter of course to be clerks and enjoyed the privileges of clerkship. She had the right of public meeting and free debate. Thus when Paris under Etienne Marcel became the real seat of power and the only counteracting force to corrupt government, the university became a political power, and under the Valois policy of depressing the nobility and conciliating the support of the clerical and legal classes she gained a place in the councils of the National Church and in the States General.

[1] A D.D. is sconced a quart of wine for picking a pear off a tree in the College garden, again for forgetting to shut the chapel door, and again for taking his meals in the kitchen. Finally, the head cook is sconced for cooking the meat badly and not putting enough salt in the soup.

VIII

The End of the Middle Ages

BEFORE the Hundred Years' War, France had enjoyed a state of material prosperity that had not been appreciated until it was lost. Before the Black Death of 1348 when, Froissart tells us, 'la tierce partie du monde mourut', the population of France was more than enough to develop its agricultural wealth. Food was cheap; if the nobles indulged in rich and extravagant dress, even the peasant could afford to furnish his house in a manner not so very different from that of to-day. Just before the war considerable advance had been made in the science of agriculture, and the improved methods had reached even the outlying parts of France. In Artois, for instance, records of 1328 show the yield of corn to have been between seven and eleven measures from land from which the most scientific modern agriculture can only get between eleven and thirteen. In many ways one is reminded of the state of rural England in the happiest years of the eighteenth century; there is the same general prosperity, the same modest comfort among the poor, the same magnificence among the rich, the same gradual decline in spiritual as against temporal things.

All this well-being came to an end with the war. The countryside was pillaged, the towns were sacked and burned, transport and communication were at an end, and prosperity and security vanished. The chronicler[1] tells us that after Poitiers 'the affairs of the realm went from bad to worse, the public weal came to an end and brigands appeared on every side. The nobles hate and despise the villeins; they care no more for the good of the King or of their vassals; they oppress and despoil the peasants of their villages. They no longer trouble to defend the country: to tread their subjects under foot and to pillage them is their only care. From this day the land of France, hitherto glorious and honoured throughout the world, became the laughing-stock of other nations.' The peace of Bretigny left mercenary soldiers all over the country: English, Walloons, Gascons, Dutch, Spaniards, Bretons, Welshmen, Germans, whose only trade was war, and whose leading passion was to live like the great lords in extravagant luxury. Neither truce nor peace brought an end to their devastations; no church nor castle was safe from their attack. Allied

[1]The Continuator of de Nangis.

English and Navarrese companies surrounded Paris, and were only with great difficulty driven away. They held sixty fortresses in the Île de France in 1358, and only nine in 1360, but order was not yet restored; King John on his way back to Paris from his captivity had to pay a large sum to a band of brigands to be allowed to pass through his own territory into his own capital city, and in 1363 the Bishop of Paris did not dare to venture outside the city walls to receive the homage of his tenants. Jean de Venette laments that 'the sweet sound of bells was no longer wakened by the praises of the Lord, but by enemy attacks. "People, take shelter!"' Bertrand du Guesclin was the one man who successfully fought against the depredations of the Companies in the three years following the Peace of Bretigny, and thus he earned rank as a national hero. Deschamps tells us,

> *Toute desolacion*
> *Guerre et tribulation*
> *Fut ou règne à sa venue*
> *Mais en consolation*
> *Mist par sa provision*
> *Le peuple et la gent menue;*
> *La guerre leur a tollue*
> *Et gardé d'oppression*
> *Dont toute leur oraison*
> *Estoit pour lui espandue.*[1]

But even when du Guesclin had cleared the Companies from the provinces, he had not reconstructed France. Two powerful elements alone remained: the monarchy, and the newly developed national consciousness. Charles V, as Voltaire says, 'justement surnommé le Sage, réparait les ruines de son pays par la patience et par les négociations'. He inherited a poor and dismembered realm, and left a kingdom both stable and prosperous. Stronger in character than in health, he was addicted to study rather than to the feudal pursuits of hunting and warfare. He did much to increase the monarchical power, but it was done first by encouraging the study of political theory and secondly by securing the integrity of the royal domain, by entailing it on the King's next heir and enacting that the rest of the royal family should receive not land, but money. He was an organizer, not an innovator; he took up the traditional

[1]'There was desolation, war, and tribulation on the whole kingdom when he came, but by his foresight he consoled the nation and the lesser folk; he saved them from war and kept them from oppression, so that all their prayers were lavished upon him.'

royal policy, and pursued it with courage. He asserted the royal monopoly of granting communal charters and of conferring nobility, and used
these prerogatives to break up the remains of feudal power and to
consolidate the alliance between monarchy and bourgeoisie. In innumerable ways the prestige of the feudal nobility was lessened, while every
attempt was made by dignified ceremonial and sober magnificence to
increase the prestige of the royal court. But much of the progress that he
made was brought to nothing after his death. The war between Burgun-
dians and Armagnacs made France a nation divided against itself, and
under Henry V England attained to real national consciousness. For the
first time an English war with France was an international matter and not
an affray between a vassal and his lord. France was beaten at Agincourt,
and the Treaty of Troyes left Henry V heir of France; but once Bedford
appeared as Regent for his son French national feeling was ready to be
fired by any spark of patriotism. Jeanne d'Arc heard the angel's voice:

> Jeune pucelle bien heureuse
> Le Dieu du ciel vers vous m'envoie;
> Ne vous montrez de rien peureuse,
> Prenez en vous parfaite joie.
> Sa volonté et son plaisir
> Est que alliez à Orléans
> En faire les Anglais saillir
> Et lever le siège devant.
> Puis après il vous conviendra
> A Reims mener sacrer le roi . . .
> Et Dieu vous conduira toujours.[1]

Her enthusiasm fired the country; the English were driven from Orléans,
and

> L'an mil quatre cent vingt neuf
> Reprint à luire le soleil.

Gradually the stability of France was restored upon a new basis: the whole
policy of Charles VII is a policy of commercial expansion.

The Hundred Years' War had ruined French trade. Brigands on the
highways and pirates in the Mediterranean had closed all trade routes.
Flanders and Italy were in communication through the valley of the
Rhine, and trade and wealth had passed from France to Geneva and
Burgundy, which the brilliance of the court of Philippe le Bon, Duke of

---

[1] *Mystère du siége d'Orléans.*

Burgundy, made a fifteenth-century Versailles. Few foreign merchants remained in the country, and the Fairs of Champagne, Lyons, and Saint Denis were no longer held. But as soon as the English and the bands of predatory mercenaries had been driven out of the country the fairs were re-established by the King and dealings with Geneva prohibited. Communication throughout the kingdom was made easier by developing the system of river transport, deepening the channels and removing the tolls. The port of La Rochelle had its harbour improved, and received special privileges. Further, negotiations for the establishment of commercial treaties were entered into with Germany, Switzerland, Denmark, Castille, and Egypt. In all this the King worked hand-in-hand with his minister Jacques Cœur, himself a bourgeois, the son of a tanner of Bourges. His motto was 'À vaillants cœurs rien impossible'; and through commercial enterprise he gained the position of 'Argentier de la couronne' and a place in French politics second only to the King's. Through this position he gained complete control of the commerce of the Midi, and from his chief offices at Montpellier and Marseilles organized a fleet importing Levantine stuffs from Alexandria and Beirut, carpets from Persia, perfumes from Arabia, spices from the Far East, furs from the North, and slaves from Africa, until it was said that there was not a European ship in Eastern seas that did not fly the fleurs-de-lis. His activities were not confined to maritime trade; he owned a silk manufactory at Florence, dyeworks and paper mills in France, and began to exploit the French mines.[1] Even when he fell from political power and was banished from the kingdom his activities in the Eastern Mediterranean did not come to an end. Whether he acted from motives of patriotism or of commercial gain, with his help the trade of France was reorganized and her prosperity re-established. It is to him as well as to Charles VII that Chastellain's praise should be paid: 'From his realm, laid waste, torn and tattered, like a ship derelict and open to the waves on every side, ruined to its foundations and with all its beauty and magnificence in ruin; without work, without inhabitants, without trade and without justice, without rule and without order, full of thieves and brigands, full of poverty and discomfort, full of violence and exaction, full of tyranny and inhumanity, with his royal throne lying cast upon the ground—he, with great labour, brought it back to riches and freedom.'

Yet the France that was re-created after the Hundred Years' War was not the France of the Middle Ages. Every institution of Capetian France

---

[1] It was an age of metal, of armour and artillery; clay was even replaced by pewter and latten in making household utensils.

declined after the dynasty of Valois ascended the throne in 1328: feudalism, chivalry, the Church, the university, the cities, the guilds, were all
no longer the direct result of the needs of the times. Roman and hence
Canon Law had given the Middle Ages its four dominating political ideas,
the Empire, the Papacy, the Monarchy, and the Corporation. By the
fourteenth century these four corner stones of the medieval State all
showed the two infallible signs of decay: extravagance on the one hand,
and weakness on the other. The theoretical claims of the Emperors were
most fully enunciated by their lawyers when Italy had finally slipped
from their hands and the nations of Europe had reached full knowledge
of their national integrity; the Papacy, through its inquisitors, was most
active[1] at a time when most sermons were stock homilies read out of
books. The monarchy, having absorbed much of the power of its nobles,
was most scornful of the unchivalrous people at a time when it was
powerless to check popular revolt; and the corporations were increasing
the power they claimed over their members at a time when men had
begun to realize that strength lay in individual freedom. Alain Chartier
was justified by fact when in his *Quadriloge invectif* he showed that all four
orders of the State were equally responsible for the grievous woes that God
had sent upon his country. Even the focus of the life of France had moved
away from Paris; in the fifteenth century French activities were better
represented at the courts of Philip the Bold of Burgundy[2] and of Jean
Duke of Berri than by the King in his capital. The great artists and sculptors of the fifteenth century did their best work not in Paris but in
Burgundy; the historians Georges Chastellain, Olivier de la Marche, and
Comines all belong to the Burgundian court; the *Cent nouvelles nouvelles* is
written for the Duke of Burgundy; and Gerson, the greatest theologian of
the age, is a Burgundian.

Feudalism had been profoundly modified by the increasing centralization of authority in the monarchy on the one hand and by the rise of the
bourgeoisie and the admission of the *tiers état* to political life in the States-
General on the other. The nobles had lost the right of striking money in
1346, of levying troops in 1349, of waging private war in 1357; their
judicature and their patronage alike were limited. Charles V conferred
nobility on many mayors and communal and royal officers, and even sold
it for a hundred livres tournois. The bourgeois of Paris were granted the
knights' privilege of wearing gold spurs; Jean-sans-Peur had given them

---

[1] The fourteenth-century Dominican Inquisition in Champagne burned 183 heretics in one day.
[2] The Duke of Burgundy was ruler of a great expanse of territory, including Franche Comté and the Low
Countries.

the right to hold 'noble fiefs'. Profound misunderstanding existed between all the orders of the nation: nobles, bourgeois, and peasantry were all at daggers drawn, and the old lateral weakness of feudalism was evident in the fact that each class was further divided against itself; province against province, castle against castle, regular against secular, town against town, and each peasant against every one. Chivalry, long divorced from religion, was dying a romantic death; before the war an absurd profusion and extravagance of jousting had been unchecked in France, though ordinances had been passed against tournaments in England. This extravagance had been further intensified by the 'galanterie romanesque' inspired by the Romans de la Table Ronde. Under their influence even the old epic legends were weakened in the fourteenth century by the introduction of enchantments, fairies, quests in search of adventure, monsters, and other irrelevancies. Their effects are seen in the 'Order of the Star' founded by King John in 1351, which both Froissart and its founder declared to be inspired by Arthurian legend. The domination of romance over common sense is shown in one of its statutes, 'Et leur convenait jurer que jamais ils ne fuiraient en bataille plus loins que quatre arpents à leur estimation, mais mourraient plutôt ou se laisseraient faire prisonniers'.[1] Six months later Guy de Nesle and a hundred of his knights kept this rule in battle, and were all killed. Moreover, the upholders of this *chevalerie romanesque* were against the employment of the bourgeois militia. Philippe de Valois, Froissart tells us, said in 1347 that he only wished to fight side by side with gentlemen. To take communal forces into battle, he declared, was only loss and encumbrance, for such would melt away in a *mêlée* like snow in sunshine. He allowed the principle first admitted by Philippe le Bel, that while every Frenchman in case of danger should defend France, those who wished should be permitted to defend it with money only, and to buy exemption from active service. From those who were not nobly born, he wished for money to pay the expenses of his gentlemen, but for nothing more. They could stay at home and look after their wives and families, their business and trade. This sole reliance on a feudal chivalry that was already showing signs of decay was disastrous to the military power. The standing mercenary army which du Guesclin had to establish by the *Ordonnance de Vincennes* of 1374 marked the end of military feudalism. By 1445 there was a permanent paid army of fifteen companies of a hundred 'lances', each lance, accompanied by three bowmen, a page, and a light-armed soldier, all mounted.

[1]'And it behoves them to swear that they will never fly in battle more than six hundred yards, as nearly as they can guess, but rather die or be taken prisoner'.

Du Guesclin heralded an age of condottieri, using both force and ruse; the last and most martial representative of feudal chivalry, Charles the Bold of Burgundy, died at Nancy in 1477.

The older religious chivalry, too, was gone; in 1307 Philip IV had arrested all the Templars for blasphemy, idolatry, and immorality, and his tool the Pope suppressed the Order because it stood in such bad repute that it could perform no further mission. The suppression of the Order marked not only its own decay but the moral decay of royal justice; the legal process used against them is a monument of the barbarity of French criminal procedure. Torture was freely used; false witnesses were deliberately engaged on the royal side. Fifty-nine Templars were burnt at Paris, and nine at Senlis. The great wealth which the Order had amassed in land, and, through shipping and banking, in money, was nominally transferred by the Pope to the Hospitallers, but much of it stuck to Philip's fingers. Further, the system of seigneurial justice, already weakened by the royal courts, broke down, and all below feudal rank questioned feudal order. The fourteenth century was an age of demagogues and of popular risings in every country of Europe; in France the Vaudois, the Turlupins, the Society of the Poor, the Jacquerie, the Marlottins, were all driven by different currents of the universal flood of restlessness. In Paris in 1358 the citizens wore for the first time the revolutionary cap of red and blue, and for the first time showed that citizenship is not patriotism. As the *tiers état* rose to power the communal institutions of the Middle Ages decayed. The bourgeois oligarchy, no longer content with local power, identified itself with the royal judicature and administration, and civic democracy was dead.

A real middle class gradually arose, of successful merchants and country gentlemen. The line between bourgeois and noble was less definitely drawn; there were *nouveaux riches*, who bought fiefs and patents of nobility, and there were *nouveaux pauvres*, who applied to be enrolled as bourgeois of the trading cities, tried to gain a living by intelligent agriculture, or entered one of the more respectable trades.[1] In Provence we hear of *nobiles medicantes*, and there is a story of a widowed relative of the Duke of Burgundy who kept an inn.

The country was a much changed as the towns. The immediate consequence of the war was extreme misery in the rural districts; insecurity, famine, and depopulation caused much land to fall out of cultivation: 'Les bois sont venus en France avec les Anglais.' Some districts to the

[1] The new trades of mining and glass-making were considered the most suitable.

north of Lyons, once fertile, still remain waste as a result of this agricultural decline. To counteract it there was much enfranchisement of serfs; the Abbot of Saint Germain des Prés, for instance, at one time enfranchised three villages held by his monastery, 'en considération des guerres, pestes et autres fléaux'. A gradual substitution of contracted service for the servitude of earlier centuries made the shortage of agricultural labour result in the raising of the labourer's wage under Charles VII to a height never previously attained. In some parts of Provence the proprietor only received an eighth of the produce of his land, and a quarter was deemed a high proportion. Further, since uncultivated lands were often ceded in perpetuity, a class of small proprietors arose and seigneurial rights were still further diminished.

Thus men were no longer bound to the land they tilled, and among those who did not themselves own land there was an increasing tendency to wander further afield in search of better paid work. To these wandering labourers were added bands of wandering journeymen, who were travelling from one city to another in search of a new 'patron'. To these, again, were added the merchants themselves, travelling from their provincial city to the capital, or to one of the great fairs. Besides these legitimate travellers there was a vagabond population, the result of the war— students whose colleges were ruined, priests whose prebends no longer yielded an income, mercenaries of all nationalities thrown out of employment by the peace, gipsies, and beggars. Villon is the King of the Vagabonds, *le roi des gueux*. He has recorded their *argot* in seven of his ballads, and in it all the elements of the vagabond kingdom are represented— foreign words from the mercenaries, archaic French from the peasants, clerical phrases from the vagabond priests, dog-Latin from the students, as well as regular thieves' jargon from the professional criminals. It is true that this floating population gradually became absorbed into the growing prosperity and order of the kingdom, but there can be little doubt that the restlessness, movement, and freedom from local ties which it typified helped further to disorganize the local basis of feudal aristocracy. The social hierarchy was modified by economic fact: a money basis replaced a land basis, and the *Mystère de la Passion* of 1451 declares with justice, 'Il n'est chose qu'argent ne face'.

The Church itself was weakened. The Papacy suffered vitally and permanently from the Avignonese Captivity and the Great Schism. It lost much of its spiritual character and trafficked commercially in spiritual things; it lost its universal character and became sectarian. The falling away of England and Germany from the Avignonese Papacy foreshadowed the Reformation. The older monastic orders were no longer fruitful, and the new had lost the inspiration given by their founders. The secular priesthood had reached its lowest ebb since the Gregorian movement. The tonsure gave them the privileges of the cleric and put them under ecclesiastical law, but everywhere they are found to have married and pursued worldly avocations. In Normandy there are records of rich peasants who were at once clerics and vavassors; at Louviers and Tournai the names of clerks are to be found in the list of dyers and dyer's apprentices.

The wars seriously affected the intellectual life of France. Students could not safely attend the universities; the Archbishop of Bordeaux, writing in 1439, declared, 'Those who wish to seek the pearl of knowledge can no longer go to the universities in safety; many have been taken on their way, imprisoned, stript of their books and their goods, held for ransom, and sometimes, alas! slain.' In that very year grass is recorded to have grown in the streets of Paris and wolves to have lurked in the suburbs. Yet academic life went on; and this mere continuance is as remarkable at such a time as fruitful activity shown in a more settled age. Yet as the century advanced there was a gradual change. Scholastic philosophy had overbalanced itself and tottered on crutches of orthodoxy, and though new life was manifested in the study of science,[1] the logical speculation of the Middle Ages was dead.

The literary *genres* of the Middle Ages each reflect some aspect of medieval society: the *Chansons de geste* represent the life of pilgrimage and Crusade, the Romances that of the castle hall; the love song the knight, and the *lais* and the *chansons de toile* the lady. The *fabliau* is the creation of the town; the *Mystère* of the Church, the *Miracles* of the confraternity, the *Summa* of the university. These came to an end with the society that had created them; and the literary influence of France declined with the development of a national literature in Italy and England. Lyric verse and historical prose remained to reflect the life of the fifteenth century. Villon is the first modern poet; Comines the first philosophic historian. He writes for the generation that inherited the *sagesse* of Charles V, and used that moderate wisdom to interpret events and judge character with both subtlety and common sense. The court he knows is that which René of Anjou describes, where a man must

> *Tout regarder, et faindre riens ne veoir;*
> *Tout escouter, monstrant riens ne sçavoir,*
> *Mot ne sonner des cas qu'on sçait et voit.*

[1] At Montpellier, for instance, dissection began to be practised, and the improved state of medical knowledge led to the separation of the professions of physician and apothecary.

He wrote for men whose minds were occupied not with the valiancy of romantic chivalry but with the political calculations of a Machiavellian diplomacy, seeking the relation of cause and effect, viewing all things with curiosity but without enthusiasm, men who find their embodiment in Louis XI. Just as St. Louis is the type of the culminating century of the Middle Ages, so Louis XI is that of the century that marks their close; as the Crusade is the war of the one period, so the struggle between France and Burgundy is that of the other.

None the less, out of decay sprang life. The Emperor had been deprived of any shadowy claim to supremacy; the Pope had been driven from his international position; feudalism, bourgeoisie and monarchy alike had changed; Empire and city were superseded by the nation, and France took her place in the modern world of politics—in a new Europe, a multiplicity of nations believed to be free and equal, governed by a body of doctrine known as International Law. Wars of rights were superseded by wars of interest; the hierarchy was succeeded by the balance of power, and individual experience and opinion overruled the systematic theory of the Middle Ages. Science ceased to be a form of apologetics, and became experiment; scholasticism was gradually eclipsed by the new spirit of classicism. Symbolism in all its functions was superseded by more direct if less beautiful forms of expression. Dante had claimed four meanings for his Divine Comedy: the literal, the allegorical, the moral or philosophical, and the anagogical or mystical significance; Rabelais, in his Preface to the *Gargantua*, wrote, 'Croyez vous en votre foi qu'onques Homère, escripvant l'Iliade, l'Odysée, pensast es allegories . . . Si le croyez, vous n'approchez ni de pieds ni de mains à mon opinion qui décrète icelles aussi peu avoir été songées d'Homère que d'Ovide, en ses Métamorphoses, les sacrements de l'Evangile. . . .'[1] Petrarch and Boccaccio had begun by transferring allegory from theology to poetry, and it only remained for Renaissance criticism to justify the existence of purely imaginative literature. An aesthetic basis for its re-establishment was ready; though the Poetics of Aristotle had been known in the later Middle Ages they had been neglected, until the publication in 1498 of Valla's Latin translation gave them the prestige of fresh discovery. They gave the rational justification of poetry, as aiming at the reality of an eternal probability. The difference between the poetic aims of the Middle Ages and the Renaissance can be shown by comparing Eustache Deschamps's *Art de dictier* of 1392 with Joachim du Bellay's *Défense et Illustration de la langue française* of 1549.

---

[1] 'Do you faithfully believe that Homer, writing Iliad or Odyssey, thought about allegories?. . . If you do, you will be very far from my opinion, which decides that allegories were as little thought of by Homer as Ovid in his Metamorphoses thought of the Sacraments of the Gospel.'

The didactic function of symbolism could not be left unfulfilled: moreover, a new devotion to an old teacher, Horace, justified the didactic aim of art. A definite moralizing tendency had made itself felt as soon as the duty of preaching had descended from the scholarly Augustinian to the less learned mendicant, and the various *Bibles moralisées* of the fourteenth and fifteenth centuries show the steady destruction of the ancient parallel interpretation of the Old and New Testaments by this didactic system. With the Renaissance the duty of moral teaching was transferred from the cathedral to the printing press, whence issued an enormous number of little books—such as Gerson's *Montagne de Contemplation*—which fulfilled the purpose once achieved by the great windows and the sculptured façades of the cathedrals. Similarly the representation of the individual grew more and more exact, as his relation with the hierarchical scheme of the universe became less defined. Tomb figures, which had been in the thirteenth century ideal and impersonal, became more and more strictly portraits: for the tomb of Charles VI not only the head, but also the hands and feet, were cast from moulds taken actually upon his corpse. Gradually too, the effigy ceased to be at peace, and knelt to pray; and then—about 1545—began to rest upon cushions like one who thinks out the solution of the unsolved problem of life. Art passed gradually from symbolism to history; the art of the fifteenth century was narrative art, telling stories of saints, Christ, the Virgin, and martyrs with narrative richness and naturalism. Finally, by the middle of the sixteenth century, the Christian scheme was applied to human history. In the chapel of Champigny-sur-Veude (built about 1559) the whole Bourbon family is sculptured, from Robert the son of St. Louis down to Charles, grandfather of Henry IV. The windows show in great detail scenes from the life of St. Louis; it is the apotheosis of the eponymous hero of the dynasty.

Medieval art was inspired by ideals of humility: suffering, sadness, resignation, Passion and Crucifixion. Even in its decline in the fifteenth century it approximated the types of Christ, the Virgin, and the saints to those of the poor and humble folk who represented them in the Mysteries. But the Renaissance found another ideal to express: man, sufficient unto himself, fighting his own battles, shining with strength and beauty, and rising by force of his own power to unknown heights. From representing man's earthly struggles, his ordeal of judgement, and his pardon and redemption in heaven, from expressing before all other things his religious faith, art turned to record his moments of victory and to serve his desire to impress his human personality upon material things. The hidden principle of Renaissance art is pride; its avowed aim is earthly glory, and its moral teaching is the *danse macabre*.

PLATES

I. AUGUSTINIAN ABBEY OF SAINT JEAN DES VIGNES, SOISSONS
13th to 15th century

2. RHEIMS CATHEDRAL. *West front, between 1231 and 1290*

3. ROUEN CATHEDRAL. *Detail of façade, 1370–1420*

4. DRAWING FOR THE CATHEDRAL OF RHEIMS
by Villard de Honnecourt, middle of the 13th century. Paris, Bibliothèque Nationale

5. THE TITHE BARN, PROVINS, SEINE ET MARNE
Early 13th century

6. BENEDICTINE 'ABBAYE AUX DAMES', CAEN
West front, about 1100

7. GOTHIC CATHEDRAL
Pen and ink drawing, late 15th century. Erlangen, University Library

8. PALAIS DE JUSTICE, ROUEN. *Built between 1499 and 1509*

9. HOUSE OF JACQUES COEUR, BOURGES. *Turret on East façade, 1443–1451*

10. MONT ST. MICHEL
Miniature, middle of the 15th century. Paris, Bibliothèque Nationale

11. THE KING'S PALACE AND THE SAINTE CHAPELLE OF PARIS
from the Très Riches Heures *of the Duc de Berry, about 1416. Chantilly, Musée Condé*

12. VIEW OF PARIS

Detail of the Retable from the Chapel of the Parlement de Paris, about 1480. Paris, Louvre

13. THE ROYAL CASTLE OF SAUMUR

from the Très Riches Heures *of the Duc de Berry, about 1416. Chantilly, Musée Condé*

14. CASTLE OF COMBOURG, ILLE-ET-VILAINE
About 1420

15. PORTE SAINT-JACQUES AND THE OLD BRIDGE, PARTHENAY,
DEUX SÈVRES. *End of the 13th century*

16. A STREET IN SARLAT, DORDOGNE

17. COURTYARD OF A 15TH CENTURY HOUSE, MONTFERRAND PUY-DE-DÔME

18. THE GREAT HALL OF THE PALAIS DUCAL OF POITIERS
Early 13th century

19. THE GREAT HALL OF THE HOUSE OF JACQUES COEUR, BOURGES. *1443–1451*

20. DETAIL OF THE FIREPLACE FROM THE HOUSE OF JACQUES COEUR, BOURGES.
1443–1451

21. FAÇADE OF THE HOUSE OF JACQUES COEUR, BOURGES
1443-1451

22. CHIMNEY PIECE. *About 1420. Paris, Musée de Cluny*

23. SILVER CASKET. *About 1340. Paris, Musée de Cluny*

24. COPPER-GILT CASKET
Probably Limoges, 1290–96. London, Victoria and Albert Museum

25. RELIQUARY OF THE HOLY THORN
Made for the Duc d'Orléans, 1389–1407. London, British Museum

26. CHALICE OF ABBOT SUGER
About 1140. Washington, National Gallery of Art

27. JEANNE DE BOULOGNE, WIFE OF JEAN, DUC DE BERRY
Statue, about 1385. Great Hall, Palace of Poitiers

28. WIND-VANE FORMED AS AN ANGEL
Bronze by Jehan Barbet de Lyon, 1475. New York, Frick Collection

29. LOUIS DE CHÂTILLON

Statue from the Sainte Chapelle, Bourges, about 1405. Church of Marognes, Cher

30. ST. JOHN
Wooden statue, early 15th century. Paris, Louvre

31. LOUIS II OF ANJOU
Water-colour, about 1400. Paris, Bibliothèque Nationale

32. LOUIS XII OF FRANCE
Painting attributed to Jean Perréal, about 1500. Windsor Castle, Royal Collection
Reproduced by gracious permission of Her Majesty the Queen

33. PORTRAIT OF A PAPAL LEGATE

Drawing attributed to Fouquet, about 1470. New York, Metropolitan Museum

34. BERTRAND DU GUESCLIN

Marble by Thomas Privé and Robert Loisel, 1390–1397. Saint-Denis

35. A FALCONER
Fresco from the Palace of the Popes, Avignon. Middle of the 14th century

36. LADY WITH FALCON AND DOG
Water-colour drawing, about 1400–1410. Paris, Louvre

37. THE ESPOUSAL

Miniature from the Très Riches Heures *of the Duc de Berry, about 1416. Chantilly, Musée Condé*

38. GASTON PHÉBUS, COMTE DE FOIX, GIVING ORDERS TO HIS HUNTSMEN
Miniature, early 15th century. Paris, Bibliothèque Nationale

39 · A BANQUET. *Miniature, 1377. Paris, Bibliothèque Nationale*

40. PHILIP-LE-BEL AND HIS COUNCIL, 1322. *Miniature. Paris, Bibliothèque Nationale*

41. A BALL. *Miniature from the Roman de la Violette, about 1465. Paris, Bibliothèque Nationale*

42. THE PEACE OF VENDÔME, 1458. *Miniature by Fouquet. Munich, Staatsbibliothek*

43. LADY IN FRONT OF HER TENT
Detail from the tapestry Dame à la Licorne, *about 1510. Paris, Musée de Cluny*

44. THE VINTAGE
Detail of a tapestry, about 1490. Paris, Musée de Cluny

45. THE CONCERT BY THE WELL. *Tapestry, about 1510. Private Collection*

46. MAN PLAYING BAG-PIPES. *Detail of a tapestry, about 1500. Paris, Louvre*

47. THREE TRUMPETERS

Detail from a miniature, second half of the 15th century. Paris, Bibliothèque de l'Arsenal

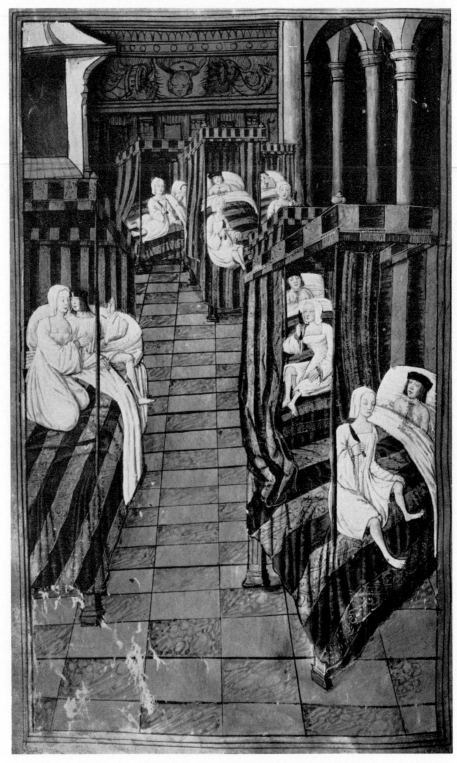

48. THE WEDDING NIGHT OF THE FIFTY DANAIDS
Miniature, early 16th century. Paris, Bibliothèque Nationale

49. A SHOPPING STREET
Miniature, about 1510. Paris, Bibliothèque de l'Arsenal

50. WOMAN PAINTING A STATUE OF THE VIRGIN

Miniature, second half of the 15th century. Paris, Bibliothèque Nationale

51. THE ARTISAN

Miniature by Bourdichon, about 1500. Formerly Amiens, Jean Masson Collection

52. THE LEATHER WORKER
Wooden statue, late 15th century. Homberg Collection

53. THE MAKER OF SABOTS
Wood sculpture, middle of the 15th century. Berlin, Museum

54. THE BLACKSMITH AT HIS ANVIL
Detail of Choirstall from the Abbey of Saint-Lucien, 1492–1500. Paris, Musée de Cluny

55. WOMAN CARDING WOOL. *13th century. Chartres, Cathedral*

56. WOMAN WASHING WOOL. *13th century. Chartres, Cathedral*

57. THE FRUIT GATHERER. *About 1230. Amiens, Cathedral*

58. THE DIGGER IN THE VINEYARD. *About 1230. Amiens, Cathedral*

59. BUILDING A HOUSE
Detail from a miniature, 15th century. Paris, Bibliothèque de l'Arsenal

60. HARVESTING AND SHEEP-SHEARING

Miniature from the Très Riches Heures *of the Duc de Berry, about 1416. Chantilly, Musée Condé*

61. THE MASKED MUMMERS

Miniature from the Roman de Fauvel, *14th century. Paris, Bibliothèque Nationale*

62. MAN HOLDING A BOARD FOR THE GAME OF NINE MEN'S MORRIS
Detail of a tapestry, about 1510. Paris, Louvre

63. MAN AND WOMAN PLAYING CHESS
Ivory carving, about 1300. Paris, Louvre

64. SIEGE OF THE CASTLE OF LOVE
Ivory carving, about 1360. London, Victoria and Albert Museum

65 AND 66. THE SHOWING OF THE HELMS BEFORE THE TOURNAMENT

Miniature from the Livre des Tournois du Roi René, *about 1460–1465. Paris, Bibliothèque de l'Arsenal*

67. A BATTLE

Miniature, early 16th century. Paris, Bibliothèque Nationale

68. SHIP OF JACQUES COEUR

Tympanum of a door, between 1443 and 1451. Bourges, Hôtel Jacques Coeur

69. THE ENTRY OF CHARLES IV INTO SAINT-DENIS
Miniature, about 1490. Paris, Bibliothèque Nationale

70. TRAVELLERS
Detail from the Choir Screen, about 1520. Amiens, Cathedral

71. THE KING OF SICILY ENTERING PARIS
Miniature, about 1470. Breslau, Staatsbibliothek

72. THE SIEGE OF RHODES, 1480. *Miniature. Paris, Bibliothèque Nationale*

73. VIEW OF JERUSALEM. *Miniature, 15th century. Paris, Bibliothèque Nationale*

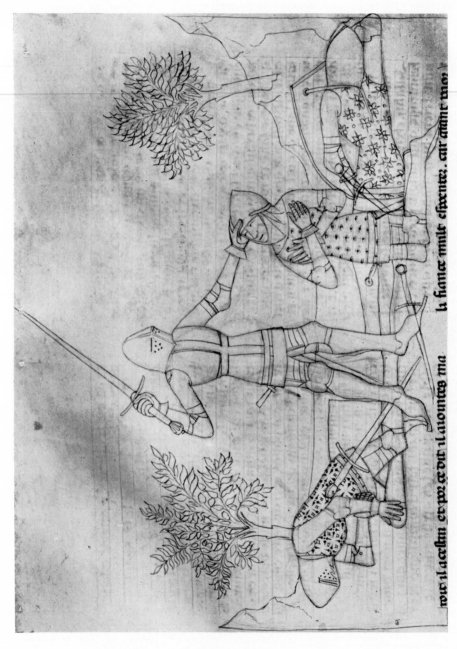

74. KNIGHT RECEIVING THE ACCOLADE ON THE FIELD OF BATTLE
Miniature from the Roman de Lancelot du Lac, early 14th century. Paris, Bibliothèque Nationale

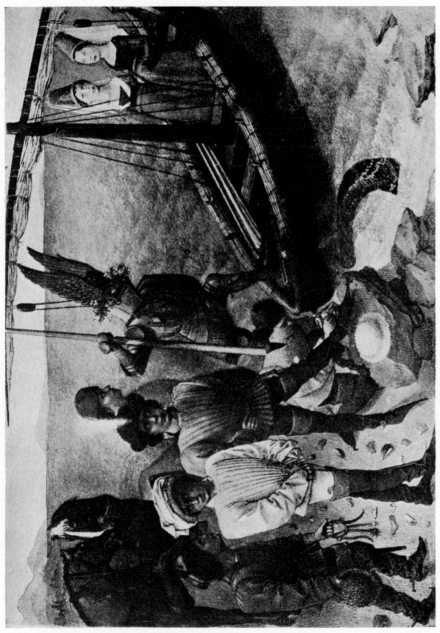

75. 'CUER' AND 'DESIR' EMBARKING FOR THE ISLAND OF THE 'OSPITAL D'AMOURS'
Miniature, 1457. Vienna, Staatsbibliothek

76. THE SIEGE OF DAMIETTA IN 1169. *Miniature, 1462. Paris, Bibliothèque de l'Arsenal*

77. THE ASSASSINATION OF JEAN-SANS-PEUR, DUKE OF BURGUNDY
Miniature, middle of the 15th century. Paris, Bibliothèque Nationale

78. A BATTLE

Miniature by Fouquet, middle of the 15th century. Paris, Bibliothèque Nationale

79. YOUTH STANDING IN A TREE. *Relief, about 1290. Church of Saint Jean de Joigny*

80. KNIGHT STANDING BEFORE A PRIEST. *Relief, end of the 13th century. Rheims, Cathedral*

81. A PROCESSION OF FLAGELLANTS

Miniature, second half of the 14th century. Brussels, Bibliothèque Royale

82. DEVILS LEADING THE DAMNED TO HELL. *Frieze, middle of the 13th century. Rheims, Cathedral*

83. A FUNERAL. *Miniature by Fouquet, about 1465. Chantilly, Musée Condé*

84. ST. SEBASTIAN INTERCEDING FOR THE PLAGUE-STRICKEN
Painting by Josse Lieferinxe, 1497–99. Baltimore, Walters Art Gallery

85. THE PROCESSION OF THE SACRAMENT

Miniature, early 16th century. Paris, Bibliothèque de l'Arsenal

86. WEEPERS FROM THE TOMB OF THE DUC DE BERRY
About 1449. Bourges, Museum

87. ISAIAH

Detail from the Moses Fountain by Claus Sluter, 1397–1405. Dijon, Chartreuse de Champmol

88. THE CONSULTANT PHYSICIAN
Miniature, middle of the 15th century. Brussels, Bibliothèque Royale

89. JEAN MIÉLOT TRANSLATING THE MIRACLES DE NOTRE DAME
Miniature, about 1456. Paris, Bibliothèque Nationale

90. THE ASTRONOMER, THE SCRIBE AND THE COMPUTIST
Miniature, about 1220. Paris, Bibliothèque de l'Arsenal

91. SCENES OF STUDENT LIFE
Relief, about 1220. Paris, Cathedral of Notre Dame

NOTES ON THE ILLUSTRATIONS

Notes on the Illustrations

1. AUGUSTINIAN ABBEY OF SAINT JEAN DES VIGNES, SOISSONS. The ruins of the West Front. (Photographed before World War I.) 13th to 15th centuries.

2. CATHEDRAL OF RHEIMS. The West Front dates from between 1231 and 1290 (up to the string course above the rose window); the upper part from 1290 to 1490. It was intended that the two towers should each be surmounted by lofty spires.

3. CATHEDRAL OF ROUEN. Detail of the façade, 1370–1420.

4. CATHEDRAL OF RHEIMS. Drawing of the system of flying buttresses, by the medieval architect Villard de Honnecourt. Middle of the 13th century. Paris, Bibliothèque Nationale, Ms franç. 19093, fol. 32v.

5. THE TITHE BARN, PROVINS, Seine et Marne. Early 13th century.

6. BENEDICTINE ABBAYE AUX DAMES (or de la Trinité), CAEN. The West Front. About 1100. (The portals restored 1851.)

7. GOTHIC CATHEDRAL AND A STATUE OF ST. MICHAEL. Pen and ink drawing. Probably French. Late 15th century. Erlangen, Universitäts-Bibliothek. B.28.

8. PALAIS DE JUSTICE, ROUEN (photographed before 1939). Built between 1499 and 1509 for the Exchequer of Normandy by Roger Ango and Roland le Roux. (Staircase modern.)

9. HOUSE OF JACQUES COEUR, BOURGES. The stair-turret on the east façade. 1443–51.

10. MONT ST. MICHEL. Miniature from a manuscript account of miracles performed at the shrine of the Saint. Four pilgrims kneel in the foreground; a fifth goes on his way. They carry the staff of pilgrimage and the men wear the wide brimmed pilgrim's hat. Middle of the 15th century. Paris, Bibliothèque Nationale, Ms franç. 9199, fol. 37v.

11. THE KING'S PALACE AND THE SAINTE CHAPELLE OF PARIS. Hay-making. Calendar scene for June from the *Très Riches Heures* of the Duc de Berry. About 1416. Musée Condé, Chantilly.

12. VIEW OF PARIS. Detail from the Retable from the Chapel of the Parlement de Paris. About 1480. Paris, Louvre.

13. THE ROYAL CASTLE OF SAUMUR. (Rebuilt towards the end of the 14th century.) Calendar illustration for September from the *Très Riches Heures* of the Duc de Berry, painted by Pol de Limbourg in 1416. Chantilly, Musée Condé.

14. CASTLE OF COMBOURG, ILLE-ET-VILAINE. A castle formed by the junction of three circular donjons. Mainly about 1420.

15. THE PORTE SAINT-JACQUES AND THE OLD BRIDGE, PARTHENAY, DEUX-SÈVRES. End of the 13th century.

16. A STREET IN SARLAT, DORDOGNE.

17. COURTYARD OF A 15TH CENTURY HOUSE AT MONTFERRAND, PUY-DE-DÔME. (11 rue Jules Guesde.) The arms over the door show that its owner was of noble birth.

18. THE GREAT HALL OF THE PALAIS DUCAL OF POITIERS. Built early in the 13th century. The triple fireplace at the end was built by Jean Duc de Berry between 1384 and 1386.

19. THE GREAT HALL OF THE HOUSE OF JACQUES COEUR, BOURGES. 1443–51.

20. DETAIL OF THE FIREPLACE IN A ROOM IN THE DONJON OF JACQUES COEUR'S HOUSE AT BOURGES. The upper frieze is carved with figures of huntsmen and of knights riding donkeys in a mock tournament. Below, three sham windows. Each holds figures of a man and woman playing chess or chequers. Between 1443 and 1451.

21. MAN LOOKING OUT OF A SIMULATED WINDOW. Façade of the House of Jacques Coeur, Bourges. 1443–51.

22. CHIMNEY PIECE. Carved stone, with pairs of lovers holding shields and garlands. About 1420. Paris, Musée de Cluny.

23. SILVER CASKET WITH GROTESQUE MEDALLIONS. French. About 1340. Paris, Musée de Cluny.

24. CASKET OF COPPER GILT, ornamented with heraldic decoration in champlevé enamel. Made for William of Valence, Earl of Pembroke, between 1290 and 1296, probably at Limoges. London, Victoria and Albert Museum.

25. RELIQUARY OF THE HOLY THORN, of enamelled gold set with pearls and jewels. The central panel contains a figure of Christ, seated on a rainbow, with the orb of the world under His feet. The Thorn rises before him from a large sapphire. Christ and the Virgin kneel beside it and angels hold a crown of thorns over His head. The outer frame is formed of figures of the Apostles.

The whole is crowned by a seated figure of God the Father in a rayed glory on the base. Angels sound the last trump and the dead rise from their coffins. Made for Louis, Duc d'Orléans, between 1389 and 1407. London, British Museum, Waddesdon Bequest.

26. CHALICE OF ABBOT SUGER. The cup of sardonyx mounted in gold, adorned with filigree and set with pearls and precious stones. From Saint Denis. About 1140. Widener Collection, National Gallery of Art, Washington, D.C.

27. JEANNE DE BOULOGNE. Wife of Jean Duc de Berry. From the chimney-piece of his great hall in the Palace of Poitiers. About 1385.

28. BRONZE WIND-VANE, FORMED AS AN ANGEL. From the Château du Lude, Sarthe. By Jehan Barbet de Lyon. 1475. New York, Frick Collection.

29. LOUIS DE CHÂTILLON. Statue from the Sainte Chapelle of Bourges. About 1405. Church of Marognes, Cher.

30. STATUE OF ST. JOHN. From a Crucifixion group at Loches. Wood, early 15th century. Paris, Musée du Louvre.

31. PORTRAIT OF LOUIS II OF ANJOU. About 1400. Paris, Cabinet des Estampes, Bibliothèque Nationale.

32. LOUIS XII OF FRANCE. He wears the gold medallion of a pilgrimage in a slit in his hat and the collar of the Order of St. James. Ascribed to Jean Perréal. About 1500. Windsor Castle, Royal Collection.

33. PENCIL DRAWING OF A PAPAL LEGATE. Ascribed to Fouquet. About 1470. New York, Metropolitan Museum of Art.

34. EFFIGY FROM THE TOMB OF BERTRAND DU GUESCLIN. By Thomas Privé and Robert Loisel. 1390–97. Saint Denis.

35. A FALCONER. From a fresco in a tower of the Palace of the Popes at Avignon. Middle of the 14th century.

36. LADY WITH A FALCON AND A PET DOG. Water-colour drawing. About 1400–1410. Paris, Musée du Louvre.

37. THE ESPOUSAL. Calendar Scene for May from the *Très Riches Heures* of the Duc de Berry, painted by Pol de Limbourg in 1416. Chantilly, Musée Condé.

38. GASTON PHÉBUS, COMTE DE FOIX, GIVING ORDERS TO HIS HUNTSMEN. Miniature from the *Livre de Chasse de Gaston Phébus*. Paris, Bibliothèque Nationale, Ms franç. 616, fol. 13. Early 15th century.

39. THE BANQUET GIVEN IN 1377 BY KING CHARLES V OF FRANCE TO THE EMPEROR CHARLES IV AND HIS SON, THE KING OF THE ROMANS. Miniature from the *Grandes Chroniques de France*. Paris, Bibliothèque Nationale, franç. 2813, fol. 473v.
The King of France sits at table between his two guests, together with three bishops or archbishops. A cloth of state powdered with fleurs-de-lys hangs behind each royal personage. On the table are three *nefs*, gold vessels shaped like ships to hold the table napkins. Before the table the *écuyer tranchant* is carving a dish, while actors perform a drama of the assault on a castle. To the left a ship, with a Benedictine and a knight as crew, indicates that it was an exploit of crusade.

40. KING PHILIP AND HIS COUNCIL. 1322. Miniature from the *Actes du Procès de Robert d'Artois*. Paris, Bibliothèque Nationale, Ms franç. 18437, fol. 2.

41. A BALL. Miniature from the *Roman de la Violette*. Made for Philippe le Bon, Duke of Burgundy. About 1465. Paris, Bibliothèque Nationale, Ms franç. 24378, fol. 5.

42. THE PEACE OF VENDÔME. 1458. Frontispiece to the Ms of Boccaccio's *Des Cas des Nobles Hommes et Femmes*, painted by Fouquet and an assistant probably in that year. Munich, Staatsbibliothek, Ms fr. 6.

43. LADY IN FRONT OF A TENT. Detail from the set of tapestries of the *Dame à la Licorne*, made for a member of the family of Le Viste, probably Claude de Viste. About 1510. The Lady stands within a jousting pavilion with the motto *Mon Seul Desir*, her attendant holds her casket of jewels. Paris, Musée de Cluny.

44. THE VINTAGE. In the foreground a man is treading the grapes; behind him a wine press is at work, while men and women convey the juice to casks for fermentation. Detail of a French tapestry. About 1490. Paris, Musée de Cluny.

45. THE CONCERT BY THE WELL. French tapestry. About 1510. Private collection.

46. A MAN PLAYING THE BAG-PIPES. Detail of a verdure tapestry. About 1500. Paris, Musée du Louvre.

47. THREE TRUMPETERS SOUNDING THEIR INSTRUMENTS FOR DINNER. Detail from the miniature *The Betrothal of Clarisse and Renaud de Montauban* from the Ms franç. 5073. Paris, Bibliothèque de l'Arsenal. Second half of the 15th century.

48. THE WEDDING NIGHT OF THE FIFTY DANAÏDS. Miniature from the French translation of the *Heroides* of Ovid. Early 16th century. Paris, Bibliothèque Nationale, Ms franç. 874, fol. 170.

49. A SHOPPING STREET. On the left is the tailor's; a workman sits cross-legged on the bench and another cuts out with a pair of shears. In the middle to the right a barber shaves a man in a shop hung with barber's bowls. To the right a grocer has a sign on his awning 'bon ipocras', an infusion of spices in wine. He has two open tarts and a sugar loaf fixed on a block for cutting on the counter, and jars of spices on shelves behind. All the shops are open to the street. The houses are gabled and timbered except for the barber's which is built of stone. Miniature from the Ms of the *Gouvernement des Princes*. Paris, Bibliothèque de l'Arsenal Ms franç. 5062, fol. 149vo. About 1510.

50. CYRÈNE PAINTING A STATUE OF THE VIRGIN. Miniature from Boccaccio's *Les femmes nobles et renommées*. Second half of the 15th century. Note the palette, the palette knife and the tray for brushes laid out on the stool. Paris, Bibliothèque Nationale, Ms franç. 12420, fol. 92v.

51. THE ARTISAN. Miniature by Bourdichon or a member of his school in the Ms of *Les Quatre Etats de la vie de l'homme*. About 1500. Formerly Amiens, Jean Masson Collection.

52. THE LEATHER WORKER. A 15th century statue in wood, once painted, of St. Crispin, patron of shoemakers. French, end of the 15th century. Homberg Collection.

53. THE MAKER OF SABOTS. A wooden sculpture of St. Crispinian. Middle of the 15th century. Berlin Museum.

54. THE BLACKSMITH AT HIS ANVIL. Detail of choirstall from the Abbey of Saint-Lucien near Beauvais, 1492–1500. Paris, Musée de Cluny.

55. WOMAN CARDING WOOL. She brushes it on a board held on her foot, to make it ready to spin. Detail of the left door of the North Portal, Chartres Cathedral. 13th century, after 1224.

56. WOMAN WASHING WOOL. She has a bucket by a flowing stream in which she rinses the shorn fleece. Detail of the left door of the North Portal, Chartres Cathedral. 13th century, after 1224.

57. THE FRUIT GATHERER. The figure represents September in the series of the labours of the Months on the exterior of the Cathedral of Amiens. About 1230.

58. THE DIGGER IN THE VINEYARD. The figure represents March in the series of the labours of the Months on the exterior of the Cathedral of Amiens. About 1230.

59. BUILDING THE HOUSE. Detail of miniature from Pierre de Crescent's *Livre des profits champêtres*. Paris, Bibliothèque de l'Arsenal, Ms franç. 5064. 15th century.

60. THE CASTLE OF MEHUN-SUR-YÈVRE. Harvesting and sheep-shearing. Built by the Duc de Berry between 1367 and 1390. Calendar illustration for June from the *Très Riches Heures* of the Duke, painted by Pol de Limbourg in 1416. Chantilly, Musée Condé.

61. THE MASKED MUMMERS. A miniature from the Ms of the *Roman de Fauvel*. Paris, Bibliothèque Nationale, Ms franç. 146, fol. 34. 14th century.

62. TAPESTRY WITH TWO SHEPHERDS AND A SHEPHERDESS. One carries a board for the game of Nine Men's Morris. Woven in the Valley of the Loire, About 1500. Paris, Musée du Louvre.

63. MAN AND WOMAN PLAYING CHESS. Back of an ivory mirror-case, showing a tent in which a man and a woman are playing chess. He is accompanied by a falconer and she by a squire holding a wreath. French. About 1300. Paris, Musée du Louvre.

64. THE SIEGE OF THE CASTLE OF LOVE. Back of an ivory mirror-case. The ladies on the battlements defend the castle by throwing roses at the knights who attack it. French. About 1360. London, Victoria and Albert Museum.

65 & 66. THE SHOWING OF THE HELMS BEFORE THE TOURNAMENT. The helms and banners of the knights are arrayed on counters set up in the four walks of a cloister with their owners' squires behind them. To the right, the Duchess enters, followed by her ladies. To the left a number of the knights, in mufti, look at the armour and converse. In the centre four chamberlains with long white wands of office examine the helms. One has thrown a helmet down with his staff; a page in a tabard of the ermine of Brittany stoops to pick it up and remove it. A miniature on two pages of the *Livre des tournois du roi René*. About 1460–5. Paris, Bibliothèque de l'Arsenal, Ms franç. 2698, fols. 67v and 68.

67. A BATTLE. Miniature early 16th century. Paris, Bibliothèque Nationale, Ms franç. 6440, fol. 163.

68. GALLEY. From the tympanum of a door, in the Hôtel Jacques Coeur, Bourges. It stands as the symbol of Jacques Coeur's trading fleets. Between 1443 and 1451.

69. THE ENTRY OF CHARLES IV INTO SAINT DENIS. Miniature by Jean Fouquet from the *Chroniques de Saint Denis*. About 1490. Paris, Bibliothèque Nationale.

70. TRAVELLERS. Detail from the choir screen. Amiens Cathedral. About 1520.

71. THE KING OF SICILY ENTERING PARIS. Miniature from a Ms of Froissart's *Chroniques*. About 1470. Breslau, Staatsbibliothek.

72. THE SIEGE OF THE CITY OF RHODES BY THE TURKS, 1480. A miniature from the *Relation du Siège de Rhodes*, by Caoursin. Paris, Bibliothèque Nationale, Ms franç. 6067, fol. 55v.

73. VIEW OF JERUSALEM. Miniature from a 15th century manuscript. Paris, Bibliothèque Nationale, Ms franç. 9087, fol. 85v.

74. A KNIGHT RECEIVING THE ACCOLADE ON THE FIELD OF BATTLE. Miniature from the Ms of the *Roman de Lancelot du Lac*. Paris, Bibliothèque Nationale, Ms franç. 343, fol. 79. Early 14th century.

75. 'CUER' AND 'DESIR' EMBARK FOR THE ISLAND OF THE 'OSPITAL D'AMOURS'. Miniature from the Ms of René d'Anjou's *Le Cuer d'amours épris* 1457. Perhaps by Barthélemy Leclerc. Vienna, Staatsbibliothek, Ms 2597.

76. THE SIEGE OF DAMIETTA BY AMAURI II, KING OF JERUSALEM, IN 1169. Miniature from the Ms of the *Chroniques des Empereurs*, made by David Aubert for Philippe le Bon, Duke of Burgundy, in 1462. Paris, Bibliothèque de l'Arsenal, Ms 5090, fol. 86.

77. THE ASSASSINATION OF JEAN SANS PEUR, DUKE OF BURGUNDY, ON THE BRIDGE OF MONTEREAU. Miniature from the *Chronicle of Engnerrand de Monstrelet*. Paris, Bibliothèque de l'Arsenal, Ms 5084, fol. 1. Middle of the 15th century.

78. THE BATTLE BETWEEN JONATHAS AND SIMON MACCABAEUS AGAINST BACCHIDE, from the *Antiquités et guerre des juifs* of Josephus illustrated by Jean Fouquet. Paris, Bibliothèque Nationale, Ms franç 247, fol. 270. Middle of the 15th century.

79. YOUTH STANDING IN THE TREE, at whose roots gnaw the monsters of age and mortality. The end panel of a tomb, probably of Adelaïs of Champagne. About 1290. Church of Saint-Jean de Joigny.

80. A KNIGHT STANDING BEFORE A PRIEST WHO OFFERS HIM A CHALICE. Bas-relief from the interior wall of the western façade of Rheims Cathedral. End of the 13th century.

81. A PROCESSION OF FLAGELLANTS. All wear the robe, hood and hat of the confraternity. The foremost carries a crucifix. Before them three boys carry staves and a banner. MS of Gilles le Muisis, *Annales*. Brussels, Bibliothèque royale 13076/7, fol. 16v. Second half of the 14th century.

82. DEVILS LEADING THE DAMNED TO HELL. Frieze of the Main Door, Cathedral of Rheims. Middle of the 13th century. (Before war damage.)

83. A FUNERAL IN THE CLOISTER OF THE INNOCENTS AT PARIS. The mutes wear draperies of uncut cloth and carry candles with shields of the initials of the dead man R.E. The coffin is carried by white cloths passed underneath it. To the right a coped priest sprinkles it with holy water. A miniature by Jean Fouquet. About 1465. Chantilly, Musée Condé.

84. ST. SEBASTIAN INTERCEDING FOR THE PLAGUE-STRICKEN. Probably painted after the plague raged in Provence 1497-9, by Josse Lieferinxe. Oil on panel. Baltimore, Walters Art Gallery.

85. THE PROCESSION OF THE SACRAMENT. The mitred bishop carries the Host in a monstrance under a canopy embroidered with the arms of the royal fiefs. Paris, Bibliothèque de l'Arsenal, Ms 601, fol. 326v. Early 16th century.

86. WEEPERS FROM THE TOMB OF THE DUC DE BERRY AT BOURGES. By Jacques Morel. About 1449. They represent members of his household in mourning cloaks. Bourges Museum.

87. THE HEAD OF ISAIAH. Detail from the *Puits de Moïse* at the Chartreuse de Champmol, near Dijon. By Claus Sluter, 1397-1405.

88. THE CONSULTANT PHYSICIAN. The messenger has brought the physician a specimen of the patient's urine in a covered basket. The physician sits in his doctor's gown on a settle before the fire and holds it up to inspect it against the light. From the *Epitre d'Othéa* of Christine de Pisan. Brussels, Bibliothèque royale, Ms franç. 9392, fol. 42v. Mid 15th century.

89. JEAN MIÉLOT OF GAISSART, Canon of Saint-Pierre at Lille, translating the *Miracles de Notre Dame*. About 1456. Paris, Bibliothèque Nationale, Ms franç. 9198, fol. 19.

90. THE ASTRONOMER, THE SCRIBE AND THE COMPUTIST. A miniature from the Psalter of Saint Louis and Blanche of Castille. An astronomer in the centre, holding a tube, precursor of the telescope, examines an astrolabe. On his right a man holds a set of tables apparently written in Arabic. To his left a younger man takes down his findings in a book. About 1220. Paris, Bibliothèque de l'Arsenal, Ms 1186, fol. iv.

91. SCENES OF STUDENT LIFE. From a relief on the Cathedral of Notre Dame de Paris. About 1220.

COLOUR PLATES

Frontispiece

THE STORY OF THE GIFT OF THE FLEURS DE LYS TO FRANCE. According to a romantic legend, referred to by Raoul de Presles, that seems to date from the second half of the 14th century, God sent an angel bearing a cloth embroidered with three fleurs-de-lys to a hermit. Clotilde, wife of Clovis, gave him alms; in return he handed her the cloth, telling her to give it to her husband, who put it on the shield he bore against the Saracens. The story is fully told in this miniature from the *Bedford Book of Hours*, written in Paris for John, Duke of Bedford. About 1415. London British Museum, Add. Ms 18850, fol. 288b.

Facing page 8

PORTRAIT OF CHARLES VII OF FRANCE. By Jean Fouquet. About 1445. Paris, Musée du Louvre.

Facing page 28

CHARLES VI, SALMON AND PRINCES. By the Boucicaut Master 1412. Geneva, Bibl. Publique et Universitaire, Ms. fr. 165, fol. 4.

Facing page 36

WOMAN SHEARING A SHEEP; HER DOG SITS BESIDE HER. Detail of a tapestry, made in the Valley of the Loire. About 1500. Paris, Musée du Louvre.

Facing page 88

ST. JOHN AND THE PRIESTLY DONOR. Detail from the Pietà of Villeneuve-lès-Avignon. Provençal. About 1460. Paris, Musée de Louvre.

Facing page 104

THE MASS OF ST. GILES. The Saint elevates the Host, Charles Martel kneels before the altar, and an angel flies down carrying a parchment to say that thanks to the Saint's prayer the King's sin was forgiven. The scene is the high altar of the Abbey of St. Denis; the retable, the cross, and the other altar trappings are historic pieces. The panel comes from a large retable. The kneeling man in a furred merchant's gown, holding a candle, is perhaps the donor. By the unnamed Master of St. Giles. About 1480. London, National Gallery.

Select Bibliography

This bibliography is intended as a reading-list rather than an indication of sources. It does not give a list of original texts, literary or historical. It has been brought up to date, but the books published after 1924 were not available to the author when *Life in Medieval France* was written. Most of the books cited contain useful bibliographies. Unless otherwise stated books written in French are published in Paris, and in English in London.

FRENCH

Acloque, G. *Les corporations, l'industrie et le commerce à Chartres.* 1917.

Adhémar, J. *Influences antiques dans l'art du moyen âge français.* 1939.

Ahsmann, H. P. J. *Le culte de la sainte Vierge et la littérature française profane au moyen âge.* 1930.

Aubert, M. *L'architecture cistercienne en France.* 2 vols. 1947.
    L'art français à l'époque romane. 4 vols. 1929–50.
    Suger. 1950.
    La sculpture française au moyen age. 1947.

Bédier, J. *Les Légendes épiques.* 1914.
    Les Fabliaux. 1911.
    Les Chansons de Croisade. 1909.

Belperron, P. *La Croisade contre les Albigeois et l'Union du Languedoc avec la France,* 1209–1249. 1944.

Berlière, U. *L'Ordre monastique.* 1921.

Bloch, Marc. *Les caractères originaux de l'histoire rurale française.* 1965 (revised version of 1931 edition).

Blum, A. and Lauer, P. *La miniature française au XIVe et XVe siècles.* 1930.

Boissonnade, P. *Du nouveau sur le Chanson de Roland.* 1923.

Borodine, M. *La femme et l'amour au XIIe siècle d'après les poèmes de Chrétien de Troyes.* 1909.
    Le roman idyllique au moyen age. 1913.

Boutaric, E. *La France sous Philippe le Bel.* 1861.

Bouvier, R. *Un financier colonial au XVe siècle: Jacques Coeur.* 1928.

Bréhier, L. *Les Croisades,* 1923.
    L'art en France, 1930.

Bruffault, R. *Les troubadours et le sentiment romantique.* 1945.

Bruel, A. *Romans français du moyen âge.* 1934.

Calmette, J. *La Société féodale,* 1923.
    Derniers étapes du moyen âge français. 1944.
    Reveil capétien. 1948.

Champion, P. *Splendeurs et misères de Paris,* 1431–84. 1933.

Clément, P. *Jacques Cœur et Charles VII.* 1866.

Cohen, G. *Le théâtre en France au moyen âge.* 2 vols. 1928–31.
    Histoire de la mise en scène dans le théâtre religieux français du moyen âge. 1906.
    La grande clarté du moyen âge. 1943.
    Histoire de la chevalerie en France au moyen âge. 1949.
    Vie littéraire en France au moyen âge. 1949.

Defourneaux, M. *La vie quotidienne au temps de Jeanne d'Arc.* 1952.

Doyen, G. and Hubrecht, P. *L'architecture rurale et bourgeoise en France.* 1942.

Duby, G. *L'économie rurale et la vie des campagnes dans l'occident médiéval (France, Angleterre, Empire) neuvième-quinzième siècle.* 1962.

Dupont, J. *Les primitifs français.* [1937].

Enlart, C. *Manuel d'archéologie française.* 1929–32.

Fagniez, G. *Etudes sur l'industrie et la classe industrielle à Paris.* 1877.

Faral, E. *Les jongleurs en France au moyen âge.* 1910.
La vie quotidienne au temps de Saint Louis. 1944.

Fawtier, R. *Les Capétiens et la France.* 1942.

Flipo, V. *Memento Pratique d'archéologie française.* 1930.

Focillon, H. *Art d'Occident.* 1938.
Peintures romanes des églises de France. 1938.

Gastone, A. *Les primitifs de la musique française,* 1922.

Gautier, L. *La chevalerie.* [1883].

Gerould, T. *La musique au moyen âge.* 1932.

Guilhiermoz, P. *L'origine de la noblesse en France.* 1902.

Hanotaux, G. *Histoire de la nation française,* 1920–29.

Hautecoeur, L. *L'architecture française,* 1950.

Hubert, J. *L'art préroman.* 1938.

Kleinclausz, H. *Histoire de Bourgogne.* 1909.

Langlois, C. F. *La Vie en France au moyen âge,* 4 vols. 1924–28.

Lasteyrie, R. de. *L'architecture religieuse en France à l'époque gothique.* 2 vols, 1926.
L'architecture religieuse en France à l'époque romane. 2nd ed. 1929.

Lavisse, E. (ed.). *Histoire de France.* Vols. I–IV, 1901–2.

Lecoy de la Marche, A. *Le roi René.* 2 vols. 1875.
La chaire française au moyen âge. 1886.
La France sous Saint Louis et sous Philippe le Hardi. 1893.

Lefrançois-Pillion, L. *Les sculpteurs français du XIIe siècle.* [1931].
Les sculpteurs français de XIIIe siècle. [1931].
Maîtres d'œuvre et tailleurs du pierre des Cathedrales. 1949.

Longnon, A. *Atlas historique de la France.*
Les noms de lieu de la France. 1920–9.

Lot, F. *La France.* 1941.

Luce, S. *Histoire de Bertrand du Guesclin et de son temps.* 1893.
La France pendant la guerre de Cent Ans. 2 vols. 1890.

Luchaire, A. *Les communes françaises.* 1890.

Mâle, E. *L'art religieux en France au moyen âge.* 3 vols. 1908–1910.

Molinier, A. *Les sources de l'histoire de France.* 1901–6.

Mortet, V. and Deschamps, P. *Recueil de textes sur l'histoire de l'architecture et la condition des architectes.* 2 vols. 1929.

Mourey, G. *Tableau de l'art français des origines à nos jours.* 1938.

Oursel, C. *L'art roman de Bourgogne.* Dijon and Boston. 1928.

Paris, G. *La littérature française au moyen âge.* 1913.

Pernoud, Régine. *Histoire de la bourgeoisie en France.* 1960.

Pirenne, H. *Les villes du moyen âge*. Brussels, 1927.

Petit Dutaillis, C. *La monarchie féodale*. 1933.

Rambaud, A. N. *Histoire de la civilisation française*. 1887.

Réau, L. *La peinture française du XIVᵉ siècle*. 1939.
    L'art gothique en France. 1950.
    L'art religieux au moyen âge. 1946.

Rey, R. *L'art roman et ses origines*. Toulouse, 1945.
    La sculpture romane languedocienne. Toulouse and Paris, 1936.
    Les vieilles églises fortifiées du Midi de la France. 1925.
    L'art gothique du Midi de la France. 1934.

Saulnier, V. L. *Littérature française du Moyen Age*. 1948.

Stein, H. *Les architectes des cathédrales gothiques*. [c. 1910].

Sterling, C. *La peinture française: les primitifs*. 1938.

Ungureanu, Marie. *La bourgeoisie naissante. Societé et littérature d'Arras au XIIᵉ et XIIIᵉ siècles*. Arras, 1955.

Vaultier, R. *Le folklore pendant la guerre de Cent Ans d'après les lettres de rémission du Trésor des Chartes*. 1965.

Vielliard, J. *Le guide du Pèlerin de Saint-Jacques de Compostelle*. Mâcon, 1938.

Vivent, J. *La Guerre de Cent Ans*. 1954.

ENGLISH

Adams, H. *Mont Saint Michel & Chartres*. Cambridge, Mass. 1911.

Aubert, M. *French Sculpture at the beginning of the Gothic Period*. Florence and Paris, 1929.

Barker, E. *The Crusades*. Oxford, 1923.

Baum, J. *Romanesque Architecture in France*. 2nd ed. 1928.

Bony, J. and Hürlimann, M. *French Cathedrals*. 1951.

Bloch, Marc. *French rural history. An essay on its basic characteristics, trans. Janet Sondheimer* (translation of *Les caractères originaux de l'histoire rurale française*. 1965 ed.).

Bridge, J. S. C. *History of France, 1482–93*. 1921–24.

Cambridge Mediaeval History. Vols. IV–VII, 1923–32.

Cartellieri, O. *The Court of Burgundy*. 1929.

Crosland, J. *Old French Epic*, 1951.

Deschamps, P. *French Sculpture of the Romanesque Period*. Florence and Paris, 1930.

Duby, G. *Rural economy and country life in the medieval west*. 1968 (translation of *L'économie rurale et la vie des campagnes . . .*).

Evans, Joan. *Monastic Life at Cluny, 910–1157*. Oxford, 1931.
    Romanesque Architecture of the Order of Cluny. Cambridge, 1938.
    Art in Mediaeval France, 987–1498. 1948.
    Cluniac Art of the Romanesque Period. Cambridge, 1950.
    Dress in Mediaeval France. Oxford, 1952.

Fawtier, R. *The Capetian Kings of France, trans. L. Butler and R. J. Adam*. 1960 (translation of *Les Capétiens et la France*).

Fowler, Kenneth. *The age of Plantagenet and Valois. The struggle for supremacy, 1328–1498*. 1967.

Frank, G. *Mediaeval French Drama*. 1954.

Funck Brentano, F. *The Middle Ages*. 1922.
    The Earliest Times. 1927.

Gardner, A. *Mediaeval Sculpture in France*. Cambridge, 1931.
    Introduction to French Church Architecture. 1938.

Haskins, C. H. *The Renaissance of the Twelfth Century*. Cambridge, Mass., 1927.
    Studies in the History of Mediaeval Science. Cambridge, Mass., 1924.

Holmes, U. T. *History of Old French Literature to 1300*. 1938.

Huizinga, J. *The Waning of the Middle Ages*. 1924.

Keen, Maurice Hugh. *The Laws of War in the Late Middle Ages*. 1965.

Ker, W. P. *The Dark Ages*. 1904.

Kilgour, R. L. *The Decline of Chivalry*. Cambridge, Mass., 1937.

Labarge, Margaret Wade. *Saint Louis. The Life of Louis IX of France*. 1968.

Leff, Gordon. *Paris and Oxford Universities in the Thirteenth and Fourteenth Centuries*. 1968.

Lemoisne, P. A. *Gothic Painting in France*. Florence and Paris, 1931.

Lewis, Peter S. *Later Medieval France. The Polity*. 1968.

Lodge, E. C. *Gascony under English Rule*, 1152–1453. 1926.

Michel, P. H. *Romanesque Wall-paintings in France*. 1951.

Morison, J. C. *The Life and Times of St. Bernard*. 1863.

Panofsky, E. *Abbot Suger on the Abbey Church of Saint Denis and its Art Treasures*. Princeton and London, 1946.

Pegues, Franklin J. *The Lawyers of the Last Capetians (1270–1328)*. Princeton, 1962.

Poole, R. L. *Illustrations of Mediaeval Thought*. 2nd ed., 1920.

Power, E. (trans.). *Le ménagier de Paris*. 1928.

Rashdall, H. *Universities of Europe in the Middle Ages*. ed. F. M. Powicke and A. B. Emden. 3 vols. Oxford, 1936.

Ring, G. *A Century of French Painting*, 1400–1500. 1949.

Taylor, H. O. *The Mediaeval Mind*. 1911.

Tilley, A. (ed.). *Mediaeval France*. Cambridge, 1922.
    The Dawn of the French Renaissance. Cambridge, 1918.

Vinogradoff, P. *Roman Law in Mediaeval Europe*. New York, 1909.

Vitry, P. *French Sculpture during the Reign of Saint Louis*. Florence and Paris [1930].

Wescher, P. *Jean Fouquet and his Time*. 1947.

Young, K. *The Drama of the Mediaeval Church*. Oxford, 1933.

Acknowledgements

WE WISH to express our gratitude to all Museums and Libraries which have provided us with photographs and given us permission to reproduce their works.

In particular we should like to thank the Walters Art Gallery in Baltimore; the Bibliothèque Royale in Brussels; the University Library in Erlangen; the British Museum, the National Gallery and the Victoria and Albert Museum in London; the Staatsbibliothek in Munich; the Frick Collection in New York; the Louvre, the Bibliothèque Nationale and the Bibliothèque de l'Arsenal in Paris; and the National Gallery of Art in Washington.

We are also most grateful to Dr. Joan Evans for providing some of her own photographs. Other photographs were obtained in Paris from Archives Photographiques, Photo Bulloz, Photo Giraudon, Photo Roubier and Photo Viollet.

THE PHAIDON PRESS

The illustrations on pages 15 and 72 are from the Album of the medieval architect Villard de Honnecourt, middle of the 13th century. (Paris, Bibliothèque Nationale, Ms. franç. 19093, fols. 5 and 23v.) The miniature on page 52 is from the *Roman de la Rose*, a 15th century French manuscript in the École des Beaux-Arts in Paris (fol. 29v). The woodcut on page 240 shows the Royal Hawking Party, from Guillaume Tardif's *L'Art de Faulconnerie*, Paris, 1492.

Index

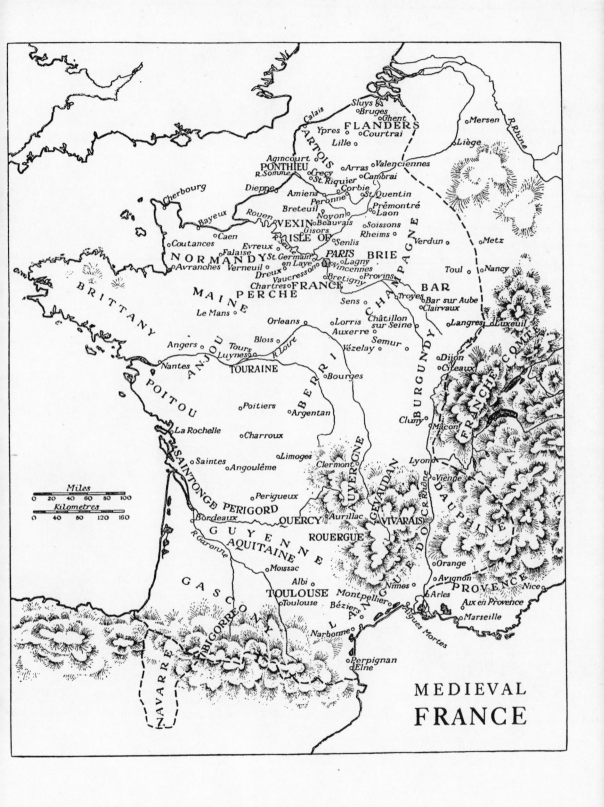

MEDIEVAL
FRANCE